D0463791

DIRECTIONS FOR HISTORICAL LINGUISTICS

A Symposium

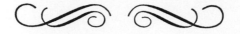

DIRECTIONS FOR

HISTORICAL LINGUISTICS

A Symposium

Edited by

W. P. LEHMANN and YAKOV MALKIEL

UNIVERSITY OF TEXAS PRESS, AUSTIN & LONDON

Dedicated to the memory of
URIEL WEINREICH

PREFATORY NOTE

By the middle of the 'sixties the two editors of this collection had for some time been discussing the inadequate attention to historical linguistics and the need to restore historical studies to their position of leadership among the primary linguistic disciplines. A symposium concerned with some of the central theoretical topics seemed the proper device for renewing interest. An occasion for the symposium presented itself with the establishment of The University of Texas' program in linguistics as a separate department in the academic year 1965–66. After selection of the principal speakers—reflecting the tastes of three "generations"—and extensive correspondence with them on the most desirable topics in a context so defined, the symposium, supported by The University's Excellence Fund, convened on April 29–30, 1966. Tentative versions of all five major communications by the authors of the essays published here were preprinted and distributed among the hundred or so participants, making it possible for the writers to present a shorter version orally and to reserve ample time for discussion. The papers were subsequently revised, partly on the basis of comments by participating linguists. For the authors we express our gratitude to the discussants, especially for such contributions from them as may have been tacitly incorporated in the present expanded version of these essays. We hope that the topics seem as central to others concerned with historical linguistics as they did to the principals on that memorable occasion—which we hope may be the first in a series of such colloquia.

The first topic involved the task of putting current work in perspective with that carried out when the historical viewpoint virtually monopolized the field of linguistics. The ability and the intention to treat language as a structure may be the chief differences between the approach of the great nineteenth-century pioneers and our own activities.

However many linguists contributed to the structural approach, the impetus for it derives mainly from Ferdinand de Saussure. In achieving for linguistics the status of a structurally oriented discipline Saussure sharply distinguished descriptive from historical analysis. Today, when Saussure's ideas have been fairly well assimilated, it may be advisable to examine the extent to which his dichotomy has affected historical linguistics. Among most modernists, language is viewed as a series of levels or strata, in particular the phonological and the morphosyntactic. Accounting for sound change has, of course, been one of the chief concerns of historical linguists. By standard theory sound change takes place at the phonological level; as a result, the entire edifice may then be rearranged through new patterning at the morphosyntactic or semantic planes. Yet the assumption of such neat strata, with carefully specified directions of interaction, possibly reflects a grasp of language simplified for pedagogical presentation. An unbiased examination of more intimate relationships between the various strata conducive to sound change, with full allowance for an occasional reversal of the accepted sequence or hierarchy, ranks among the key problems of historical linguistics, as suggested in the second essay.

But if nonphonological components may have an effect on phonological development, how should we define the relationship between the morphological and the phonological components of language? What sort of entities must we posit? Linguists have generally operated with a prime phonological entity, the phoneme, and a prime morphological entity, the morpheme, without achieving agreement on the interfacing of the two strata. The assumption of an intermediate entity, as Jerzy Kuryłowicz indicates, might leave the theorist's standard strata essentially untouched, while providing the mechanism for deepened understanding of phonological and morphological change.

In contrast to the generous share of attention which change at the phonological level has traditionally received, change at the morphosyntactic level has by and large been examined from the angle of "chain reactions," that is, rearrangements of morphological and syntactic forms entailed by phonological change. Modification of morphosyntactic categories—gender, case, syntagms built around function words—and the rise of new patterns to express them for the most part remain to be explored. A theoretical framework for such examination, as traced by

Émile Benveniste, constitutes one critically urgent need for historical probings. With such a framework at our disposal, morphosyntactic change and its effects can be studied as intensively as has been phonological change.

The material on which historical linguistic theory is based has been taken in most instances from preurban societies, often preliterate and even prehistoric speech communities. Proto-Germanic must have been spoken by a small group; similarly proto-Indo-European. When historical linguists began to concern themselves with languages eventually emerging from groups such as classical Greek, they generally focused attention on subgroups, such as Attic Greek. The resultant techniques and the theory itself must now be tested against the situation observable in complex urban groups. For in complex societies the stimuli for change, and the constraints on it, may be more diversified, as must be the techniques for dealing with them. Besides accounting for current changes in language, only refinements of method which may result from such study are bound to clarify problems left unsolved in historical linguistic study of the past. Among the most imaginative studies of change in contemporary linguistic communities are those carried on by Marvin Herzog and William Labov, in conjunction with the late Uriel Weinreich. The conclusions they have reached may provide the starting point for inquiries into the dynamics of other contemporary communities.

It is no diminution of the shares of Professors Herzog and Labov in this study to state that much of the original impetus for their research came from Uriel Weinreich. Few would deny that his work, carried on without fanfare in a tragically short lifespan, has provided some of the most noteworthy contributions to linguistics of the past decade and a half: on the varieties of language; on language in its relation to other facets of culture; on exploratory approaches to semantics. With a feeling of the great loss for linguistics caused by the untimely death of a splendid scholar, who was also a dear personal friend, we dedicate this book to his memory.

The Editors

CONTENTS

LIST OF FIGURES

DIRECTIONS FOR HISTORICAL LINGUISTICS

A Symposium

Saussure's Dichotomy between Descriptive and Historical Linguistics

W. P. LEHMANN

The University of Texas at Austin

The shape of linguistics today was set in large part by Ferdinand de Saussure. We agree with some of his principal insights into the make-up of language: its functioning as a semiotic system in which oppositions and interrelationships are of prime importance. On his views, whether these are original with him or carried on from previous scholars of language and sign systems, the generally observed subdivisions of linguistics are based: synchronic and diachronic, or as they are more generally labeled, descriptive and historical, as well as some of the offshoots of our discipline, such as sociolinguistics, which now are burgeoning. In his homage to Saussure, Meillet says that Saussure wished above all to mark the contrast between two manners of dealing with linguistic facts: the study of language at a given moment, and the study of linguistic development through time.[1] More matter of factly, Bloomfield states that Saussure "had for years expounded . . . the natural relation between descriptive and historical studies."[2] Hjelmslev quotes with satisfaction the letter of Bally which applauded him for following the ideal formulated by Saussure.[3] Whatever the deviations in further parts of their theory, they with other linguists followed Saussure in their approach to language as a sign system which can be studied from a synchronic or a diachronic point of view. It is the aim here to examine the dichotomy which Saussure propounded between syn-

[1] A. Meillet, *Linguistique historique et linguistique générale*, II (Paris: Klincksieck, 1938). His statement on the work of Ferdinand de Saussure is given on pages 174–183. The excerpt is on page 183: "l'étude de la langue à un moment donné, et l'étude du développement linguistique à travers le temps."

[2] L. Bloomfield, *Language*, pp. 18–19 (New York: Holt, 1933).

[3] L. Hjelmslev, *Essais linguistiques*, p. 31 (Copenhague: Nordisk Sprog- og Kulturforlag, 1959).

chronic and diachronic linguistics, to note the implications of it for him, and to observe some effects of the dichotomy on subsequent linguistic work until the present.

Classifying linguistics with other studies of *valeur*, like economics, which we refer to as the social sciences and humanities, Saussure ascribes to them two axes of study: one an axis of *simultanéités*, the other an axis of *successivités*.[4] Because of the great number of signs in language and because of their diversity, linguistics above all other studies cannot investigate simultaneously the relationships in time and those in the contemporaneous system. It is therefore necessary to distinguish two linguistics (*Cours,* p. 116). After considering several possible terms—historical linguistics or evolutionary linguistics for the one and static linguistics for the other—Saussure gives his preference to the terms cited above, synchronic and diachronic.

Without doubt the dichotomy leads to oversimplification, even to awkwardness in the investigation of language. Saussure was far too capable a thinker to fail to see these; but he also recognized that in much scientific work progress requires simplification. In view of his impact on linguistics the simplifications he adopted, and bequeathed to succeeding linguists, must be specified, as must the difficulties themselves for which he proposed the simplification.

When we investigate any given language, such as German or French, the same material is handled twice, once by synchronic, once by diachronic linguistics. But how? The commonly adopted solution is to set up stages: Old French, Modern French, Old High German, Middle

_____

[4] Ferdinand de Saussure, *Cours de linguistique générale.* Third edition, edited by Charles Bally and Albert Sechehaye with the collaboration of Albert Riedlinger, p. 115 (Paris: Payot, 1949). References will be to this text. Commentary on Saussure's views is voluminous, and apparently will continue. Although additional materials of his have been published, such as *Les sources manuscrites du 'Cours de linguistique générale' de Saussure,* by Robert Godel (Genève: Droz, and Paris: Minard, 1957), I am dealing only with the *Cours* and its influence on linguistic work of the time after Saussure. Other points of view of his, and his way to them, may be valuable in providing further insights into language, and into the perspectives which are essential for work of lasting importance in linguistics, but especially into his own intellectual development. For a statement on his fundamental views which is unlikely to be surpassed see É. Benveniste's essay, "Saussure après un demi-siècle," now published as Chapter III of his *Problèmes de linguistique,* pp. 32–45 (Paris: Gallimard, 1966).

High German, New High German, and so on. For these stages Saussure provided an elegant name: *espace de temps* (*Cours*, p. 142). Admitting that one state of a language is not a point in time, he suggested that an *espace de temps* might be as long as ten years, a generation, an age, or more. The assumption of a "space in time" seemed tenable to him because of the manner in which languages undergo change: during some periods they may evolve little or undergo few changes, at any rate changes of little importance; during other periods they undergo a considerable number of changes rapidly. Periods with few changes would be handled as states; those of many changes would be selected for diachronic study, as the evolutionary phases of a language between its quiescent states. Even if there were a few changes in a period selected for synchronic study, these might be disregarded in somewhat the same way as mathematicians neglect infinitesimal quantities in some of their operations.

Obviously this identification of quiescent as opposed to evolutionary stages in language is artificial. It reminds us of a cyclical view of history, of Scherer's approach to literature with its alternation between stages of excellence and long periods of quiescence. Possibly it is unjustified to identify selected linguistic stages with periods of literary eminence. Yet the ideal *langues* which historical linguists have been using for their selected *espaces de temps* coincide remarkably with periods of literary glory. The high point of the Middle High German *langue* may be dated around 1200, the time at which the great medieval German poets were flourishing—with the apex of New High German and Old High German separated from it by approximately six hundred years. If we accept a cyclical view of human history, and if our literary standards agree with those of Scherer and his contemporaries, work in historical linguistics is greatly simplified. But our historical grammars then are regulated by nonlinguistic criteria. We produce a grammar for the Periclean Age of Greece, for the Augustan Age of Rome, for classical Sanskrit. Somewhat bluntly, historical linguists may center their activities around such periods because the *langue* at the time was indeed static—but for nonlinguistic reasons. A strong literary tradition had established a conventional language which was widely followed: Wolfram von Eschenbach would discard his East Franconian dialect divergences from the norm, as would an Alemannic Gottfried von Strassburg and a Bavarian Walther von der Vogelweide. The resulting *langue* gives the data for our Middle High German grammars; it is one of the *espaces de temps* in German.

In the welter of changing language we must obviously make some selection, especially when we need to get a tradition like the German language under control, and for pedagogical purposes; but we must also examine the basis for our simplification. Was the period from 1175 to 1225 really a period of linguistic calm in South Germany? Do we really find periods of linguistic calm coinciding with periods of literary excellence? Is our understanding of language in its development best obtained by selecting a number of stages which are defined by nonlinguistic criteria and using these as stages of reference?

The procedure of selecting *espaces de temps* came to be troubled when further investigation was made of language, notably by the dialect geographers. By concerning themselves with all types of language, not merely that of the eminent works of literature, they made it clear that even selected stages are not classically simple. The Middle High German around 1200 is not as neat as our elementary grammars may suggest. Nor is a precise distinction possible between various stages of language. Middle High German and New High German, Middle English and New English seem to merge at various times, depending on the criteria used to identify them—and similarly the stages of other languages.

Equally troublesome, forms of language contemporaneous with the ideal stages also share features with earlier and later stages. Language does not seem to evolve cyclically. Grimm's Law did not operate during one evolutionary period in proto-Germanic, to be quiescent for another period, and then resume its disruption of the German phonological system at another troubled period. Similarly, umlaut in the Germanic dialects, or the great English vowel shift, was not a momentary phenomenon, occurring between two static periods of *langue*. It is not necessary to pursue the details of these phenomena in the history of the Germanic dialects to establish this point. But it is important to observe that the linguistic data concerned are phonological. In distinguishing between various stages of a language, in pursuing diachronic linguistic study of any linguistic tradition, Saussure centered his attention around the phonological component of *langue*.

The discussion to this point has dealt largely with externals. Definition of stages of language by externals, by nonlinguistic cultural criteria, may be justified, for possibly we can grasp language only within a culture. If so, there is no great point in arguing about the basis of selection of any *espace de temps* used in historical linguistic study. Because literary and language study have been closely associated, we may take as our selected points in the history of a language those at which eminent literature was produced. Alternatively we might select periods of great religious interest, such as the Cluniac reform, the Protestant revolution; or of technological change, such as the improvement of communication systems through the Carolingian reform of the writing system, the introduction of the printing press, and so on. If language is indeed treated as a subordinate component of culture, and if our criteria for selecting *espaces de temps* had no intimate relationship with language itself, the classification we arrive at after agreeing on our criteria would not distort our views of it. But for Saussure the basis of selection of important diachronic stages was intimately related to his view of language. His distinction between synchronic and diachronic study was directly associated with his understanding of language. It is because of this intimate connection between his understanding of language and the two types of study, synchronic and diachronic, that a scrutiny of his dichotomy is of fundamental importance in linguistics.

For besides proposing two manners of study for dealing with linguistic facts, Saussure saw in the mechanism of language, in the *signifiant,* two strata, or levels: a phonological and a morphological.[5] Whatever terms we adopt for the two levels, or whatever terms he himself used, the *signifiant* of language is made up of two types of components: one, the components of sound, phonemes; the other the components of form, morphemes. And each set of components makes up a system.

For Saussure each set can be studied variously. The set of sounds may

---

[5] Saussure's views on the treatment of sounds in language are too complex for detailed discussion here. Moreover, they have been discussed in detail, as by R. Wells, "De Saussure's System of Linguistics," *Word* 3.1–31 (1947); reprinted in M. Joos, *Readings in Linguistics*, pp. 1–18. It is almost ironic to read today Wells' unhappiness about Saussure's inconclusiveness concerning phonemics, though with Wells' other comments these illuminate widespread linguistic views of the nineteen-forties as well as Saussure's.

be examined under *phonologie*—which has no relation to time; one may deal with the production of sound, the physical events, and the auditory effects. Sounds may also be studied from the point of view of their role for the native speakers of any language; of the three types of phonological study, this type most resembles subsequent phonemics. A third type of study, *phonétique* proper, deals with sounds as they change in time, belonging in contrast with the other two types to diachronic linguistics.

Grammatical statements on the other hand are synchronic. They may display the result of diachronic changes, as in Latin *facio: conficio* (*Cours*, p. 219); but it is even dangerous to use for such pairs the term *permutation*. For such a term may provide a "false notion of movement where only a state is present" (*Cours*, p. 219).

It is static (descriptive) linguistics, or the description of the state of a language, for which Saussure reserves the term *grammar* (*Cours*, pp. 185ff.). Grammar deals with *langue* as a system of means of expression; "grammatical" is equivalent to synchronic and significant . . . there is for us no "historical grammar."[6] Grammar, accordingly, the study of the morphology and syntax of a language, must be assigned to descriptive linguistics, excluded from diachronic linguistics.

The primary aim of diachronic linguistics is therefore *phonétique*. *Phonétique* does not deal with significance, nor with a grammar; in giving the history of the sounds of a word, one can disregard its meaning. And if the evolution of a *langue* is reduced to that of sounds, the opposition between the objects proper to the two divisions of linguistics becomes clear: diachronic is equivalent to nongrammatical as synchronic is to grammatical (*Cours*, p. 194). There is a precise dichotomy.

In concluding his general chapter on diachronic linguistics, however, Saussure states that *phonétique* may not account for all the developments in a language; after one has applied it, one finds a residue which seems to justify the notion of a "history of the grammar" (*Cours*, pp. 196–197).[7] But the intricate explication which a detailed statement of the distinction between diachronic and synchronic would require is be-

[6] *Cours*, p. 185: "qui dit grammatical dit synchronique et significatif . . . il n'y a pas pour nous de 'grammaire historique'."

[7] It may be this residue which is yielding to subsequent study that contrasts

yond the scope of the *Cours*. (The footnote of the editors at this point ascribing the problem to Saussure's lack of consideration of *la linguistique de la parole* probably attempts too simple an explanation. For Saussure's subsequent discussion embraces the possibility of competing forms in the *parole* before they are incorporated in the *langue*). The *Cours* itself maintains the distinction, examines the mechanism of interplay between *phonétique* and *grammaire*, and firmly establishes two linguistics: synchronic and diachronic.

We may clarify the distinction by examining the topics discussed in the third part of the *Cours*, for they follow from Saussure's view on the change of language. First, phonetic change takes place. This may have an effect on the grammar, disrupting grammatical ties. The ties are then restored, often rearranged, by the workings of analogy; analogy is at once a source of renovation and of conservation. Through analogy, then, the grammar of a language may be rearranged, but "analogical phenomena are not changes"; they correspond rather to creations in a synchronic stage of language. Even though analogy acts as an agent in modifying *grammaire*, the action belongs on the synchronic plane. The dichotomy between *phonétique* and *grammaire*, between diachronic and synchronic linguistics remains firm. It not only establishes two manners of dealing with linguistic facts, two types of linguistic study; it also divides language itself into two components.

Like most positions in a science which later become fixed as dogma with their own inadequacies, Saussure's dichotomy represented an advance over that of his predecessors. In a fine passage (*Cours*, pp. 118–119), Saussure objects to the linguistics of his time, which he ascribes largely to Bopp, as being entirely absorbed in diachrony. Moreover, it never defined its aims. Comparison was only a means of reconstructing the past. Its basis too was poorly defined. With comments particularly relevant today, Saussure contrasts nineteenth-century linguistics with that it ousted, traditional grammar, whose most notable work he recognizes as the grammar of Port-Royal. This Saussure esteems because it attempted to describe the state of French at a given time, the period of Louis XIV. Further, although it erred in neglecting parts of lan-

---

with the approach of Saussure, as in the work of J. Kuryłowicz and Y. Malkiel, among others.

guage, such as derivation, and in being normative rather than determining the facts, its basis is less subject to criticism and its aim better defined than are those of nineteenth-century linguistics. Accordingly there were few grounds for the reproach that it was not scientific. Saussure forecasts that linguistics will return to the static view of traditional grammar, after its rejuvenation by historical linguistics. Presumably it was to carry out this aim that he composed his course of lectures on general linguistics.

Unquestionably Saussure achieved his aim. But we have suggested that he did so at a cost: in the resulting linguistics, stages of language were artificially set up which were relatively static, with intervening periods of considerable change. Though pedagogically useful, this view of language also has its shortcomings. And we may now be at a point when, having profited from the contributions of historical linguistics, we can resume relations with eighteenth-century linguistics, and build on the new static linguistics a new historical linguistics.

The historical linguistics which Saussure proposed tremendously emphasized phonology. By it the essential change in *langue* is at the phonological level. To be sure, this change disrupts the grammatical system, leading to adjustments at the morphological level. But these adjustments are of a different order from phonological change. They are readjustments rather than innovations. Moreover, in Saussure's historical linguistics semantic change goes almost completely unmentioned. The *signifiant* of language makes up the central concern of Saussurean linguistics, and in historical linguistics the phonological component of the *signifiant*. It is scarcely surprising that subsequent work has moved to modify this view. But as yet there has been none of the explicit, general formulation which made Saussure so influential. The time may now be at hand for such a formulation, based on the notable work that has been carried out after the publication of the *Cours*.

To illustrate views which are departures from Saussure one may cite a segment from Szemerényi's statement on recent etymological research; Szemerényi sees in etymological work from about the beginning of our century a "break away from the pursuit of original forms and/or meanings, a shift of emphasis to historical processes" (p. 177).[8] This break

[8] O. Szemerényi, "Principles of Etymological Research in the Indo-European Languages," *Innsbrucker Beiträge zur Kulturwissenschaft*, Sonderheft 15, Inns-

may partially accord with Saussure's views; but the shift to a concern with processes indicates that etymologists are no longer chiefly concerned with determining items or states, rather with the procedures by which interrelations in language are achieved. We may exemplify the shift of interest with one of Saussure's comparisons, that between an observer of language and an observer of a game of chess (*Cours,* pp. 126–127). Saussure points out, and we agree, that for anyone observing a game of chess at any given point it is unimportant to know how a given position of the pieces has been arrived at. For a description of the position at the moment, the history of previous moves is unessential. Similarly, if a linguist were an external observer of language, a synchronic description accompanied by a subsequent diachronic statement would be adequate. But the role of observer no longer satisfies linguists. For just as an observer of a chess game at any one point obtains only a partial view of the total game, so observation of selected points in the development of a language yields an inadequate account of language in its development. In historical as well as in descriptive linguistics an approach is now favored which deals with language from the point of view of the participant, to whom the moves are of central importance, whether in following the course of a game or in interpreting the situation at the moment.

It has been noted above that Saussure's view of a linguist as an observer leads to a concern for language as a state. Today there is a far greater concern for language in operation, as will be discussed below. An observation on some of the current work in linguistics, that dealing with linguistic theory, indicates briefly the shift of concern: "The current controversy in linguistics is largely concerned with the question of what is the best method of describing both states and operations."[9] Although Thomas was referring to work in descriptive linguistics, the quotation from Szemerényi illustrates that the concern extends to historical linguistics as well.

Interest in operations is evident at the morphological and semantic level, as well as at the phonological. But if we occupy ourselves pri-

---

bruck 1962. Sonderdruck aus II. Fachtagung für indogermanische und allgemeine Sprachwissenschaft, pp. 175–212.

[9] O. Thomas, *Transformational Grammar and the Teacher of English,* p. 15 (New York: Holt, Rinehart and Winston, 1965).

marily with operations, not states, language is highly fluid. To a great extent the procedures we apply are also less general; the term *law* for example differs from its use for physical sciences even more than it did for Grimm. And *change* may refer to minute shifts. Any new presentation dealing largely with operations, a new course of general linguistics, will be far less neat than is Saussure's, but it may also comprehend more details of linguistic events.

The shift to a more fluid phonology has been so prominent that it needs little elaboration. Jakobson proposed guidelines for a more flexible handling of phonology in the early years of the Prague Circle.[10] His "principles of historical phonology" lead to a view of regarding successive mutations in language from either a synchronic or a diachronic point—and at any time, either before, during, or after the mutation, we may look at the language synchronically or diachronically. Already in his article of 1930 Jakobson introduces such terms as *chain*, which was exploited at length in possibly the most extensive discussion of the sound systems of language regarded from the point of view of the processes underlying their changes.[11]

The greater fluidity in handling phonology may be the theoretical deviation from Saussure's approach which has been most widely discussed by historical linguistics, but it is also one of the least. Rather than adopt major stages for synchronic description, it suggests seizing any period of language. It may therefore be primarily substituting linguistic realism for pedagogical selectivity. But as in Saussure's diachrony, the major concern of this historical linguistics is with phonology as the innovating segment of language—maintaining in this way Saussure's link between diachronic linguistics and the phonological level of language. Since an assumption of change rather than rearrangement at other levels of language would be a far greater departure from Saussure, these will result in a far more different approach to language than is Jakobson's "integral method."

The most explicit attempt to set up principles of a dynamic morphol-

---

[10] See his "Principes de phonologie historique," *Selected Writings I*. Phonological Studies, pp. 202–220 ('s-Gravenhage: Mouton and Co., 1962). The essay was first published in 1931, though presented in 1930.

[11] André Martinet, *Économie des changements phonétiques*. Traité de phonologie diachronique (Berne: Francke, 1955).

ogy in historical linguistics is that of J. Kuryłowicz.[12] In this article analogy is viewed as a dynamic mechanism: the morphological patterns of language seem to stand in some kind of tension, which may be resolved in accordance with six rules. Some of these rules predict that one of two or more parallel forms may replace another; they are general principles, virtually laws on potential change in morphology.

In contrasting the views of Kuryłowicz and other contemporaries[13] with those of Saussure we may recall how explicit Saussure was about the ineffective role of the speaker in initiating, and even in controlling, change in language. His comparison between language and chess reflects this view, for he states that "the chess player has the *intention* of carrying out a shift and of effecting an action on the system; but language does not premeditate anything."[14] And at the end of the section he speaks of a blind force operating against the sign system. Kuryłowicz in contrast views the speaker as deciding between alternate forms, and through such decisions controlling the selection of two or more competing forms. We may characterize the aim of Kuryłowicz as an attempt to specify how the speaker controls the effects of change in language. Others, as do Weinreich, Labov, and Herzog in their contributions to this volume, are attempting to specify the mechanisms of the "blind force" that operates against the system of signs.

The study of operations, or processes in historical linguistics may then have enlarged on Saussure in dealing with problems of language change that he left untouched. A clearer specification of analogy and, even more, attempts at identification of the source of language change within the system modify considerably the position of Saussure. They also promise to illuminate questions left untouched by earlier historical linguists, and to enlarge our understanding of language in its change.

[12] These principles are outlined in his article "La nature des procès dits 'analogiques'," *Acta Linguistica* 5 (1945–1949), 15–37. They have been elaborated in Chapter I of *The Inflectional Categories of Indo-European* (Heidelberg: Winter, 1964). See especially pp. 38 ff. Examples of their application by Professor Kuryłowicz may be found in this book, and others to which he refers in his discussion.

[13] O. Szemerényi, *Studies in the Indo-European System of Numerals* (Heidelberg: Carl Winter, 1960).

[14] *Cours*, p. 127. "Il n'y a qu'un point où la comparaison soit en défaut; le joueur d'échecs *a l'intention* d'opérer le déplacement et d'exercer une action sur le système; tandis que la langue ne prémédite rien ..."

If we contrast an excellent grammar of the past, such as W. Streitberg's *Urgermanische Grammatik* (Heidelberg: Carl Winter, 1896), we may note that it primarily describes states, and confronts a succeeding state with one that had preceded it. When for example we compare with Streitberg's treatment of the Germanic consonant shift that of E. Prokosch in *A Comparative Germanic Grammar* (Philadelphia: Linguistic Society of America, 1939), we note in it a much greater concern with processes. For Prokosch, however, the chief interest lay in extralinguistic processes, such as the social setting at the time of the shift and articulation of the sounds. Subsequent study, following in great part J. Fourquet in *Les mutations consonantiques du germanique* (Paris: Les Belles Lettres, 1948), has attempted to specify the linguistic processes involved in the Germanic consonant shift. It would require a great deal of space to give in detail the changing approach to the Germanic consonant shift and to other problems of historical linguistics; of prime concern here is that, as in the study of etymology, increasing emphasis has been placed on processes, in the attempt to account for change in language.

A comprehensive attempt to broadly examine language in change has been displayed in the work of Malkiel. Dealing in an impressive set of studies with language at all of its levels, he has introduced flexibility in the interpretation of change. His approach agrees to a large extent with that of Saussure, for some of the topics he discusses—weak sound change, trajectories—suggest basic concern with phonological change. Yet for Malkiel analogy may launch developments, the pressure of a morphological pattern may block or wipe out developments, grammatical as well as phonological structure may bring about change. As his essay in this volume illustrates, he is directly concerned with a dynamic effect of grammar, and with this concern he departs from a strict Saussurean approach.

A greater departure, however, will be introduced by linguists who relate all parts of language to syntax—who rigorously determine interrelationships between all linguistic elements and the unit they see as central to language, the sentence. The assumption that the sentence is the basic entity of language is not new; Saussure commented on it (*Cours,* pp. 148–149, 172–173), but rejected it on the grounds that the sentence belongs to *parole*, not *langue*.[15] An approach to language ascribing such a role to the sentence would therefore bring about a considerable change from Saussurean linguistics. If the total emphasis is further placed on processes, not states, the departure from a Saussurean approach will be far greater than is that in the work of Malkiel, Kuryłowicz, and others. Since little work in diachronic linguistics has been undertaken with a transformationalist approach, however, the possible great distinction between some historical studies of the future and that basing itself on Saussure is merely indicated now. Yet until such works are published, there is little point in discussing theoretical problems which will confront a syntactically based phonology.

The usefulness of these approaches will vary from one instance to another. Possibly each approach will clarify specific problems in language, and, following Malkiel's study "Each Word Has a History of Its Own," we may even suggest that fractions of various problems in one language may yield to each approach.

By a distinctive feature analysis, for example, we may specify more precisely the twofold development of PGmc *au* to OHG *ou* before labials and velars, to *ō* before dentals and PGmc *h*: An acute distinctive feature in the following consonant is accompanied by lowering of the second formant and fixing of both formants; the grave consonants regulate lowering of the first formant in the early part of the diphthong. Such an interpretation would require us to specify OHG *r* as acute, as well as PGmc *h*. This specification of the process underlying a sound change makes use of distinctive features on a syntagmatic plane. Other specifications, such as those of processes in the Germanic consonant shift, would primarily use distinctive features on a paradigmatic plane.

Still other procedures, at this time much more tentative, might deal with problems that have eluded analysis from a Saussurean dichotomy between phonology and morphology. It has been proposed, for ex-

---

[15] See especially *Cours*, p. 172: "On pourrait faire ici une objection. La phrase est le type par excellence du syntagme. Mais elle appartient à la parole, non à la langue." J. J. Katz and P. M. Postal, in *An Integrated Theory of Linguistic Descriptions* (Cambridge, Massachusetts: The M. I. T. Press, 1964), state on page ix that it is necessary to distinguish sharply between language and speech, referring to Saussure; but in dealing with "language" they take as their unit the sentence.

ample, that the problematic -ē of the Gothic genitive plural may be ascribed to analogy.[16] For it is found in nouns with front vowel characterizing the genitive singular, for example, *dags,* gen. sg. *dagis* (gen. pl. *dagē*), while -ō is found with back vowels in the genitive singular, for example, *giba,* gen. sg. *gibōs* (gen. pl. *gibō*). This situation arose in a phonological system with four long vowels:

$$\begin{array}{llll} \bar{\imath} & \bar{u} & \text{contrasted with three short:} & \text{i} \quad\quad \text{u} \\ \bar{e} & \bar{o} & & \text{a} \end{array}$$

Speakers might then have regarded the two low long vowels as not distinctive in the environment of the genitive suffix and may have distributed them in accordance with the pattern of the vowels in the genitive singular.

Accordingly, besides expecting modifications in the strict Saussurean dichotomy, and solutions to problems which it left unsolved, we may now be at a point of dealing with areas of language that seemed unpromising to Saussure, such as the area of semantic change. For Saussure, changes in meaning were individual, and accordingly incapable of general treatment.

We may illustrate with his example, *poutre* (*Cours,* p. 132), which at some time was changed in meaning from 'filly' to 'beam, support.' Apparently this change cannot be related to other semantic changes, particularly if we regard the meaning of 'filly' as an indissoluble unit. Similarly, other examples, such as NE 'horse,' which is also used for supports, as in 'carpenter's horse, clotheshorse.' Yet although we may not provide generalizations for such changes in meaning, we find it difficult to believe that some entities of the language might be extended in meaning as was *horse* in these ways, for example, *lungs* or *water* or *three* or *'s*. Noting such examples, we may suggest that eventually general statements on change of meaning may be found in a more thorough analysis of units selected for study of meaning. If we determine for *horse* the distinctive features of meaning, and their place in the meaning structure of a given language, we may be able to specify semantic shifts in somewhat the same way as we do phonological shifts.

---

[16] W. P. Lehmann, "The Gothic Genitive Plural -ē: Focus of Exercises in Theory," *Papers in Linguistics in Honor of Léon Dostert.* edited by William M. Austin, pp. 108–111 (The Hague—Paris: Mouton, 1967).

Just as we specify a modification of *p* to *f*, or *e* to *i*, on the basis of a distinctive feature approach, applied to the structure of a specific language in its development, so we may account for a modification of 'sturdy animate quadruped' to 'sturdy inanimate quadruped' and the like in a given semantic system. To be sure, in accounting for changes in a phonological system, a small number of distinctive features are adequate, whereas in a semantic system thousands would be necessary. Yet this approach to locating general principles in a further area of language shift is not contrary to Saussure's views; rather, it is an extension of them.

When modifications in historical theory are proposed, their proponents might with advantage examine the views of Saussure. Such a course may be useful because Saussure may already have examined the proposed modification. Further, highly careful studies, such as Benveniste's on Saussure's views on the arbitrariness of the linguistic sign (*Acta Linguistica* 1 [1939]), have not overturned the position of Saussure, though they have refined it.[17] Other more recent studies may represent somewhat further departures from Saussure's principles, particularly from his insistence on a strict dichotomy. But much of the activity in descriptive linguistics, whatever it is labeled, is merely leading to a finer analysis of language, and will in this way permit more precise definition of phenomena of concern to historical linguistics, finer accounting of change in language. Other areas of vigorous activity in linguistics are concerning themselves with relatively unstudied segments of language. Still other activity is closely examining language in its social setting. If like Saussure we may attempt a clarification of linguistic activities by comparing those in another science—without suggesting parallelism in techniques or subject matter—we may note a great amount of work parallel to that in molecular biology, on the one hand, and to ecology, on the other, in the linguistic examination of minute entities and the role of language for the learner, the speaker, and society. While this work, and the mode of specifying language, is bringing about modifications in linguistics, and accordingly departures from Saussure, it does not nullify his entire theory. The departures which

[17] "Nature du signe linguistique," Chapter IV, pp. 49–55, of his *Problèmes de linguistique générale* (Paris: Gallimard, 1966).

have been introduced, particularly in reducing the distinctions between his dichotomies, may lead to elimination of shortcomings of his linguistic theory, in somewhat the same way as were those of Bopp and his successors by Saussure, without leading to positions which disregard the achievements of past theory.

The Inflectional Paradigm
as an
Occasional Determinant of Sound Change

YAKOV MALKIEL

University of California, Berkeley

I

Introduction: *Some Prospects of Research in General Diachronic Linguistics*

Through the last two or three decades the balance sheet for diachronic linguistics has been predominantly negative. One notes no dearth of competent and even very respectable monographs written along traditional lines, inquiries which have clarified a number of important issues left previously in abeyance; such benefit as has accrued to general linguistics from these studies, however, has been meager, not necessarily because these inquiries displayed little imagination, still less because the data collected and distilled were incapable of stirring any fruitful discussion, but chiefly because the new and deeper insights, real or potential, which investigations of this kind could have afforded were buried underneath a mass of material of limited appeal, except to narrow specialists. To produce a truly beneficial large-scale effect, the matters of general import and broad applicability with which such studies are fortunately interspersed should have been, somewhere along the line, separated, explicated, possibly restated, and certainly made available, in a different context, on a different level of discourse, and through a different medium.

True, the picture confronting us is not all gray, let alone black; one discerns a few bright spots. Major advances have been scored either in terms of enhanced generality through cross-cultural, cross-temporal, cross-spatial analyses providing us with models and formulas, or in terms of more sophisticated, more experimental, less conventional analyses of unique historical situations high-lighted with exemplary finesse in terms of accomplishments which invite emulation. Along an independent axis, a third measurable token of progress has been the awakening of fresh interest among laymen and students, and the ability of several scholars to satisfy this hunger without resorting to rote and repetition.

To briefly illustrate these points: On the positive side of the ledger, we now have at our disposal, by way of broadly slanted methodological distillation, such tools as Uriel Weinreich's *Languages in Contact* (1952), André Martinet's *Économie des changements phonétiques* (1955), and Henry M. Hoenigswald's *Language Change and Linguistic Reconstruction* (1960). Among such trail-blazing monographs as exemplify rather than codify refined methods one may adduce, on the one hand, a number of weighty studies from the seasoned pen of Jerzy Kuryłowicz, bridging *L'accentuation dans les langues indo-européennes* (1952; 2d ed., 1958), *L'apophonie en indo-européen* (1956), and *The Inflectional Categories of Indo-European* (1964), with incisive prongs into comparative Semitics; and, on the other, Émile Benveniste's masterly *Études sur la langue ossète* (1959) and *Hittite et indo-européen* (1962), planned as inducements to reappraise the comparative method. Finally, the progressive trend in teaching is signaled by Winfred P. Lehmann's *Historical Linguistics: An Introduction* (1962), a book very much in demand among our tyros, and quite properly so.

Heartening as such symptoms are, it remains a fact that these advances have remained, by and large, unco-ordinated—involving virtuoso performances by brilliant, dauntless individuals rather than large-scale break-throughs achieved by teams of workers or schools of thought. Even more sobering is the realization that in some instances, after an energetic start, the probing has not been pushed to the hilt, counter to prognosis. To cite just one case of a job left unfinished: After Martinet, twelve years ago, concluded his stimulating *Économie,* significantly subtitled *Traité de phonologie diachronique,* one might have expected him to advance along at least one of the two roads conducive to beckoning goals: either the exploration of the principle of economy extended to linguistic domains other than that of phonology (say, inflection or syntax), or, alternatively, deeper probings, within the unvarying realm of sound development, into such discrete forces (the separate drives toward clarity and expressivism, among others) as are locked in ceaseless struggle with the trend toward parsimoniousness and symmetry. These hopes, one regrets to add, have not so far been fulfilled.

Yet economy of sound development, for all its overriding importance to the speakers and, if you wish, its esthetic appeal to the analyst, is just one of perhaps as many as five or even ten vital factors cutting across the growth patterns of individual languages, all of which clamor for dissection by experts combining the technical command of minute details with a detached view ranging, ideally, over numerous language families. Scholars meeting this dual qualification are, of course, few and far between; conceivably it is, more than anything else, this discouraging scarcity of leaders both well informed and farsighted, on whom the practitioners of our exacting discipline could depend for initiative and continued guidance, which is at the bottom of most of our current frustrations.

More cannot be undertaken here than to identify with varying degrees of brevity fifteen or so very pressing problems—broad-gauged and fundamental—whose firmer grasp would be of great assistance in grappling with a profusion of narrower, specific questions. These problems may, at this preliminary stage, be strung in noncommittal, haphazard sequence, as they come to mind. The structuring of these problems into anything approximating a single, coherent edifice of knowledge would mark the final stage of a venture upon which we are just now entering.

(1) *Conclusions from Fluidity of Usage to the Date of Upheaval.* On the whole, phonetic, morphological, and syntactic variants are known to survive side by side for an astonishing length of time (witness, for one example, the Standard Italian conjugation). Nevertheless, one might, under certain conditions, draw inferences from the intensity and the distribution of linguistic flux to its temporal distance from the event which set it in motion in the first place. Thus, in a language exhibiting, on the whole, rigidified verbal paradigms, individual spots of softness in the system of the verb might, if cautiously interpreted, yield clues to points of relative, if not of absolute, chronology.

(2) *Conclusions as to Earlier Stages from the Comparison of Trajectories of Rival Forms.* The systematic exploitation of the record of rival forms was initiated, but hardly brought to a successful conclusion, by the Italian neolinguists, who focused their attention excessively on

the configuration of geographic areas. Tentative projection into depth might also be made through comparison of frequency of use at carefully chosen cutoff points. Suppose forms a and b are near-synonyms in 1950, with a occurring many times more often than b; suppose further that a, by 1750, was used only twice as frequently as b, and that by 1600 the two words enjoyed parity. Could one, barring external interferences, extrapolate from this gradual expansion of a at the cost of b the original prevalence of b over a and even its ultimate anteriority?

(3) *Questioning of Specious Regularity.* The older technique of dividing an inventory of historically analyzed forms into a "regular" and an "irregular" column (and, in the process, of almost mechanically attributing irregularity either to borrowing or to analogical pressure) has long been open to question. For one thing, that approach did not sufficiently take into account the speakers' active participation in the changes (folk etymology, camouflaging of borrowings); for another, the "exceptions" were embarrassingly numerous. There now emerge additional possibilities of exposing, through microscopic inspection, instances of apparent regularity as so many belated corrections of an earlier deviation. Thus, one (minor) analogical pressure within a verbal paradigm can deflect a few of its members from the expected path, onto which they may, three or four generations later, be pushed again through a stronger pressure exerted from a different direction. How can such adjustments (backspins) be detected where the early record is fragmentary or seems irretrievably lost? How many exceptions to sound laws may, on the assumption of such a zigzagging state of affairs, be reinterpreted as due to over- or undercorrection? How, above all, are we to explain the paradox that the (supposedly) stronger influence asserting itself in the end did not at once block the agency of its weaker counterpart, but tolerated it for a while before vigorously counteracting? (Cf. Point (17) below.)

(4) *Paradigmatic Resistance to Sound Change.* One of the most trivial sequences of events in language history involves a sound change (or a cluster, or else a chain, of such changes) which leads to such violent disruption of a close-knit morphological system (e.g., a declensional or a conjugational paradigm) as to entail a number of remedial adjustments, the obvious alternative being the abandonment of the impaired system itself. In some instances the succession of observable

happenings seems to be inverted: an impending sound change that threatens to isolate a word from a morphologically meaningful context is, in the first place, discernibly delayed or completely warded off. The details of this shunting-off and its psychological roots remain to be determined.

(5) *The Paradigm as a Stimulus for a Sound Change.* It is unlikely that numerous sound changes are produced by morphological conditions; and it is further improbable that the few which may have been so produced display a conspicuously wide range. However, consider this possibility: a less than very common consonant cluster may for some reason occur pre-eminently in a characteristic group of verb forms and may thus become subject to the impact of a demonstrably influential leader verb. Once the outcome of this cluster has been affected through this primary analogical influence, at first strictly to the extent that it represents a recurrent segment of sharply delineated verb forms, further interplay of secondary analogical pressures, particularly at the point of transition from one generation to another, may extend the modification in question to nouns, adjectives, and other parts of speech. It is this particular hypothesis, applicable, above all, to some such situations as standard diachronic phonemics is unable to cope with satisfactorily, which will be examined in the main portion of the present paper.

(6) *Multiple versus Simple Causation in Language Change.* While it is well known that students of explicative historical linguistics tend to lean either in the direction of "substratum theories" (external influence) or in the direction of "structural modifications" (internal influence), little attention has been paid to the wisdom of positing, under certain conditions, the agency of complex, as against simple, causation, which might bridge the resultant gap. Such fundamental possibilities as habitual complementarity, bare compatibility, or mutual exclusiveness of potentially concurrent factors deserve systematic exploration.

(7) *Primary versus Secondary Determinants of Language Change.* Whereas the preceding point concerns simultaneously interacting forces, there exists an equally pressing need for the study of typical concatenations of such forces along the temporal axis. Mention has already been made of the (analogical) inflectional adjustments which

are likely to occur in the wake of powerful sound shifts; in this context the two sets of changes, though diverse in essence, are of comparable magnitude. The situation is different if two dialects are sharply polarized, in their respective core regions, by, say, the limitation to either of one neatly profiled sound change, while the interjacent, transitional zone shows signs of confusion through osmosis. Gradually, very minor differentiating factors (neighboring sounds, number of syllables, place of stress, width of semantic scope, social or stylistic level) will allow speakers of that area—provided they lean neither toward bolder leveling nor toward the indefinite toleration of semantically unnuanced doublets—to break up the sum total of words potentially affected by the critical sound law into small groups, each typically dominated by a leader word. In such a progression of events the original sound change marks a primary determinant, while the adventitious differentiating factors must rank as secondary determinants.

(8) *Interference of Nonlinguistic Factors with Language History.* There has never been any doubt—least of all among lexicologists—of the important rôle played by certain overt external factors (say, invasions, seasonal migrations, commercial traffic, intermarriage) on the vicissitudes of languages. Far more difficult of even oblique observation, especially at past stages, are certain hidden external factors relating to the structure of the given society: the degree of cohesion of its members, the identifiable strata that can be set off on the scales of education or prestige, and the intensity of the imitative drives as against the resistance to such temptations, among others. In languages where "progressive" and "conservative," "aristocratic" and "rustic" variants are suggested by differences in form, no truly satisfactory interpretation is conceivable without an equal share of attention granted to the social matrix. The techniques of diachronically slanted sociolinguistics remain to be established.

(9) *Possible Relation of Lexical Frequency or of Incidence to "Regularity" of Sound Change.* Any simple direct ratio of frequency to regularity must obviously be ruled out: When, through the syncope of an unstressed vowel, there arose, in proto-Spanish, the dyadic cluster -*xr*- [šr], in all likelihood uniquely found in two tenses of a single verb (*exir* 'to go out'), it was perfectly predictable that the short-range solution would consist in the intercalation of a -*t*-: *yxtré* 'I shall go out,'

on the analogy of quite common triadic clusters encountered in comparable contexts, such as *-m(b)r-, -l(d)r-, -n(d)r-, -ç(t)r-*. On the other hand, where a very infrequent cluster fails to match a broader pattern and each word involved seems to follow its own course, sometimes casting off three or more variants, the decision as to which variant of which word represents the norm is nearly impossible. Where lexical infrequency and relative isolation in the phonological system happen to coincide, regularity is bound to be at its lowest. Assuming that a given parent language has five word-initial consonant clusters involving *l* as their second ingredient, the fact that, by virtue of distinctive features, *bl-* and *gl-* (or *kl-* and *pl-*) support each other would tend to make their outcome in some daughter languages more regular than that of *fl-*, a group difficult to pair off; the (independently) weaker lexical representation of *fl-* in the chosen ancestral language would make prognosis of its subsequent course even more hazardous.

(10) *"Strong" versus "Weak" Phonological Change.* Scholars have learned to distinguish the pure phonological change (to be known as *ph. ch.*) from other modifications of sounds undergone—often incidentally—in some such context as borrowing, blend, saltatory or sporadic shift (as a rule, hazily delimited along the axes of time and space), or analogical adjustment. The distinction is useful and deserves retention, but does not exhaust the problem. There is some point in examining and even computing separately the total outcome of a phoneme (or family, or succession, of phonemes), regardless of the specific category of change at issue. The aggregate of these modifications, both "pure" and "impure," of the sound in question may, for the sake of tidiness, be marked by capital letters: *PH. CH.* Let us assume that in the transition from Stage X to Stage Y every *p* was shifted to *b*, while the original *b* in 60 percent of the ascertainable cases yielded *v* and in 40 percent disappeared. Whichever explanation for the discrepancy we may offer, there is merit in discriminating between $p > b$ as an eloquent example of a strong *PH. CH.*, and $b > v \sim$ zero as an equally cogent illustration of a weak *PH. CH.* The weakness of a *PH. CH.* may have a direct bearing on the infiltration of sporadic changes, lexical blends, and other modifications; it may also serve as an index of dialect mixture.

(11) *Reformulation of the Age-and-Area Hypothesis.* In the rad-

ical form in which "areal" or "spatial" linguistics was propounded by
a few Italian extremists as a downright substitute for the comparative
method, it led to a violent overreaction in many quarters, much as has,
through its comparable exclusivism, glottochronology and lexicostatis-
tics on this side of the Atlantic a decade or so later. But surely a cautious
study of the extent to which temporal inferences can be drawn from
present-day territorial distribution is, per se, a perfectly legitimate un-
dertaking. It might be particularly rewarding for diachronically oriented linguists to compare notes on this subject with geologists, paleon-
tologists, and paleobotanists, on the one hand, and with sociologists,
anthropologists and folklorists, on the other.

(12) *Allowances for the Purposefulness of Language Change.* Any
involvement of assumptions redolent of "teleology" is bound to produce unusually sharp divisions among linguists—divisions along philosophical lines, accompanied by very strong emotional orchestration. It
will be remembered that on this point L. Bloomfield, as the author of
two book reviews, clashed violently with Jespersen (whom he otherwise greatly admired), in an attitude which did not prevent him from
accepting (1933), tacitly and practically without qualification, some
of Gilliéron's most celebrated etymological findings based squarely on
the assumption of the speakers' free and active participation in the
shaping of their speech (avoidance of homonymy, striving toward
clarity, preference for prestige forms, indulgence in humor). The level
of consciousness and the degree of volition mark the overlap of linguistics and psychology and raise problems which cannot be shirked
or shrugged off by the diachronicist—indeed, which every generation
of linguists must pose and seek to answer anew. Perhaps it would be
helpful to separate the broad and highly explosive issue of "progress
in language" from less controversial appeals to speakers' (semi)con-
scious involvements in narrower decisions.

(13) *Complexity of Conditions Presiding over a Sound Change.*
One conceivably useful typology of sound changes might be organized
around the number of isolable factors controlling each. Thus, a classic
contrast between Old French (except for one dialect, Walloon) and Old
Spanish, viewed in their simultaneous estrangement from the common
parental language, consists in the fact that the diphthongization of Lat.
Ĕ and Ŏ hinges in the former on three conditions: (a) word stress, (b)

brevity of the vowel at the Latin stage, (c) openness of the syllable, but only on the first two in the latter. A parallel example is provided by the varying comportment, in French but not Spanish, of stressed vowels before nasals as against all other consonants. In general, Hispano-Latin sound changes are characterized by their simplicity, by Romance standards at least, while the Gallo-Latin equivalents strike one by their complexity. Granted the validity of this contrastive general characterization, it is noteworthy that a few isolated sound changes in Spanish depend on the concurrence of several factors; this is particularly true of the monophthongization of *ue* to *e*—as in *fr(u)ente* 'forehead,' *fl(u)eco* 'fringe, ragged edge,' where *f-*, qua labial, and *-r- /-l-*, qua liquids, seem to exert separate pressures—and of *-ie-* to *-i-*, as in *avi(e)spa* 'wasp,' *mi(e)rlo* 'blackbird,' *pri(e)sa* 'haste,' *pri(e)sco* 'kind of peach,' *ri(e)stra* 'string,' *si(e)glo* 'world, century,' and *vi(é)spera* 'eve', where ill-defined random combinations of (a) *s-*, especially before consonant or word-initially, (b) *r* and (c) *l*, in varying position vis-à-vis the diphthong, and (d) a preceding labial consonant (*m, p, v*) seem to produce the effect at issue. What conclusions —chronological, territorial, social, structural—can be drawn from such an atypical complexity of strictly phonological factors? (For a partial answer, see Section VII, below.)

(14) *Clarity as a Driving Force, Viewed in Isolation and in Counterpoise to Economy.* One shortcoming of the Gilliéronian school, known more advantageously for its detective flair than for any propensity toward theorizing, was its failure to integrate the much-vaunted avoidance of homonymic conflicts with the general dynamics of language change; add to this limitation the excessive stress on lexical— as against, say, phrasal—homonymy, and the neglect of semanticosyntactic ambiguity, along with polysemy. The entire problem, once broadened, may be reopened, and could be dramatized by gauging the impact of clarity against the power of economy matched as two rival prime determinants of language change.

(15) *Reconciliation of the Family Tree and the Undulatory Projections of Language Change.* Despite the wealth of scattered writings on this topic, there still exists no authoritative balance sheet, as regards either the theory or the recommended procedure.

(16) *Onomatopoeia, Expressivism, Sound Symbolism, and Depar-*

ture from Saussure's Classic Postulate of "L'Arbitraire du Signe." This
entire interlocking area clamors for fresh re-examination. Whereas the
topic of phonic evocation of acoustic realities (noises produced in inanimate nature, animal cries, modulations of the human voice) may
have been excessively—and at times inexpertly—labored, the no less attractive subject of phonic suggestion of events rhythmically segmented
but inaudible (ripples on the surface of a pond, vibration, trepidation)
remains a stretch of terra incognita. There arises the possibility of
elevating playfulness to the same kind of pedestal as economy and
clarity, particularly on the strength of linguistic developments where
emotional coloration has been achieved at the expense of economy, or
of clarity, or of both.

(17) *Varying Intensity, as against Regularity, of Sound Changes.*
Within the large corpus of writings on the character of sound changes,
heavy emphasis has traditionally been placed on the problem of regularity of recurrence, at the expense of the equally weighty and equally
legitimate problem of a sound change's variable intensity at different
periods of its ordinarily protracted agency. When we affirm that a
sound change in Language A was operative over a stretch of, say, four
centuries at least, we can tentatively measure its duration through
several mutually complementary techniques. We can seldom pinpoint
the actual start, but we are free to observe that the earliest records of
the shift, within the purview of Language A, fall into the first century
of its suspected activity. At the opposite end of the line, certain borrowings from Language B into A, on which the shift under study has
left its imprint, cannot, for cultural or historical reasons, antedate the
fourth century of its existence. The concluding segment of the line will
have the benefit of an extra-neat "break" if it can be demonstrated that
the next wave of borrowings no longer participated in the sound shift
at issue. Without impugning the validity of this series of familiar arguments we can still wonder whether the intensity of the shift was really
invariable over the entire period of four hundred years, or whether—
to indulge in just one flight of the imagination—it quickly reached its
all-time peak, then gradually lost momentum, tapered off, and, in the
end, became extinct. We can expect to gauge the changing degrees of
this intensity by pitting Sound Change X against other, contrastable
forces in language growth. Let us assume that some such neatly deline-

ated sound shift as diphthongization (X) clashes, at various successive steps, with rival forces—for instance, dissimilation in contact (Y) or at a distance (Y'), or else metaphony (Z). Let us further suppose that diphthongization succeeds in overcoming the resistance of these opposing forces, overwhelmingly in the first and barely in the second century of its existence, but fails to break their deadlock in the two concluding centuries of its four-hundred-year span (cf. Point (3), above). Granted the comparability of all the conditions involved, would it not be cogent to argue that the impact of the sound change under scrutiny has gradually weakened? Might not this hypothesis, in turn, help us to understand an otherwise paradoxical situation, namely, why a given change is allowed to occur at a certain moment, yet may, at a later juncture, be canceled by a league of the very same forces which could not, at the outset, prevent it from taking place, although they were already present and geared for action?

II

Exemplification of Point (5) through a Glance at Lat. -*RǴ*-, -*LǴ*-, and -*NǴ*- in Paleo-Romance Perspective. *The General Picture*

Advances in scientific insights have frequently been scored through scrupulous re-examination of all the loose ends left over after the successive or combined application of previously established methods. To formulate and exemplify one assumption seldom made in Romance quarters (and possibly elsewhere), namely that morphological conditions—specifically, characteristic or recurrent features of the verbal paradigm—may, in the last analysis, be held responsible for a baffling sound shift (see Point (5), above), the highly idiosyncratic Old Spanish development of Lat. -RG^{ei}-, LG^{ei}-, and -NG^{ei}- will here be thrown open for discussion. Section II is designed to furnish a bird's-eye view of the entire problem, to set off the erratic, self-contradictory trajectory of the three clusters in Spanish from their normal, perfectly transparent evolution in most if not all cognate languages (Old Provençal being another "outsider"), and to sketch in a very schematic causal explanation of the deviation thus isolated. In subsequent sections the varying degrees of anomaly in Old Spanish and Old Provençal will be gauged within the framework of the hypothesis advocated, attention will be given to the peculiar emergency situation—the *détresse phono-*

logique—which, in the first place, makes morphological interference with sound change more readily understandable, and a few tentative generalizations will be drawn concerning detection and diagnosis of such suspected interferences. Only by way of afterthought will a sampling of rival explanations be listed and discussed, as succinctly as possible, in an effort to show the source of their inadequacy.

In its narrowest projection and at first deliberately viewed out of context, the problem at hand can be described in the following terms:

The Old Spanish development of the Latin medial consonant groups (a) -RG-, (b) -LG-, and (c) -NG- before front vowels is puzzling within the edifice of Hispano-Latin phonology. An additional difficulty accrues to the outcome of the -NǴ- group inasmuch as, apart from the particular transmutation which places it in the neighborhood of the group listed under (a) and (b), its record shows traces of growth in two other directions; no neat hierarchy between these three slants (α, β, γ) has so far been established.

The parallelism between -RǴ-, -LǴ-, and -NǴ- consists in the shift of palatalized g (= ǵ) to z, a unit phoneme pronounced with or without affrication, depending on period, locus, and position within the word: [dz] or [z]. Examples from medieval sources (except for an occasional modern dialect form) include:

(a) ARGERE 'enclosure' (× MARGINE 'edge, boundary') > *ar-zén > mod. -cén 'margin,' ARGILLA 'potter's clay' > *arzilla*, BERGIDU > *Bierzo* (a territory in Leon), Late L. BURGĒNSE 'pertaining to a township' > *burzés* 'burgher,' ĒR(I)GERE 'to raise' > *erzer*, EXTERGERE > *estarzer* > *estarcir* 'to stencil, pounce,' SPAR-GERE 'to scatter, strew, sprinkle' > *esparzer*, TERG-ĒRE or -ĔRE 'to wipe (off), dry, clean, polish' > *terzer* 'to dry' (top. and anthrop.), VERGĒGIU > *Berzeo*;

(b) Ē- and *EX-MULGĒRE 'to milk (to the last drop)'—beside MULCĒRE 'to stroke (gently)'— > *esmuzir* > Ast. *esmucir* 'to milk' (with loss of the -L-, a circumstance causing little surprise in this context);

(c) Triple development:

(α) GINGĪVA 'gum' > *enzía*; SING-ULU, *-ELLU 'single, one alone, one each' > *senzi(e)llo* 'simple'; *UNG(U)ICULA 'little nail' (cf. recorded UNG-ELLA, -UELLA, -ICULUS) > *onzeja, -çeja*;

(β)-(γ) LONGĒ 'far off' > *lueñe*; PUNGENTE 'pricking, piercing, puncturing' > *(barba) pun(n)iente,* compare mod. *barbiponiente* 'beginning to grow a beard, apprenticed'; QUĪNGENTŌS 'five hundred' > *quin(n)ientos.*[1]

These latter outcomes, -nn- (i.e., *ñ*) and -n-, show such a degree of fluctuation before *ie* that, at least in this position, they seem to represent either two prongs or, still better, two phases of a single development, with -*ñié*- doomed, or tending, to yield ground to -*ñe*-.

Very frequently within the ranks of Group (c), and only by way of exception elsewhere, one observes the wavering between the three possible treatments: (α) change of *ǧ* to *z*, (β) merger of *ǧ* with the preceding consonant, conducive to the crystallization of a new consonant, and (γ) loss of *ǧ* without any concurrent change in the preceding consonant. Perhaps not insignificantly, the high rate of fluctuation in Group (c) coincides with the predominance of verbal families in that group, while the lower rate of fluctuation in Group (a) matches the nominal character of many, possibly most, of its constituents; Group (b) is too exiguous to invite any parallel comment on the spread of form classes. Thus, the rival reflexes of FRANGERE 'to break, shatter, dash to pieces' in the oldest texts were *franzer* and *frañer,* of which the latter before long emerged as the stronger. In the germane cases of CINGERE 'to gird, surround' and TANGERE 'to touch, seize, strike, play (an instrument),' the victory of -*ñer,* -*ñir* over **-zer* precedes the dawn of vernacular literature, and there is no lack of passages in archaic texts where, before -*ié*-, *n* replaces *ñ*: *cinientes* (Alexandre), *taniendo* (Ruiz). The reverse outcome of the competition between variants can be tidily documented in at least one instance: from IUNGERE 'to join, yoke' standard Spanish has inherited *uncir* (<-*zir*),

---

[1] The data adduced at this preliminary stage have been culled chiefly from R. Menéndez Pidal's writings: *Manual de gramática histórica española,* 6th ed. (Madrid: Espasa-Calpe, 1941), § 47:2*b,* and *Orígenes del español,* 3d ed. (Madrid: Espasa-Calpe, 1950; *Obras,* Vol. VIII), § 49, with a measure of extra attention to the tidiness of Latin bases. The author also cites the top. *Castil Anzul* (between Antequera and Aguilar, i.e., in Andalusia, not too far from Málaga and Cordova), tracing it to ANGĒLLAS; if this is so, has there occurred any secondary association with *azul* 'blue'?

while *uñir* 'to yoke,' along with its offshoot *uñidura* 'yoking,' is at present relegated to dialect speech (Extremadura, León, Salamanca, Valladolid, Zamora). Finally, a sharp split within a single family has occurred in the case of *RING-ERE, Class. Lat. -Ī 'to show the teeth, snarl, growl' > *reñir* 'to quarrel' as against the corresponding noun *renzilla* 'quarrel'; at older stages the latter, confusingly enough, was flanked by the var. *reñ-illa*.

It must be understood that in the medieval paradigm of verbs traceable to prototypes in -NGERE there survived certain forms, directly representative of the sequences -NGŌ or -NGA-, in which *-ng-* was temporarily left intact. Thus, the present indicative of the descendant of FRANGERE ran: 1 *frango*, 2–3 *franze(s)*, 4 *franzemos* or *frañemos*; and the subjunctive was *franga(s)*. The situation was further complicated by the accompanying gradual absorption of the given *-er* (<-ĒRE, -ĔRE) verbs by the vigorously expanding *-ir* (<-ĪRE) class, which, quite unlike the *-er* class, exercised a powerful metaphonic influence on the radical (hence mod. *riño* ~ *reñimos*). Add to this, as a separate factor of intricacy, the postmedieval unvoicing of *z* [dz] to *ç* [ts], later deaffricated to [θ] or [s], according to the region involved. It was the speakers' reaction to multidimensional complexities of this kind which, in the end, provoked widespread leveling, in the course of which the remaining *-ng-* forms were wiped out in favor of *-ñ-* or, occasionally, of *-nz-*, *-nç-*: *tango* > *taño* 'I touch,' *unga* > *unza* 'let me (or him, her) yoke.'[2]

The one nontrivial instance of wavering outside the domain of -NG- involves ARGENTU 'silver,' which yielded either *ariento* (cf. top. [Leon.] *Arintero*, [Gal]. *Arenteiro* < ARGENTĀRIU) or *arzinto (vivo)* = Hisp.-Ar. *azogue* 'quicksilver'; the *-rz-* form was favored, though not to the point of exclusiveness, indubitably in Mozarabic and possibly in Aragonese. Characteristically, the derivative ARGENTEU 'made of, covered with, silver; of the color of silver'—later substantivated in the vernacular: 'small weight, small coin'—followed a radi-

---

[2] Outside the verbal paradigm the leveling could, under certain circumstances, proceed in the opposite direction; cf. *burgués,* which hugs more closely the radical of *burg-o* than do the older forms *burz-és* (vernacular) and *burgés* (certainly an old Gallicism rather than a "cultismo," as J. Corominas, *DCELC,* I, 548*a,* rashly assumes).

cally different course. Its Hispanic product, whose inventory shows a good deal of fluctuation in regard to minor features, was in the main *arien-zo, -ço* (with the satellite formation *aren-, aran-çada* *'merchandise, terrain worth that coin'). Clearly, the alternative outcome **arzenço*, involving an affricated dental spirant at the start of two consecutive syllables, would, if it ever came into existence (say, in Mozarabic), have succumbed to the powerful dissimilatory trend.[3]

The transmutation of -NG- into [ɲ] and its further occasional shift to [n] before *-ié-* pose no serious problem within the total context of Romance phonology.[4] On the other hand, the emergence of *-z-* as the second ingredient of the cluster exposed to fronting is conspicuous in the extreme, whichever measuring rod the analyst favors to gauge the degree of irregularity.

For one thing, the broad trend in Romance has been to treat the second element of a dyadic medial group, especially if it was a stop, like its word-initial counterpart, leaving them both preferably intact; compare, with respect to *t*, APTĀRE 'to fit, adapt, get ready' > Sp. *atar* 'to tie' beside TŌTU 'whole' > *todo,* where apparent exceptions are detectable (as with MULTU 'much' > *mucho,* STRICTU 'tight' > *estrecho* 'narrow'), the erratic form is usually at least two steps removed from the base (cf. the intermediate stages preserved in Ptg. *muito, estreito*). The fact that, in the case under investigation, *l, n,* and *r* happen to constitute the first ingredient of such a cluster does not, of itself, lead one to expect any departure from the general tendency,

---

[3] This dissimilatory treatment calls to mind the preservation of the initial cluster in Sp. *clavija* 'pin, peg,' *playa* 'beach,' and the atypical shift FL- > *l* (FLACCIDU 'flabby, weak' > Sp. *lacio* 'withered, faded'), as explained in my article "The Interlocking of Narrow Sound Shift, Broad Phonological Pattern, . . . ," *ArL,* XV (1964), 144–173; XVI (1965), 1–33. See also J. R. Craddock's parallel comment ("A Critique of Recent Studies in Romance Diminutives," *RPh,* XIX [1965–1966], 286–325, esp. 315–318) on F. González Ollé's discovery of an important pattern in the distribution of *-uelo* and *-i(e)llo.*

[4] One is free to interpret the shift *-ñie-* > *-nie-* as an alternative to the widespread reduction of *-ié-* to *-e-* after a palatal consonant, in conjugation and in suffixal derivation: *dix(i)eron* 'they said,' *amarill-ento* 'yellowish' beside *gras-iento* 'greasy.' These two processes are quite different, with regard to the attendant circumstances, from the tendential monophthongization of *-ie-* to *-i-* and of *-ue-* to *-e-* in the transition from Old to Modern Spanish. (See Section VII, below, and the corresponding footnotes.)

compare the unvarying comportment of so capricious a phoneme as D
in DOMINU 'master' > *dueño*, on the one hand, and in CAL(I)-
DĀRIA 'kettle, stove' > *caldera*, SOL(I)DU 'solid (substance)' >
sueldo 'copper coin, soldier's pay,' VENDERE 'to sell' > *vender*,
MORDĒRE 'to bite' > *morder*, on the other. Quite a few departures
from this standard of preservation are on record, true, but they usually
either (a) have a bearing on the first element of the cluster, which in
the process may altogether disappear, (α) leaving traces (ALTERU
'one of two' > *otro* 'other' via *outro*, cf. Portuguese) or (β) failing to
do so (MORSU 'bite, biting' > *mueso*—as in *atar,* above) or, if they
affect the second element at all, (b) entail a minor adjustment
(BARBA 'beard' > OSp. *barva*, HERBA 'grass' > OSp. *yerva*; the
adjustment is here defensibly called minor against the background of
the well-known Hispano-Latin *b* ~ *v* fluctuation). Since word-initially
neither Ǵ- nor the consonantized I of, say, IĀ-, IĒ-NUĀRIU 'January'
with which Ǵ- tended to coalesce in late provincial Latin ever yielded
/z/, but rather disappeared—compare GELĀRE 'to freeze' > *elar,*
GERMĀNU '(half-)brother' > *ermano, IĒNUĀRIU* > *enero*[5]—
the three clusters *-nz-*, *-lz-*, and *-rz-* must, on this score of broad patterning, rank as highly idiosyncratic.

This judgment is unlikely to become subject to revision if we include
in our field of observation a few cognate languages. In closely related
Portuguese, for instance, events took a markedly different, far less astonishing course. Except for a dwindling lexical nucleus which stands
apart (GERMĀNU > *irmão*, [gloss] IECUĀRIA 'giblets,' lit. 'dish
made of liver' [IECUR] > *iguaria* 'tidbit,' cf. OSp. *yegüería*),[6] the re-

---

[5] There are a few details to observe regarding the adjacent vowel: IĒIŪNU
yielded *ayuno* (cf. also *desayuno* 'breakfast') rather than **eyuno* by virtue
of the vacillation between IĒ- and IĀ- which has left vestiges in Latin literature and may have been more sharply profiled in provincial speech, in all likelihood; the loss of I- was extra early here, as in *uncir* < IUNGERE, by way
of recoil from medial -I-. GENUCULU > OSp. *inojo* 'knee' recalls, in its
raising of *e* to *i*, the case of GERMĀNU > Ptg. *irmão*; the var. *finojo* owes its
f-either to confusion with *fe-, fi-nojo* 'fennel' < FĒNUCULU or to the transfer
of *f-* from the verb figuring in the stereotyped phrase *fincar los inojos* 'to kneel
down,' on the strength of the partial identity of *fin-* and *in-*. (For further elaboration see "La F inicial adventicia en español antiguo," *RLiR*, XVIII [1954],
161–191, esp. 185–190.)

[6] On *iguaria* see my article in *Language,* XX (1944), 108–130, and the post-

flex of Ǵ- and J alike was /ž/, presumably affricated at the earliest stage: GELĀRE > *gear* (cf. *geada* 'frost'), GENERU 'son-in-law' > *genro,* GENUCULU '(little) knee' > *jẽolho* > *joelho,* IACĒRE 'to lie, rest' > *jazer,* IĀNUĀRIU > *janeiro* (beside IĀN-ELLA [dim. of IĀNUA 'outer door, entrance'] > *janela* 'window'), IĒIŪNĀRE 'to fast' > *jejuar,* DIĀRIA [dj-, j-] 'daily (quota of work)' > *geira* 'yoke of land,' lit. 'day's plowing of a yoke of oxen.' Word-medially, after a consonant, the same /ž/ appears, even following an N, especially in the ranks of the -NGERE verbs: SPARGERE > *espargir,* orig. *-er,* TANGERE > *tanger* 'to ring (bells), play (an instrument), goad (a herd),' LONGĒ > *longe*; characteristically, despite the obvious temptation to dissimilate the two *g*'s appearing at the start of two successive syllables, speakers of Portuguese have allowed GINGĪVA to survive in its pristine shape almost unaltered, as *gengiva.*[7]

On the Italian side, to briefly adduce the Tuscan evidence: The situation in and around Florence is very much as in Portugal, except that the affrication of /dž/ has here been more faithfully preserved. Once again, we encounter the expected parallelism of the two positions: on the one hand, GENERU > *genero,* GENUCULU > *ginocchio,* IĒNUĀRIU > *gennaio*; on the other SPARGERE > *spargere,* SURGERE > *sorgere,*[8] TERGERE > *tergere,* MULGĒRE > *mungere* 'to milk, extract, sponge on,' EXPINGERE 'to push out' (from PANGERE 'to fix, drive in, undertake, agree upon') > *spingere* 'to push, thrust'; and, eloquently paired off in a single word, in defiance of the ubiquitously latent dissimilatory trend, we find G[i] and -G[i] in GINGĪVA > *gengiva.*[9]

---

script, *ibid.,* XXI (1945), 264–265. Despite the sporadic criticism that these writings aroused, I am still convinced that the solution advocated was correct.

[7] For simplicity's sake, in dealing with Portuguese and French data I disregard the fact that, at a certain evolutionary phase, syllable-final *n* began to dissolve, with varying speed and results, into the preceding vowel.

[8] The difficulty is compounded by the fact that certain Latin bases have been locally transmitted in different strata; thus, being vernacular, Fr. *sourdre* and It. *sorgere* are endowed with evidential force which is absent from Sp. *surgir,* visibly a crude Latinism.

[9] At first blush the segment *-nc-* of Fr. *gencive* < GINGĪVA is reminiscent of its OSp. near-equivalent *-nz-* in *enzía.* But the resemblance may be specious; in all likelihood the OFr. var. *gengive,* at present peculiar to the southern belt of Oïl dialects (see E. Gamillscheg, *Etymologisches Wörterbuch der fran-*

French offers an entirely different picture, inasmuch as the early syncope of the weakest vowel here produced a series of unattractive consonant clusters which speakers later smoothed over by intercalating homorganic "buffer consonants," particularly -d-: IUNGERE > *[džoɲrə] > joindre [žwɛ̃drə], PLANGERE 'to beat one's breast' (in token of pain or mourning) *[plaɲrə] > plaindre 'to lament.' It will be remembered, from a celebrated article by J. Gilliéron, that MUL-GĒRE was on its way to becoming moudre, but swerved from the straight path, because speakers shied away from the threat of this verb's coexistence with the homonymic progeny of MOLERE 'to grind.' The trajectory of -RǴ- is exemplified by SURGERE 'to rise up' > sourdre. Word-initially the outcome of Ǵ-, J- was [dž], eventually deaffricated: GENERU > gendre, IĀNUĀRIU > janvier, DIURNU 'daily' > jour 'day.' Because it is hazardous to reconstruct the preliterary form that underlies, say, sourdre, it seems wisest to withhold judgment on the extent to which proto-French may have abandoned the broad phonological trend in Romance, a trend so clearly discernible in Portuguese and Tuscan.

Old Provençal, in striking contrast to Old French even though on a distinctly more modest scale than Old Spanish, did occasionally exhibit the change of postconsonantal -Ǵ- to -z-, alongside the rivaling shift to /ž/ (spelled g). Thus, (a) ARGENTU here yielded argen; (b) BUR-GĒNSE cast off both bor-ges and -zes; (c) FUL-GUR, *-GER 'lightning' plus the verbs SPARGERE and SURGERE emerged on the local scene as fólzer, espárzer, and sórzer, respectively. The prevalence of verbs in Group (c), as against the predominantly nominal character of Groups (a) and (b), seems, to say the least, noteworthy. It is the first of these three developments which matches most neatly the local course of word-initial Ǵ-: GENTE 'clan, breed, people' > gen, Gr.-Lat. GYRĀRE 'to turn, revolve' > girar. As regards -NǴ-, however, Provençal displays the same development as Spanish in lueñe < LONGĒ: compare fránher < FRANGERE and plánher < PLANGERE (with the digraph -nh- signaling [ɲ]).

---

zösischen Sprache [Heidelberg: C. Winter, 1928], p. 465a, with clues to further literature), represents the original regular outcome, while the innovation gencive may be due to a lexical blend triggered by consonant dissimilation, or to the dissimilatory trend pure and simple.

This partial coincidence of native strata in Old Spanish and Old Provençal—two languages geographically noncontiguous, each boasting a lexicon interspersed with easily recognizable mutual borrowings—is a matter of considerable importance. Whichever explanation of the rise of Cons. $+ z$ we may favor, the hypothesis endorsed must snugly fit two different contexts.

To revert to Spanish: given all these complications, it is baffling that an expert of the stature of R. Menéndez Pidal should—as late as 1950 (after abjuring a different interpretation, long championed by himself in the wake of others)—have referred to an *evolución perfectamente comprensible.* Quite the contrary: phonologically the development represents a genuine crux. It is only after running into a blind alley in our strictly phonological operations that we can, with a clean conscience, solicit help from a neighboring subdiscipline.

In this impasse the history of Spanish verbal inflection seems to offer the missing link. Every scrap of evidence points to the powerful analogical influence exerted, in the two moods of the present tense, by DĪCŌ, -ĔRE, a verb whose paradigm is characterized by the neatly patterned interchange of -*g*- and -*z*-: (ind.) *digo, dize(s)* . . ., (subj.) *diga(s).* The influence here posited is visible in the attraction OSp. *dizer* exerted on *fazer* < FACIŌ, -ERE: while Portuguese (1 *faço,* 2 *fazes,* . . . 7 *faça*) and Italian (1 *faccio,* . . . 5 *facete,* . . . 7 *faccia*) preserve quite faithfully—after one makes the necessary phonological allowances—the configuration of the Latin prototypal forms, Old Spanish tramples upon the tradition by substituting 1 *fago* for **faço* and 7 *faga* for **faça,* thus giving rise to two perfectly parallel series, one regular: *digo, diz(es),* . . . *diga,* the other decidedly analogical: *fago, faz(es)* . . . *faga.* But the influence of the voiced velar, which acts as the central pillar of *digo, diga* (meanwhile reinforced by *fago, faga*), went much farther: the -*g*- infiltrated *oya* < AUDIA(M) and, on the dialect level (sporadically also in Golden Age texts), *huya* < FUGIA(M), leading to *oiga* and *huiga,* and made its pressure felt in many other ways; compare the subjunctives (obs.) *fierga, ponga, salga, tenga,* (obs.) *tuelga, valga, venga*—clearly echoing *di-ga, ha-ga,* also archaic *franga, tanga*—beside the corresponding infinitives *ferir, poner, salir, tener, toller* (> *tullir*), *valer, venir.*[10]

[10] This situation can again be contrastively dramatized through reference to

One need not, of course, hold DĪC-Ō, -AM > Sp. *dig-o, -a* alone responsible for the propagation of the velar. In Tuscan, where DĪCŌ yields *dico* and FACIŌ survives as *faccio,* the crystallization of *pongo, tengo,* and *vengo* must, for instance, be attributed exclusively to the combined weight of the FINGŌ, PANGŌ, PINGŌ, TANGŌ, TING(U)Ō . . . series, which also happens to be lexically more deeply entrenched in the Appenine Peninsula (cf. *spingere*). In the light of this evidence, it is wisest to postulate for proto-Spanish the combined pressure of *digo* and the gradually receding *-ngo* verbs. Once this assumption has been made, only one step separates us from the further conjecture that the present-tense paradigm of *dezir,* with its characteristic alternation of *-g-* and *-z-* (*digo, dizes, diga*), may have left an imprint of this alternation on, say, *frañer,* producing *fran-go, -zer* . . . alongside differently leveled *frañ-o, -e(s)* . . . and in preference to traditional *frango, frañes,* which for a while had proved immune to deflection. The novelty of the assumption consists solely in hypothesizing the analogical spread, from an established focus of diffusion, not of the characteristic *g* viewed in isolation, but of the striking alternation *g:z* taken en bloc. Given the well-known cohesion of all *-er* and *-ir* verbs in Spanish (a residual or closed series), it will further be readily granted that the innovation of *-nz-,* sparked by the contact of *dezir/ fazer* with the *-ñer* verbs, could have leaped to other verbs of the same conjugation classes (*-er/ -ir*), inviting the formation, under comparable conditions, of *-lz-* and *-rz-* clusters. The concluding and, theoretically, most noteworthy—if problematic—step in the chain of events here visualized would then have been the diffusion of *-lz-, -nz-, -rz-* to nonverbal components of the lexicon, culminating in the crystallization of a "sound law" unattached to any particular form-class.

---

the conservative state of affairs in Portuguese, where one finds *tenha* < TENEAM, *venha* < VENIAM (and, in their wake, *ponha* despite PŌNAM), also *valha* < VALEAM and *saia* 'I may go out' < SALIAM 'I may jump.' The analogical spread of the velar in Spanish involved, of course, a long-drawn-out process, and one is free to cite instances of late contamination such as *oiga* and *huiga* or, for that matter, *caiga* < *ca(y)a* < CADAM and *traiga* < *tra(y)a* 'I may bring' < TRAHAM 'I may drag, pull along' only on the explicit assumption that they represent distant reverberations of the same shift—observable at an early date in *faga* and *fierga*—which is here held indirectly responsible for the rise of unorganic *-lz-, -nz-,* and *-rz-.*

III.

Three Additional Considerations

These sweeping contentions are certainly in need, first, of a measure of qualification and, second, of corroborative support. Our first check must be on the comportment of Old Provençal, whose partial affinity to Old Spanish has been insufficiently stressed in the past.[11]

In the Provençal deposit of DĪCERE the alternation of radical-final -*g* and -*z* is not as sharply silhouetted as in Old Spanish, in consequence of the deeper erosion of word-final vowels—witness the 1 pres. ind. *dic* (< *digo), the inf. *dir(e)*, the 2 pres. ind. *ditz*, as against OSp. *digo*, *di-* or *de-zir*, and *dizes*, respectively. But enough of the alternation remains (pres. subj. *diga*, 4–6 pres. ind. *diz-em, -etz, -on*, impf. ind. *di-* or *de-zia*, ger. *dizen*) to give substance to the surmise that some influence—distinctly weaker than in Old Spanish—could have acted on certain -GERE verbs.[12] These expectations are fully borne out by the rather tidy record available for inspection. While the -NGERE verbs here stand consistently apart (*cénher* < CINGERE, *destrénher* 'to harass' < DIS + STRINGERE, *esténher* 'to quench' < EX- TING(U)ERE, *fénher* 'to feign' < FINGERE, *fránher* < FRAN- GERE, *plánher* < PLANGERE), the -RGERE verbs supply a few telling examples: *sorzia* < SURGĒBAT and *sórzer* < SURGERE, in their relation to *sorga* < SURGAT, may have been proportionately arrived at on the model of *dezia: diga*;[13] the same supposition holds true for *esparzer*. The point to remember is the correlation, gratifying from the vantage point of Spanish, between (a) the narrower range, in

[11] Surprisingly, W. Meyer-Lübke, in re-examining this entire issue toward the very end of his career ("Zur Geschichte von lat. *G^e G^i* und *J* im Roma- nischen," *VRom,* I [1936], 1–31), paid proper attention to the Provençal (esp. p. 28, with a reference to C. Appel's *Lautlehre*) but not to the hastily sketched Spanish facet of the elusive problem.

[12] In citing Old Provençal forms I am guided by authoritative handbooks such as O. Schultz-Gora, *Altprovenzalisches Elementarbuch.*

[13] Additional models available in Old Provençal, though not in Old Spanish, included *iaz-er* 'to lie' < IACĒRE vs. p. ptc. *iag-ut, lez-er* 'to be permitted' < LICĒRE vs. p. ptc. *leg-ut, nózer* 'to damage' <NOCĒRE vs. p. ptc. *nog-ut, plaz-er* 'to please' < PLACĒRE vs. p. ptc. *plag-ut,* etc. The characteristic -*g*- ingredient of the past participles in question has been extracted from the cor- responding preterites, in which it reflects ancestral -ŲĪ.

Old Provençal, of the /g/ ~ /z/ alternation in the paradigm here assumed to have started the entire movement, namely DĪCERE; and (b)
the narrower scope, to the north of the Pyrenees, of the shift -Ǵ- >
-z-, the dual restriction (unknown to Spanish) being phonological:
only -RǴ- is affected, and morphological: verb forms almost exclusively are involved (though nominal *borzes* beside *borges* is on record).

Another consideration—this time within the confines of Spanish—
on which the acceptance of the hypothesis here championed may be
made contingent, is whether a certain internal difficulty in the expected
sound development could have produced an emergency—or, to speak
with Gilliéron and his followers, a *détresse*—which would make the
course taken by the community's tone-setting speakers more readily
understandable in retrospect. Through a noteworthy coincidence, the
development of word-initial Ǵ-, J- from Latin to Old Spanish, an evolution which, on the strength of a broad phonological trend, might
very well have matched the controversial changes undergone by Ǵ, J
word-medially after consonant, is itself far from transparent. If ana-
logues may be borrowed from other Romance languages, the likeliest
reflexes of Ǵ- and J- would have been /j/ or /ž/. Traces of both these
developments are on record, with /j/ < J- surviving especially before
central and back vowels. It is not yet quite clear how they can be most
persuasively hierarchized; compare IUNCTA > *junta* 'junction, seam,
joint, gasket' beside *yunta* 'yoke (of animals),' the chances being that
/ž/ points toward a more aristocratic pronunciation (cf. refined *joven*
beside racy *moço* 'young'). Total loss of the initial consonant in this
environment is rare and almost invariably attributable to dissimilation
of palatals at the start of successive syllables (cf. *ayuno* 'fast' <
IĒIŪNU, *unc-ir* 'to yoke' < IUNǴ-). Before a front vowel the loss of
the consonant is, conversely, the norm: GERMĀNU > OSp. *ermano*,
while its occasional preservation ranks as a clue to learned transmission: *general* (as against truly vernacular Ptg. *gèral*). If we assume
that *yermano, *yenzía 'gum' were the proto-Castilian forms, it can be
argued—and the argument is not new—that the reduction of *ye, that
is, *ié*, to *e* was the direct consequence of the close association of the *ie*
diphthong with the stressed syllable.[14] Given the demonstrably late

---

[14] Characteristically, Old Spanish preferred *otri* and *otre* 'somebody else' to
otrie, nadi (or *ninguno*) 'nobody' to *nadie; alguien,* introduced into the literary

date of the diphthongization Ĕ > *ie*, the resultant monophthongization *ye-* > *e-* in pretonic syllable, through overreaction, would have to be assigned to a still later date. Wavering between **ye-* and *e-* in words like *(y)ermano, (y)enzía* could have produced the setting for the sporadic elimination of *(y)-* from other contexts where it was bothersome, as in *(y)unzir*—with dissimilation, sporadic or saltatory shift, and regular sound change working hand in hand, as they often do.[15]

If we now ask ourselves just what events could be posited as ideally normal on the assumption that at the outset /j/ also developed from Ǵ medially after consonant, the answer is that -LǴ- might have cast off **/lj/* and, by the same token, -NǴ- should have led to **/nj/* and -RǴ- to **/rj/*. For -NǴ- this line of reasoning assuredly holds, with /ɲ/, as in LONGĒ > *lueñe*, actually emerging as the predictable next step. For -LǴ- a parallel sequence of events, conducive to /λ/, would be self-explanatory, but the material available is too scant to yield any useful information on the rate of recurrence of this evolution. In the case of /rj/, however, a development essentially metathetic, that is, quite at variance with that of /nj/, might be anticipated if one were to take one's cue from VARIU 'variegated, spotted, changeable' > *ve(i)ro* (as in the furrier's term *vero*), -ĀRIU > *-e(i)ro*, and the like. The single and very cautious assumption, then, that Ǵ-, J- tended to yield in Castilian /j/ rather than /ž/ as in most cognate languages (including Portuguese and Catalan at its flanks) accounts for the genesis of major disruptions both word-initially (especially through the late recoil from **ye-* in pretonic position) and word-medially after consonant (particularly through the varying impact of /j/ on the preceding /n/ and /r/); also—a signal additional obstacle—for the discrepancy between the evolutionary trends in these two positions ordinarily known, at least in Romance, for their marked mutual affinity.[16]

---

language from the western dialects (where it bordered on deeply entrenched OGal.-Ptg. *alguén*), was originally stressed on the *e*, as is known from rhymes.

[15] Compare my observations in "Linguistics as a Genetic Science" (in *Lang.*, XLIII [1967], 223–245) on R. Posner's and K. Togeby's mutually exclusive views on the agency of consonant dissimilation.

[16] Inexplicably, J. D. M. Ford, *Old Spanish Readings* (Boston: Ginn & Co., 1911 and later printings), p. xxxviii, toyed with the idea that, after *n* and *r*, /j/ first became *dž*, then *dz*; for details, see the appended *historique du problème*. For one attempt to arrive at a total view of G^{e,i}, in Peninsular perspec-

To sum up: There very definitely did arise a state of acute phonological emergency in proto-Spanish with regard to Ǵ-, J-, a situation favoring, even inviting, a kind of external intervention as one avenue of escape from excessive structural fragmentation. Under these circumstances, contagious effect of DĪC-Ō, -ĔRE and of the -NGŌ, -NGERE verbs, that is to say, the extension, by force of analogy and by the interplay of the proportion $g:z$, of an inflectional pattern to the point of its elevation to the rank of a sound correspondence, gains in plausibility. One could speak of a transition from the morphophonemic to the phonemic level.

Interestingly, there exists an additional instance of the substitution of z in Old Spanish for $*j$ traceable to Ǵ; again the process awaits clarification. This time, an isolated (if important and semantically many-faceted) word is involved: *rezio* 'strong, thick, coarse, harsh, hard' (mod. *recio*), in whose prototype the -Ǵ- was surrounded by front vowels: RIGIDUS 'stiff, rough.' If we ask ourselves: What should the outcome of RIGIDU have been? and if we fall back on such classic correspondences as FRĪGIDU 'cold' > *fri(d)o* (via *friyo*), LEGERE 'to pick, read' > *leer*, MAGIS 'more' > *ma(i)s*, MAGISTRU 'master, teacher' > *maestro*, NĀVIGĀRE 'to sail' > *navear*,[17] the answer to our question will be **reyio* (or at most **reido*), a locally most unappealing form by virtue of both the falling diphthong *ei*, barely tolerated by Old Spanish (cf. the Catalanism *pleito* 'lawsuit' beside native *plazdo* < PLACITU, also disyllabic *reÿ* 'king,' trisyllabic *reína* 'queen'), and the latent instability of *-io*, a tidy suffixal marker of the far-flung adjectival series moored to -IDU:[18] *limp-io* 'clear,' *suz-io* 'dirty,' *teb-*, *tib-io* 'lukewarm.' Small wonder that on the local scene so infelicitous an outcome of RIGIDU exerted no attraction on the nearly parallel product of FRĪGIDU, in eloquent contrast to the events that

---

tive and with a structuralist slant, see E. Alarcos Llorach, *Arch.*, IV (1954), 330–342; cf. K. Baldinger, *La formación de los dominios lingüísticos en la Península Ibérica* (Madrid: Editorial Gredos, 1963), p. 24, and my own comment, infra.

[17] See R. Menéndez Pidal, *Manual de gramática histórica española*, 6th ed., § 41₃.

[18] For a panoramic view of this problem, which awaits monographic treatment, see my article "Multiple versus Simple Causation in Linguistic Change," in the Festschrift *To Honor Ramon Jakobson: Essays on the Occasion of His*

occurred in French (where OFr. *freit, froit* presuppose the influence of *roit*, the common ancestor of mod. *raide* and *roide*) and in Italian (where *freddo* points to an *-ĬGD- rather than -ĪGD- segment). One is tempted to go one step further: Far from exerting pressure on FRĪGIDU, the hypothetical proto-Spanish malformation that sprang from RĪGIDU could easily have succumbed to the influence of some other word, preferably an adjective forming part of the same close-knit series. Granted the likelihood of such a course of events, SŪCIDU 'juicy, sappy' > OSp. *suzio* might be credited with providing a model for the replacement by *rezio* of some such unviable form as **reyio*. There was no dearth of semantic contacts between the two adjectives here suspected of interaction, though one has the impression that these affinities were too weak to have of themselves provided the initial stimulus. Nevertheless such links could easily have sufficed to translate into action the speakers' recoil from **reyio*; that they are not merely a figment of one analyst's imagination follows from the reverse pressure plausibly exercised in Portuguese by the representative of RIGIDU > *rijo* on SŪCIDU > *sujo*.[19] *Rezio* differs, then, from *enzia, terzer*, both in phonological detail and in the choice of specific analogical models; it shares with the words here under consideration the secondary character of the -*z*-, its source in the parent language, and the avoidance of **/j/ in certain contexts.

IV.

The Mechanism of the Sound Changes and Their "Inner Diffusion"

It was the assumption in Section II that the striking relation *diG-o, -a : diZ-e(s)*, within the contagious paradigm of a verb independently known for its aggressiveness, could have supplied a handy model for *franG-o, -a : franZ-e(s)* in rivalry with, and eventually as a substitute for, the older *frañ-e(s)*. Similarly, *esparG-o, -a : esparZ-e(s)* may have

---

Seventieth Birthday (The Hague: Mouton, 1967), II, 1228–1246.

[19] Since intervocalic G before vowel disappears in Portuguese no less consistently than in Spanish (LEGERE > *ler*), it is advisable to start from the stage **rigju* which must have been reached on the local scene very early, given the extra-quick extinction of -D- along the Atlantic Coast. The (convergent) groups -*dj*- and -*gj*- tended to yield /ž/ in the West, but /j/ or zero in the Center unless the Center opted for a learned form; contrast Ptg. -*ejar* with Sp. -*ear* < -IDJĀRE, Ptg. *enveja* 'envy' < INVIDIA with Sp. *envidia*.

replaced an older ineffectual *esparye(s)*. The reason for the vulnerability of the latter form can be thus pinpointed: Had it been an isolated word, unfettered by any paradigmatic ties, the natural course for the speakers to follow would have been to transmute it into *espaire(s)*; compare the unimpeded development of the common suffix -ĀRIU > -*airo* > -*e(i)ro*. But since the word at issue was the captive of its membership in a verbal alliance, this smooth road was blocked by the menace of the genesis of two allomorphs such as *esparg-* ~ *espair-*, paired off in a pattern unprecedented in Hispano-Romance conjugation. With /j/ thus immobilized, through paradigmatic tightness and cohesion, in its phonologically no longer comfortable position after, rather than before, the /r/, its analogical replacement by /rz/, suggested by *digo* ~ *dizes*, must have come to speakers as a welcome alternative, as an actual relief.

Outside the domain of conjugation, but still within the realm of morphology, we discover derivational relationships that may have favored similar solutions. Granted that BURGĒNSE in all likelihood initially yielded some such product as *boryés*, the phonologically tempting further advance to *boirés* (cf. CORIU 'leather' > *coiro* [as in Ptg.] > *cuero*) was scotched by the coexistence—and continued semantic proximity—of the primitive *borgo*. A very opportune spark could at that stage of latent tension have flown from the SPARGERE to the BURGUS family, placing *boryés/ borzés* alongside *esparye(s)/ esparzes*.[20]

Once the exclusive link to the verb was loosened or relinquished, any late and unremovable /rj/, /lj/ would tend to cast off /rz/, /lz/, while the temporary rivalry of doublets involving /rj/ beside /rz/

---

[20] I realize that OProv. *bor-zés* beside -*gés* poses slightly different problems in the absence of any visible or inferable /j/. Could it be that the preservation of the *r*, vitally needed in a family headed by *borc* < *borgo*, was better ensured in the embedment of the /rz/ than of the /rž/ cluster? Another problem, lexical in nature, must temporarily be left in abeyance: While OSp. OPtg. *borgés* is clearly of Gallo-Romance provenience judging by its form (cf. Fr. *bour-geois,* orig. -*geis*)—as were later to be in semantic content the analogically reshaped *burgu-és* 'middle-class citizen' and -*esía*—the exact relation (borrowing?) of OSp. *bor-, bur-zés* to OProv. *borzés* awaits definitive clarification, on the scale of a full-fledged word biography. The preliminary analysis here subscribed to reckons with the autochthonous status of OSp. *borzés,* thus implying some kind of polygenesis of the -*rz-* < -RG- cluster in the two languages.

would, like any state of fluctuation, provoke the agency of codeterminants on a liberal scale. Thus, at the phase */arjiλa/, the descendant of ARGILLA could have profited from the ubiquitously latent dissimilatory trend in changing to *arzilla* and thus eschewing the sequence /rj . . . λ/, obnoxious through its excess of palatality. The final phase would be marked by the analogical penetration of -*rz*-, -*lz*-, -*nz*-, riding the crest of a vogue, even into nooks and crannies of the lexicon where speakers could derive no perceptible benefit from its prevalence over rival forms.

V.

Some Procedural Remarks

If the concrete cases here inspected under microscope constitute a fair sample of the problems falling under the rubric "Morphological Interference with Sound Change," a few tentative generalizations suggest themselves at this point. Diagnostically, it seems wisest to start from the axiomatic assumption that most sound changes can be accounted for in terms of a phonological system's internal balance and economy. It is only where explanations of this order fail, without undue stretching, to do justice to ascertainable facts that the analyst is well advised to try out a "second string" of possible factors of causation. This strategy has traditionally been adhered to where suspicion of borrowing from an adjoining language was at issue (lateral pressure); some scholars have further applied it to assessments of the plausibility of substratum influence (vertical pressure). It seems theoretically defensible and also feasible to attach to this second string the possibility, rare in some languages yet conceivably frequent in others, of inflectional pressure.

In many cases the first step will be the detection of an embarrassing discrepancy between (1) a broad phonological trend (such as the prevalent coincidence, in Romance, of consonantal development [a] word-initially and [b] medially after consonant) and (2) a specific sound correspondence or a set of such narrower correspondences (such as the triple shift characteristic of Old Spanish: -NǴ- > -*nz*-, -LǴ- > -*lz*-, and -RǴ- > -*rz*-). Where substratum influence and lateral borrowing cannot be invoked, the probability of a starting point concealed inside an inflectional paradigm increases very sharply. If two or more noncontiguous cognate languages show varying dosages of the same treatment, and if this significant differential can be persuasively harmonized with the discrepancies between the inflectional paradigms thought to have set these developments in motion, so much the better: witness, in our special problem, the understandably unequal scopes of adventitious *z* in Old Spanish and Old Provençal. The concluding step in the operation is to ask oneself what ideal narrow developments— only marginally on record, if at all—can be extrapolated from the known broad phonological trend. If these theoretically normal developments abounded in stumbling blocks for the speakers, the spread of the innovation (in this instance, of the *z*) from the paradigm of the verb, via certain proportional relationships fostered by fluctuation, to the core of the system of sound correspondences ceases to be erratic. By way of afterthought, one may then examine some evolutions which give the impression of embodying parallels. Even if this first impression of close resemblance evaporates upon closer inspection, as was true of *rezio* < RIGIDU, certain recurrent isolable features within each ensemble of circumstances—for example, the substitution of analogical /z/ for **/j/ in both *rezio* and *enzía* < GINGĪVA—may be worthy of sustained attention.

VI

A Bird's-Eye View of Earlier Analyses

A retrospective survey of earlier opinions is appended here, less for the sake of its intrinsic significance than *par acquit de conscience*, as it were. Incidental references to morphological pressures as a possible or probable molder of sound changes are, of course, scattered over many linguistic writings, old and new.[21] Also, suspicion of an analogical

---

[21] Thus, Ford, *Old Spanish Readings*, p. xxxiv, remarking on the unexpected loss of -*g*- before *a* and *o* in certain verb forms (*humear* 'to smoke, steam' < FŪMIGĀRE, *liar* 'to tie' < LIGĀRE, *lidiar* 'to tie' < LĪTIGĀRE, *rumiar* 'to ruminate' < RŪMIGĀRE: also 1 sg. *lío, lidio,* etc.), wondered "whether the loss of the *g* did not commence in them with the forms of the verb whose ending began with *e*: LIGENT > *lien*." On the more modern concept (H. Lausberg, R. L. Politzer) of *détresse morphologique,* see C. Blaylock, *RPh,* XVIII (1964–1965), 267. Morphological conditions as possible determinants of sound changes are very clearly isolated by R. Posner in her critique of O. Nandriş's Rumanian studies and in her skillful arbitration of the recent con-

spread of OSp. *-zir* from a few key verbs to other infinitives (or rather paradigms) is not entirely new,[22] but its original advocate stopped short of taking the vitally important second step, namely that of concluding that the analogical *-z-*, after its diffusion over certain verbal paradigms, might ultimately have wormed its way into the strictly phonological domain. Yet, on the whole, the discussion has been distinctly barren, in part as a result of several recalcitrant etymologies, which acted as so many stumbling blocks,[23] in part because scholars could afford either to disregard with impunity the rise of *-lz-*, *-nz-*, *-rz-* altogether (on account of the meager lexical representation of these clusters?)[24] or, misled by their atomistic attitude, to state it as a bare fact, left unintegrated and unexplained.[25]

---

troversy between L. Romeo and F. Schürr anent Romance diphthongization (see *RPh,* XIX [1965–1966], 450–459, esp. 454 and 457ff.).

[22] O. J. Tallgren[-Tuulio], *Estudios sobre la "Gaya" de [Pero Guillén de] Segovia* (Helsinki, 1907), p. 83, §§ 23f. Strictly speaking, Tallgren posited the joint influence of (a) *dezir, -duzir* 'to lead,' *luzir* 'to shine,' *nuzir* 'to harm' < NOCĒRE, plus *arrezir* 'to grow stiff with cold' (based on *rezio*) and (b) *esparzir, estarzir* < EXTERGERE, *unzir,* also *sar-, sur-zir* 'to darn' = mod. *zurcir* (cf. Ptg. *serzir*) on certain infinitives which might otherwise have yielded *-cir*; but since, of the two groups implicated, only (a) is entirely transparent in its phonological behavior, one may modify his hypothesis to the effect that Group (b) was itself deflected from its initially autonomous course by Group (a) before the two groups, joining forces, brought their combined pressure to bear on other verbs in the fifteenth century.

[23] Thus, the equation *senzi(e)llo* < SING-ULU, *-ELLU, introduced by J. Cornu (1880) in lieu of Diez's untenable *SIMPLICELLU, caused considerable embarrassment to the pioneers; the background of *arcén* 'border, edge, brim' (in particular, its conceivable relation to a by-form of AGGER 'rampart') provoked hot discussion (Diez, S. Bugge, and others); the wisdom of operating with *RICIDU or *RECIDU, in preference to RIGIDU, was seriously weighed (e.g., by E. Gorra in 1898 and by Tallgren in 1907), inviting an occasional side glance at Alb. *rekethe,* among others.

[24] This statement applies to A. Horning (1883), to J. Saroïhandy (1902), and to such other students of Old Spanish sibilants as moved in too narrow a groove.

[25] Compare the relevant treatises of C. Michaëlis [de Vasconcelos] (1876), P. Förster (1880), R. J. Cuervo (1895). A. Zauner, in *Altspanisches Elementarbuch* (Heidelberg: C. Winter, 1908), though perfectly aware of the coexistence of (a) *estreñer* 'to tighten' < STRINGERE, *lueñe, tañer* (§ 50) and (b) *enzía, senziello* beside *esparzer* and *burzés* (§ 71), was worried, not about this major discepancy, but about a minor detail: the appearance in a few texts

Among the explicative conjectures the following deserve to be set off:

(a) An appeal to consonant dissimilation involving the assumed unvoicing of the second member of a set in the case of GINGĪVA > Fr. *gencive*, Sp. *encía* (Meyer-Lübke, 1890).[26] The same scholar on that occasion attributed *sencillo* to the influence of SINCĒRU and, possibly, to the coexistence of *uncir/ uñir*, wondering whether the discrepancy separating *arienzo* (Ǵ > ø) from *esparcer, ercer, arcén,* and *ancilla* (Ǵ > θ) should be traced to varying vowel qualities or to a dissimilatory trend. Any such explanation, accounting for each word individually and abounding in doubts and alternatives, is unacceptable in the context of phonology; the intrinsic difficulty was here compounded by the author's inability to segregate medieval from modern graphies and forms.

(b) The contrast *riño* 'I quarrel' / *riña* 'feud' (n.) : *rencilla* 'bicker' (n.) seems to point to word stress as the differentiating feature, at least in the ranks of the *reñir* < RINGĪ family. From the observation of this one alliance of forms Menéndez Pidal for a while gained—and conveyed to others—the impression that -NǴ- > -*nz*- and the two related developments (-*lz*-, -*rz*-) crystallized only in pretonic position;[27] by the mid-'twenties, having become aware of his error, he candidly re-

of ç for z (*erçer, onçeja* and, conversely, *arzón, arienzo*), a point no longer regarded as quite so troublesome after the publication of Menéndez Pidal's *Orígenes del español* (see the introductory chapter on spelling).

[26] *Grammatik der romanischen Sprachen* (Leipzig, 1890), § 499.

[27] *Manual (elemental) de gramática histórica española,* 2d ed. (Madrid: V. Suárez, 1905; 3d ed., 1914; 4th ed., 1918), § 47.2 *b*; retracted in *Orígenes del español,* § 49.3, in the light of the newly discovered var. *reñilla.* Compare the cautious acquiescence of F. Hanssen, *Spanische Grammatik auf historischer Grundlage* (Halle: M. Niemeyer, 1910), § 19.8, and his even greater restraint in *Gramática histórica de la lengua castellana* (Halle: M. Niemeyer, 1913), § 134, as against the unqualified acceptance by V. García de Diego, *Elementos de gramática histórica española* (Burgos: Tipografía de "El Monte Carmelo," 1914), p. 44, a passage criticized by A. Castro one year later (see below); one may add, in vain, since the erroneous appeal to the stress still haunts the incorrigible author's *Gramática histórica española* (Madrid: Editorial Gredos, 1951), § 19.5, where he stubbornly parts company with Menéndez Pidal's second thinking. Menéndez Pidal's initial hypothesis fits into a pattern of conjectures suggested, at the turn of the century, by the unwarranted reverberations, in Romance, of Karl Verner's law (1876); see my note: "Quelques fausses applications de la loi de Verner aux faits romans," in the

tracted the conjecture with a bow to a dissenter (A. Castro, see below under [d]).

(c) The intermediate stage between -RǴ- and -rz- must have been */rž/: a sequence pieced together out of whole cloth first by G. Baist[28] and later by J. D. M. Ford in *Old Spanish Readings* (p. xxxviii). Was ·it suggested by the evolutionary trend in Portuguese?

(d) The difference between, on the one hand, QUĪNGENTŌS > *quiñentos* (coll. Sp., Jud.-Sp., Ptg.) and, on the other, the words displaying -*nz*-, -*rz*- (common starting point: -NG- > -NǴ- > *-ÑǴ-) involves, first and foremost, syllable juncture: thus opined A. Castro in a substantial book review (*RFE,* II [1915], 181). This is a sufficiently accurate description of the process at issue, but hardly a causal explanation of the differentiation.

(e) A richly nuanced development confronts the observer, within which certain strains can be neatly isolated. The most noteworthy of these streaks, the one involving the rise of -*nz*- and -*rz*-, allegedly shows a "perfectly understandable" shift Ǵ > *z* (see(c) above), running parallel to the more familiar shift Ḱ > *ç*, that is, /c/ or [ts]. This has been Menéndez Pidal's view since the mid-'twenties,[29] presented contagiously enough to have gained adherents[30] and formulated on the basis of a copious array of data tidily transcribed, dated, and localized. The documentation is priceless and unassailable, but the conjecture seems vulnerable: If it is true that -Ǵ- > -*z*- (say, in ARGILLA > *arzilla*) acts as a voiced counterpart of -Ḱ- > -*ç*- (say, in VINCIT > *vençe*), it is equally true that the latter result concomitantly honors the broad trend equating the growth of word-initial and -medial postconsonantal occlusives (cf. CAELU > *çielo*), while *z* fails to straddle the two developments: One encounters not the slightest trace of GERMĀNU > **zermano*.[31] One additional flaw in Menéndez Pidal's reasoning: Since

---

A. Burger Testimonial Issue of the *Cahiers Ferdinand de Saussure,* XXIII (1966), 75–87.

[28] "Die arabischen Laute im Spanischen," *RF,* IV (1891), 401–403.

[29] *Orígenes del español* (Madrid: Imprenta de la librería y casa editorial Hernando (s.a.), 1926; 2d ed., 1929; 3d ed., 1950), § 49.4.

[30] Note the inordinately heavy reliance on Menéndez Pidal in G. B. Pellegrini, *Grammatica storica spagnola* (Bari: "Leonardo da Vinci" editrice, 1950), §§ 73.3 and 74.7.

[31] On Ptg. *iguaria* 'tidbit,' OJud.-Sp. *yegüería* 'mess, dish' < (gloss)

the assibilation of Ḱ occurred early and that of Ǵ, which he posits, would have followed suit at once, it is inexplicable how this allegedly natural z could have dissolved in the following /je/, as in ARGENTEU > *arienzo*. Only on the assumption that there at first lingered on a /j̑/ : /arjenço/, which merged with the demonstrably late diphthong *ie* < ẹ < Ẹ̆, while succumbing in different contexts to an analogical z spreading from the most contagious of all verbal paradigms (*di-, de-zir*), do we fully reconcile plausible temporal sequences with narrow and broad phonological developments.

(f) At this point one wishes it were possible to report some breakthrough scored by the application of structural analysis; yet such, disappointingly enough, is not the case. E. Alarcos Llorach's paper, offering an advantageous bird's-eye view through joint consideration of G[e, i], J, DJ, GJ (and, as a foil, of K[e, i], TJ, KJ), has the merit of conjoining, for the first time, the processes under study, especially as observable between vowels, with the treatment of geminate occlusives and of -LL-, -NN-, -RR-, along imaginative lines suggested by A. Martinet;[32] while some facets of the evolution, as a result of this choice of focus, stand out in gratifyingly sharper relief, the idiosyncratic Castilian treatment of -LǴ-, -NǴ-, -RǴ-, which does not smoothly lend itself to the approach, dwindles into insignificance, being relegated to a brief and inconclusive footnote.[33] B. Pottier's passing mention of

---

IĚCUARIA 'giblets,' also on Ptg. *irmão* = OSp. *ermano* < GERMĀNU and on the proper name *Elvira* see my papers in *Lang.,* XX (1944), 108–130 and XXI (1945), 264–265, as well as R. Lapesa's comment in *Asturiano y provenzal en el Fuero de Avilés* (Salamanca: Universidad de Salamanca, 1948; Acta Salm., II:4), pp. 31–33, and E. Alarcos Llorach's reaction to these statements toward the end of the article listed in the following footnote.

[32] "Resultados de G[e, i] en la Península," *Arch.,* IV (1954; *Miscelánea . . . Amado Alonso*), 330–342. This paper clears up two points: (a) the mutual resemblance of Portuguese and Catalan and their joint departure from Castilian—a state of affairs corroborating Menéndez Pidal's general findings of 1926; (b) the marked inner consistency (i.e., regularity) of the Peninsula's lateral languages as against the extraordinary complexity of the centrally located language. Particularly praiseworthy is the distinction drawn between */j/ and */jj/ through inner reconstruction, in the absence of reliable graphemic evidence. The author is laudably cautious in assessing the Mozarabic material, seen chiefly through the prism of toponyms, and contributes a lexical vignette on the transmission of GYPSU.

[33] See p. 338 n. 24, where *esparzer, arzilla, enzía,* on the one hand, and

arcilla and *encía* is not at all helpful, and one is shocked to see him conjure up, however cautiously in comparison with V. García de Diego, the ghost of accentual interference which Menéndez Pidal had, one hoped, at long last allayed in 1926.[34] H. Lausberg, through the subtle overtones of his wording, draws the well-versed reader's attention to the diachronically erratic character of OSp. *esparzer, senziello,* and *unzir,* but is discreet enough to withhold any comment that might firmly commit him to some narrow-gauged causal explanation.[35] This triple restraint, which borders on unadmitted failure, is perhaps not entirely coincidental: It marks the limit, in explicative matters, of diachronic phonemics as it developed in the quarter century 1940–1965. Like the advocates of any legitimate and provocative method, the practitioners of diachronic phonemics, after elegantly solving a number of problems previously rebellious to analysis, have left in their wake an embarrassingly copious residue of unanswered questions. To come to grips with these residual difficulties we must make bold to shift certain emphases without further delay.

VII

One Tentative Parallel

Were the case here examined at length a severely isolated instance of the presumptive concatenation of circumstances, the credibility of the entire argument would be reduced to the narrowest of margins. For-

---

orçuelo 'sty' < HORDEOLU, *vergüença* 'shame' < VERĒCUNDIA, on the other, are subsumed under a single head, despite the clear indication, through the *z:ç* contrast, that two entirely different processes are involved. I have found little additional enlightenment in the author's *Fonología española* (3d ed. [Madrid: Editorial Gredos, 1961], pp. 229–232, 234, 244, and esp. 251–256), where Alarcos exacerbates his error by conjoining ARGILLA > OSp. *arzilla* and RADIU, *-A 'ray' > *raça* 'light stripe, crack, slit, cleft.' The book must be judged in the light of D. Catalán's strictures in *RPh,* XVIII (1964–1965), 178–191. Alcarcos disregards my study of VERĒCUNDIA (*SP,* 1944) and of -DJ- > -ç- (*UCPL,* XI [1954], passim). The recently published 4th ed. of the *Fonología* has not yet become available to me.

[34] *Introduction à l'étude de la philologie hispanique,* I (Paris: B. Pottier, 1960), § 75: *tañer, uña,* and § 119f.: *arcilla, encía, (y)ermano* (note the "Remarque").

[35] *Romanische Sprachwissenschaft,* II: *Konsonantismus* (Berlin: de Gruyter, 1956), §§ 410, 417.

tunately, striking parallels can be marshalled; in fact, one need not go
far afield to discover analogous sequences of events. The chief reason
for calling the counterpart selected for mention here "tentative" is the
less heavy documentation with which, for expedience's sake, the new
hypothesis will be surrounded.[36]

The conditions under which Lat. Ĕ and Ŏ diphthongized to *ie* and *ue*
shortly before the curtain went up on the recorded history of Spanish
are well known and relatively simple to describe. A less easy task is the
statement of those circumstances whose interplay, at a distinctly later
date, allowed *ie* and *ue* to be monophthongized to *i* and *e,* respectively
—in a radically asymmetric pattern.[37] The monophthongization occurred only in a pitifully small minority of cases, especially as regards
ue > *e,* and was slow in attracting scholarly attention, the upshot of
this delay being the absence of any workable consensus on the explanatory level.

Let us first state the raw facts. The rising diphthong *ue*—from the
outset one of the most characteristic features of the Spanish sound system—yields *e* in just a few cases which seem to demand a straight
phonological explanation: the geographic name *Bur-(u)eva,* mod. *La
Bureba* (Prov. of Burgos), plus *cul(u)ebra* 'snake' < COL-ŬBRA,
*-ŎBRA, *fl(u)eco* 'fringe, flounce, reveled edge' < FLOCCU, and
fr(u)ente 'forehead' < FRONTE. In a few additional instances alternative causes come to mind; specific sound conditions may here have
acted as mere concomitants: *estantigua* 'procession of hobgoblins; bug-
bear, badly dressed person, scarecrow' < OSp. *huest(e) antigua,* lit.
'old army' < HOSTE ANTĪQUA (either loss of primary stress
through composition, or the agency of taboo, or the combination of
these forces, may have acted as the prime mover); *estera* 'mat(ting)'
< STŎREA 'rush mat' (contamination with the common suffix *-era*
< -ĀRIA, which in this particular context showed marked functional

---

[36] For a fuller treatment of this multipronged issue see my article "Diphthon-
gization, Monophthongization, Metaphony" in Yuen Ren Chao Testimonial
Issue of *Lang.* XLII (1966), 430–472, and my forthcoming contribution to the
Mélanges Jean Frappier.

[37] We shall not here be concerned with the rival monophthongization
ié > é AFTER a palatal consonant, as in OSp. *dix(i)eron* 'they said,' mod.
dijeron, beside *tejieron* 'they wove' (analogically remodeled), or as in *amari-
llento* 'yellowish' alongside *gris-iento* 'grayish' (suff. *-iento* < -ENTU).

affinity) ; compare the parallel shift of Berceo's suffix *-duero* < -TŌRIU to *-dero*;[38] *pestorejo* 'back of the neck,' a masculine companion piece to the combination of POST 'after, behind' and AURICULA, the diminutive of AURIS 'ear' (vowel dissimilation may have been at work, brought to bear on **postorejo,* compare *redondo* 'round' < ROTUNDU; in this eventuality there arose no diphthong to begin with).

The ranks of Old Spanish words containing *i* traceable to *ie* are more sizable, and the diphthongal forms are, for the most part, documented. Typical representatives include: *aprisco* (v.) 'I gather the sheep in the fold,' (n.) 'sheep-fold,' from *APPRESSICĀRE; *avispa* 'wasp' < VESPA (conceivably with an *a-* borrowed from *abeja* 'bee' < API-CULA 'little bee'); *mirl-o,* rarely *-a* 'blackbird' < MERUL-A, rarely -U; *níspero* 'medlar-tree' and *níspola* 'medlar-fruit' < MESPILU beside-A; *pingo* 'I drip' < *PENDICŌ; *prisa* 'haste' < OSp. *pries(s)a* < PRESSA 'pressure'; *prisco* 'kind of peach' < PERSICU, lit. 'Persian apple'; *remilgo* (refl. v.) 'I am affectedly nice, squeamish,' (n.) 'affected gravity, prudery,' related to MEL 'honey'; *ri(e)stra* 'string, row, file' < RESTE, with hypercharacterization of gender and secondary *-r-* after *-st-*; *si(e)glo* 'world' < SAECULU (presumably through the instrumentality of OFr. *siegle,* as against mod. *siècle*); *vi(é)spera(s)* 'eve' < VESPERA (HŌRA) 'evening.'[39] To this larger contingent of examples one must add numerous instances of *-iello, -iella,* in the overwhelming majority of cases a suffixal element, originally diminutive (a value not infrequently blurred at the Romance stage; cf. *Cast-illa,*

---

[38] The fact that in STŌREA the expected **ue* would have been a product of Ŏ + (attracted) *j* rather than of Ŏ alone and would have presupposed an older stage **oi* (cf. CORIU 'leather' > Ptg. *coiro* beside Sp. *cuero,* more advanced) does not make the example any less relevant.

[39] It is not impossible that mod. *pértiga* 'long rod or pole,' a notorious crux, has evolved from far more transparent OSp. *piértega* < PERTICA through the intermediate stage *pírtega,* with subsequent vowel metathesis. In this event the equally baffling Ptg. *pírtiga* 'pole, shaft' could conceivably be explained as a word transplanted from Spanish soil (e.g., by seasonal workers using this tool in harvesting fruit). In my aforecited article (*Language,* 1966) an attempt is made to demonstrate that the familiar conjugational series, *yxo* 'I go out' < EXEŌ beside inf. *exir, sigo* 'I follow' < SEQUOR beside *seguir, sirvo* 'I serve' < SERVIŌ beside *servir, visto* 'I clothe, don' < VESTIŌ beside *vestir,* involves at least as strong a dosage of monophthongization of older *-ie-* forms as it does of metaphony.

OSp. *-iella* < CASTELLA, lit. 'encampments, castles'); at rare intervals the concluding segment of a root morpheme, as in *silla* 'chair (lit. stool), saddle' < OSp. *siella* < SELLA. Finally, the reduction of *ie* to *i* occurred in a number of rather obscure medieval proper names, opportunely assembled by R. Menéndez Pidal in 1926: *Liestra ~ Listra, Asieso ~ Asiso, Agierbe ~ Agirbe* (*g* = /j/), *Xavierre ~ Scavierri ~ Exavirr,* beside mod. *Javierre, Espierre, Espierlo.*

This is not the place to review the existing, woefully scattered literature on this two-edged problem.

In analyzing the reduction of *ue* to *e* one has the impression of weakness and sporadicity, qualities which, in turn, are determined by the number of conditions that must be met before the change can eventuate. Aside from the primary stress falling on the critical syllable, there must be present, in close vicinity, a bilabial consonant plus a liquid (*r* or *l*). The accumulation of so many conditioning factors reminds one of Rumanian or Old French historical phonology, rather than of Spanish, known for its bold and clear-cut architecture, devoid of all manner of "Schnörkel." Small wonder that the shift was easily blocked. Thus, OSp. *vuestro* 'your(s),' beside informal *vuesso,* met all the requisite conditions, yet failed to cast off **vestro, *vesso,* presumably because the parallelism with *nuestro* 'our' sufficed to counterbalance the tendential sound shift. Yet Latin for centuries tolerated NOSTER beside VESTER.

If, in passing on to *-ie-* > *-i-,* we take as our prime classifier not some specific neighboring sound, but—on a more abstract plane of reasoning—the number of identifiable conditioning factors, we must draw a sharp line between, on the one hand, dim. *-i(e)llo, -i(e)lla* and, on the other, all the remaining examples. In the case of the diminutives, the single source of causation seems, at first glance, to be the [λ] of *-i(e)llo* and its feminine counterpart; at any rate, the phonic, syllabic, and accentual configuration of the root morpheme and the choice of *-o* or *-a* as the final vowel seem to have exerted not the slightest influence on the long-drawn-out fluctuation between diphthong and monophthong.[40]

---

[40] It is difficult to decide to what, if any, extent the *s* of *siella* was responsible for the word's transmutation into *silla*. It is hazardous to separate *si(e)lla* from *si(e)glo*; but note that *siervo* 'serf' < SERVU successfully withstood the pressure, while *sirvo* 'I serve' < SERVIŌ owes its *i* mainly, if not exclusively,

The situation is radically different with the other members of the group: Here, as previously with the handful of -*ue*- > -*e*- cases, one observes, typically, the simultaneous agency of two separate factors, usually the appearance of (a) an adjacent or, at least, not too far removed *l* or *r* (better still, *R* and *r*) and (b) the characteristic Castilian apico-alveolar /s/ which, lying as it does between [s] and [š], gives the acoustic impression of a palatal consonant [ś]; almost invariably the *s* is either word-initial or represents the first ingredient of a medial consonant cluster. Examples include *aprisco, prisa, ristra, siglo, vísper(a)s.* One finds certain variations; thus, it would seem that the co-occurrence of *r* and *l* makes the intervention of *s* dispensable, witness *mirlo, remilgo.* Because bilabials (*b, p, m*) happen to figure prominently in several of these examples, it is not impossible that in the end they too acted, upon occasion, as a secondary conditioning factor; compare *avispa,* where the *s* was a concomitant and the analogy of *víspera(s)* might have been operative, *pirtega (if this reconstruction mediates between OSp. *piértega* and mod. *pértiga*), which paired off *p*- with -*r*-, and *pingo,* where these supporting circumstances were absent unless one credits the nasal with the power to substitute, at intervals, for either liquid. Generally speaking, *aprisco, pingo,* and *remilgo* stand apart insofar as they are members of verbal paradigms rich in arrhizotonic forms; their -*i*- may have first crystallized in pretonic syllables, as a reflex of *e* before such clusters as -*ng*-, -*lg*-, -*sc*-, a circumstance which potentially detracts from the weight of their evidence.

There is no strict parallelism, then, between the respective scopes of *ue* > *e* and *ie* > *i*, quite apart from the conspicuous asymmetry of these reductions within the system. The retrenchment *ie* > *i* affects a palpably larger number of lexical items, some of them verbal, involves a richer interplay of pairs of conditioning factors, and, in one crucially important instance—be it only on account of its exceptionally high incidence (-*illo*, -*illa*)—seems to hinge on a single circumstance.

The temporal sweep of -*ie*- > -*i*- is also noteworthy. The trend remained in operation long enough for OSp. *sieglo,* clearly a borrowing

---

to metaphonic influence. In isolation the *s*- of *sie*- certainly lacked the force to raise the front vowel, as is exemplified by *siete* 'seven' < SEPTE(M).

from Old French (much as OPtg. *segre* is a Provençalism), to have
yielded *siglo*. On the other hand, Menéndez Pidal, through scrupulous
sifting of dated documentary evidence, established the fact that in the
suffix *-iello, -iella* monophthongization occurred at a remarkably early
date, though it took speakers of Spanish centuries to rid themselves entirely of the receding *-ie-* variants (which have entrenched themselves
to this day in certain conservative Asturo-Leonese dialects).[41] Taking
into account all these circumstances of spread and impact, one is in-
clined to argue, first, that the shift *-ie-* > *-i-*, at least in its earliest manifestations, must have preceded, by a margin of centuries, the shift *-ue-*
> *-e-*, almost—but not entirely—parallel; and, second, that the stimu-
lus for the monophthongization of *-ie-* may very well have come from
-i(e)llo, -i(e)lla, judging from chronological evidence.

These temporal considerations may be reinforced by phonological
analysis. To the best of our knowledge, OSp. *-ie-* was pronounced /je/,
an assumption which makes its occasional reduction to *-e-*, as in
dix(i)eron 'they said' (cf. fn. 37, above), perfectly plausible, while
its alternative reduction to *i*, under a different set of circumstances, is
anything but readily understandable in phonic context. The difficulty
would disappear if we were to appeal to analogy: Old Spanish pitted
in stiff competition a variety of diminutive suffixes, esp. *-iello, -ino*,
-ico, -ito, and *-uelo*. It would seem that at a certain juncture stressed *i*
emerged as a characteristic marker of diminution; that in the wake of
this process the discrepant suffix *-uelo*, once very abundantly represented, was relegated to the background; and that *-iello* temporarily

[41] *Orígenes del español* see 3d ed., § 27, with a masterly summary and a
refreshing nuancing of earlier methodology in subsection 5. The author dis-
criminates sharply between the genesis of *i* < *ie* and its subsequent standard-
ization. Isolated instances of the secondary monophthong are traceable to
notarial documents of the tenth and eleventh centuries, from Old Castile; but
when the literary language crystallized in the following century, it was Leon.
-iello rather than Cast. *-illo* that initially won out in the unified *scripta*, while
diversified dialects each followed its own course. Only in the fourteenth century did writers and refined speakers reverse themselves, in favor of *-illo*.
Aragonese and Mozarabic speech communities adopted the monophthong more
slowly and, above all, more hesitantly than did their Castillian counterparts.
In modern Asturo-Leonese *-iello* predominates to this day, though certain
subdialects use instead *-iecho, -ietsu, -ichu*, and (in the extreme West) *-ello*.

survived the onslaught of its competitors at the price of exchanging its uncharacteristic *-ie-* for the highly suggestive *-i-*.[42]

One distinct advantage of the conjecture made here is that it is apt to account, as was no previous hypothesis, for the conspicuous rôle played by /l/, /r/, /R/, and /ś/ in the limited monophthongization of *-ie-*. If one recalls that, by virtue of its distinctive features, the /λ/ of *-iello, -iella* was linked, on the one hand, to /l/ and, somewhat more closely, to /r/ and /R/ and, on the other, to /ś/—in view of the latter's well-known palatality—, one can readily see why the conjunctions of at least two such phonemes partially resembling the /λ/ could sporadically produce a similar effect in transmuting the *-ie-* into *-i-*.

The labials and labiodentals were not originally endowed with comparable force, witness *fiesta* 'festival' < FESTA and *inhiesto* < OSp. *infiesto* 'steep' < INFESTU 'menacing, hostile,' which, in their resistance to change, behave exactly like *tiesto* 'flowerpot' < TESTU 'pot lid' and *siesta* 'hottest part of the day, after-dinner nap' < SEXTA (HŌRA), while the combined pressure of labial and liquid on *-ie-* may produce more impressive results: *mirlo, pingo*. However, when, through the agency of symmetry, speakers felt tempted to match the occasional monophthongization of *-ie-* with a similar treatment of *-ue-*, the most appropriate environmental feature that, in alliance with *l* or *r*, could be charged with controlling the shift *-ue-* > *-e-* was a /b/, a /v/, or an /f/. Hence *Bureba, culebra, fleco,* and *frente*.

Of the two relevant phonic ingredients of /λ/ it was thus the link to /l/ and /r/ that turned out to be the stronger, both within the ranks of *-ie-* words and, secondarily, in the far smaller group of *-ue-* words. Palatality did attract /ś/ into this process, but endowed it with much less power than that invested in /l/ and /r/; note the contrast between *ristra* and *siesta*. The contact with labials and labiovelars may have been accidental at the outset; at least, one can account for the monophthong of *aprisco, mirlo, prisa,* and *víspera* without any direct appeal to the presence of *m, p,* or *v* in the respective words. But whether or not

----

[42] For a shrewd and conscientious appraisal of current inquiries, including a searching analysis of the monographs by Bengt Hasselrot and F. González Ollé, see J. R. Craddock, "A Critique of Recent Studies in Romance Diminutives," *RPh*, XIX (1965–1966), 286–325.

merely coincidental in these particular instances,[43] the labials and labiovelars in the end became prime conditioners (though at no time sole conditioners) after the transfer of the mechanism of monophthongization from the front to the back of the mouth cavity.

One side issue worth pondering is the relative weakness of monophthongization where ascending diphthongs are involved; contrast the meager yield of this process with the rich results of the earlier monophthongization, again in Spanish, of *ei* to *e* and of *ou* to *o*. This weakness of the trend has allowed conjugational analogy to override it effortlessly, with the result that the reduction of *ie* to *i* and of *ue* to *e* operates almost exclusively in the category of nouns, including onomastic items. It might be rewarding to discover whether such sound changes as have been sparked by analogy rooted in inflectional or derivational conditions lack, as a general principle, the strength commonly found in sound changes produced by purely phonic factors.

At this latitude, a comparison of the two major problems so far examined—the one involving three medial consonant clusters (-RǴ-, -LǴ-, -NǴ-) in their transition from Latin to Romance, the other bearing on the partial monophthongization of two rising diphthongs (*ié*, *ué*) at the concluding stage of Old Spanish—may be particularly rewarding. What the seemingly quite disparate problems share is the fact that at first glance they appear to be purely phonological in content, but as soon as the analyst turns his attention to the matter of causation, strictly phonological conditions fail to provide any adequate, truly dependable clue. This qualification does not exclude the possibility that such conditions played a subordinate rôle in the two nearly parallel processes; but the single most plausible factor of causation turns out, on both occasions, to have been analogy, operating through two adjoining provinces of morphology. In the case of the three confederated consonant groups the agency that transmitted the impact was a set of crucially important, rather similar verbal paradigms; in the case of the secondary monophthong, the stimulus came from the close-knit alliance of diminutive suffixes, most of them marked by the same characteristic (if you wish, "expressive") vowel. The local intensity of analogical

---

[43] It is worth noting that in Rumanian word-initial /j/ and labials (or labiovelars) often produce the same effect on the stem vowel: cf. *iapă* 'mare' < EQUA, pl. *iepe*, and *pară* (f. sg.) 'pear' < PIRA (n. pl.), pl. *pere*.

interference, as distinct from its original direction, was determined, in the case of -RǴ-, -LǴ-, and -NǴ-, by a number of interconnected phonic conditions. The transfer of monophthongization from *ié* > *i,* where a primary cause was at work (association of *-iello* with *-ito, -ico, -ino*), to *ué* > *e,* where the application of no such direct pressure was discernible, must have been made in response to a deeply ingrained craving for symmetry.

Romance linguistics boasts a rich reservoir of problems that can potentially benefit the general methodology of diachronic analysis of language. Some of these controversial problems have been solved, though even then the reward for any scrupulous re-examination is bound to include deeper insights and improved formulations. Others —in fact, counter to widespread belief, very many—await definitive clarification. Perhaps Romance scholars, who have been somewhat negligent of this challenging commitment, should educate themselves to give priority not to those questions which relate to residual gaps in their grasp of the particular fabric of Romance culture, but to those, more urgent, which may enrich our general understanding of the anatomy of language change.[44]

[44] At proof I can, in some instances, supply fuller bibliographic references and, in others, add the barest minimum of fresh supplementary information. *Ad.* p. 25: concerning points (1) and (2), see my article "Range of Variation as a Clue to Dating," to appear in the May, 1968, issue of *RPh. Ad.* p. 27: Point (6) has been made the specific object of a searching inquiry in my article identified in n. 18, below. *Ad.* p. 28: for further details see *Lang.,* XLIII (1967), 242–245. *Ad.* p. 36: on metaphony see pp. 56–58, below, and the latest literature (1966) there adduced. *Ad.* pp. 55–63: for a far more elaborate and finely nuanced account of the problem here merely sketched in rough outline, see my paper "Le nivellement morphologique comme point de départ d'une loi phonétique: La monophtongaison occasionnelle de *ie* et *ue* en ancien espagnol," to appear in the *Mélanges Jean Frappier,* a newly announced venture of the Parisian Klincksieck firm. *Ad.* pp. 58–59: OSp. *piértega* > mod. *pértiga* poses many additional problems, of which I grew aware after concluding this paper; a few of them are taken up in my article "Latin *pedica,* **pēnsum,* and *pertica* in Hispano-Romance," to appear in the Swedish miscellany *Mélanges Alf Lombard. Ad.* p. 60: the situation in Asturian is further complicated by the sporadic infiltration of Cast. *-illo,* disguised as *-illu*; see my forthcoming paper "Patterns of Derivational Affixation in the Cabraniego Dialect of East-Central Asturian," to appear as part of a volume planned for the University of California Publications in Linguistics series. *Ad.* p. 63: I expect to show in the nearest future that at least two more phenomena usually tagged phonological, (a) the so-called

Acknowledgments

I owe a number of useful, if minor, suggestions to several scholars
who attended the Texas conference, in particular J. Kuryłowicz and
U. Weinreich, and also, among my own students, J. R. Craddock. A
few weeks after its original offering the paper was presented orally to
a group of linguists at UCLA, where it benefited from a second discussion sparked by queries from W. Bright and R. P. Stockwell.
The distribution of the preprint netted a few interesting epistolary
reactions, notably those of E. García (Columbia) and R. T. Harms
(Texas); the latter suggested a restatement, in transformational terms,
of the nuclear section of the paper. On the Berkeley campus R. Stefa-
nini has drawn my attention to several Italian parallels and near-
parallels. Thus, such northeastern dialects as Veronese and Trentino
exemplify the spread of the voiced velar from *di-go, -ga,* 'I say, may say,'
producing *fa-go, -ga, va-go, -ga, da-go, -ga, sta-go, -ga,* which match
stand. It. *faccio* (*fo*) 'I make,' *vo* 'I go,' *do* 'I give,' *sto* 'I stand,' and
the corresponding sets of pres. subj. forms, thus corroborating the
kernel of my conjecture. Also, *borg-ese* and *borgh-ese* 'burgher' coexisted in Old Italian, as they still do in anthroponymy. To Diego
Catalán Menéndez Pidal, almost my nextdoor neighbor in the year
1965–1966, I am indebted for comments on some finer points of the
Hispano-Romance material. Marilyn May Vihman gave me, as on
many similar occasions, the benefit of her incisive stylistic criticism.

---

parasitic /j/ of Asturo-Leonese and adjoining dialects (e.g., *muriu* 'wall' as
against Sp. *muro*) and (b) the Castilian shift /s/ to /θ/ before consonant (as
in *bizco* 'squint-eyed,' *mezclar* 'to mix'), likewise have their roots in morphological conditions.

The Notion of Morpho(pho)neme

J. KURYŁOWICZ

Harvard University

1. Although much has been written in the last thirty years about morphonology, we still lack a clear definition of its basic concept: the *morphoneme*. But the concepts of phoneme and morpheme have been thoroughly discussed and defined by their functions: diacritic, and semantic or syntactic, respectively. What is a morphoneme; what is its difference versus phoneme and morpheme; how does change of linguistic status from morphoneme to morpheme take place and vice versa; these are the questions we are interested in.

Besides the terms mentioned, there is another: *morph*, designating a phonemic complex (structure) with semantic or syntactical function. Without creating misunderstanding one may also speak of the phonemic structure of the morpheme. The morpheme can be represented by several syllables, by one syllable, by a nonsyllabic group of phonemes, by a single phoneme, by one or by several phonemic features, sometimes even by phonetic zero, that is, the absence of phonemic feature. On the other hand, we distinguish compound and disjunct morphemes.

Since morphemes have a semantic or syntactic function, phonemes a diacritic function, the question is whether there are any limitrophous or border problems engaging both domains, phonemics and morphology.

2. Let us start with a few premises. An essential task of phonemics is the exploration of phonemic oppositions or of phonemic features (articulatory or acoustic). Trubetzkoy distinguished several kinds of oppositions based on articulatory features, one of them being especially important, the so-called privative opposition: under certain phonemic conditions (in a given phonemic neighborhood) the marked member

is replaced by the unmarked member, the latter (the so-called archi-phoneme) being the only one admissible in the position of phonemic neutralization. Consequently, the marked member is perceived by the speaker as containing the surplus of a phonemic feature. Note for ex-ample, Polish or Russian *t* unmarked, neutral, and at the same time negative; *d* on the other hand is marked by the presence of voice (positive).

From the morphological point of view, however, another classifi-cation of phonemic oppositions must be envisaged. They seem to be either morphologically pertinent and conditioned by morphological factors, or morphologically irrelevant. For example:

(a) Privative opposition—morphologically not relevant; see the above Polish or Russian opposition *t*:*d*. The conditioning of this alter-nation is purely phonemic (a following obstruent or terminal junc-ture), never morphological.

(b) Privative opposition—morphologically relevant, for example the alternation of short and long vowels in Semitic (classical Arabic). The alternation is privative, since in closed syllables only short vowels are admissible, thus *taqulūna* but *taqŭlna*, whereas in open syllables the choice of quantity very often, indeed usually, depends on morpho-logical factors, for example, *qatala* 'he killed,' *qātala* 'he tried to kill' > 'he fought, attacked (somebody).'

(c) Nonprivative opposition—morphologically irrelevant. This is probably the most frequent model. In many languages the opposition between front and back vowels (acute and grave vowels) is totally in-dependent of phonemic surroundings and at the same time does not play a role in morphology.

(d) Nonprivative opposition—morphologically pertinent. In Ger-man the contrast between the back vowels *a, o, u, au,* and the corre-sponding front vowels, *ä, ö, ü, äu* (*eu*) appears in many morphological categories—*Bad/Bäder, Wort/Wörter, Gut/Güter, Haus/Häuser; Baum/Bäumlein; kalt/kälter; fanden/fänden*—although these two vocalic series are never conditioned by phonemic surroundings.

This transition from diacritic to semantic, as well as the opposite de-velopment, deserves special attention. We notice that a phonemic change may be governed either by phonemic or by morphological fac-tors. The replacement of *g, d, b, z, ž* by *k, t, p, s, š* in Russian or in

Polish is governed exclusively by phonemic factors, the voiced obstruent becoming voiceless before final juncture or before a voiceless obstruent; on the other hand, a voiceless obstruent becomes voiced before a voiced obstruent; for example, Polish *grad* [grat] 'hail,' gen. *gradu*; *żabka* [*žapka*] 'little frog' < *żaba* 'frog;' *kośba* [*koźba*] 'mowing' < *kosić* 'to mow.' The morphological category is not significant, and there are no exceptions. On the contrary, the alternation of front and back vowels in German, as evidenced by the examples quoted, is conditioned morphologically, hence the possibility of "exceptions," to be explained on semantic and other nonphonemic grounds. See *Wiederkäuer* < *kauen*, but *Gassenhauer* < *hauen*; *behaglich* as against *kläglich*; *anmutig* but *demütig*; *härter:zarter,* and so on.

Accordingly, we may distinguish between a phonological and a morphological alternation of phonemes differing by a distinctive feature. A phenomenon like the inherited Indo-European ablaut (front vowel *o*: back vowel *o*; *e:ē*) seems at first glance a morphological fact. The Germanic umlaut is another example, though its historical origin is quite different. We have seen, on the other hand, that the interchange of short and long vowels in classical Arabic is subject *both* to phonemic and to morphological factors.

3. Let us, however, continue our analysis of morphologically conditioned alternations. If we consider the Indo-European ablaut *e*: zero, *ei:i, eu:u* as morphological, is a contrast like German *Tag*: plur. *Tage* also to be regarded as morphological *in the same degree*? The reduced vowel of *Tage* is an ending of the plural and has therefore a semantic function. But what about the Indo-European ablaut (apophony) *full grade e*: zero? What role does *e* play as against zero in pairs like Skt. *rócate:árucat* or Gk. ἔχω:ἔσχον (**léuke-*:**luké-*; **séǵhe-*:*sǵhé-*) and so on?

A careful analysis of such contrasts proves that the morpheme of the aorist *sensu stricto* is the stressed thematic vowel *-é/ó-*, whereas the ablaut of the root vocalism represents only an accompanying, redundant morph with semantic zero function. This conclusion results from the following consideration: the zero grade of the aorist does not necessarily contrast with the full grade of the present; see a pair like Skt. *riṇákti:áricat* without change of the degree of the root vocalism. Generally speaking, the Indo-European ablaut e:zero is morphologically redundant; it only accompanies affixation. Note also the zero grade of the verbal adjectives in -tó-, for example, *lik-tó- < *leiq^u, *k̂lu-tó- < *k̂leu. Here again the zero grade of the root accompanies the morpheme proper, that is, the stressed suffix -tó-, and is essentially restricted to roots with an internal sonorant or glide. Forms like *pektó-, *settó- show no change of the vocalism of the fundamental form (*peq^u, *sed). Therefore -tó- is to be considered as the only carrier of the semantic function, whereas the ablaut, limited to roots of a certain phonemic structure, represents *from the morphological point of view* a redundant feature of the derived form.

We meet the very same situation in the German plural in -er (and other similar formations). The carrier of the semantic function is the ending -er. This ending is governed both by the phonemic form and by the meaning of the root; see, for example, plurals like *Bänder, Schilder* as against *Bande, Schilde*. Within this morphological category the umlaut, subordinate to the ending, is conditioned by the phonemic structure of the root (front or back vowel). The umlaut *depends not on the phonemic surrounding* (see *kälter* comparative versus nom. sing. masc. *kalter*), *but on the phonemic structure of the morphological surroundings*. In roots with front vowels the plural is sufficiently characterized by simple -er. Therefore *Brett:Bretter*, but *Blatt > Blätter*.

Incidentally, the same remarks may be applied to the other kinds of Indo-European ablaut, e:o, and e:$\bar{e}$ (lengthened grade). The Indo-European o-grade accompanies certain inflectional and derivational processes only in roots with fundamental vocalism e, whereas in roots with fundamental o, affixation by itself is sufficient (cf. ἀπο-τέμνω: ἀποτομή, ἀπο-κόπτω: ἀποκοπή). And the same is true for the lengthened grade. Thus the sigmatic aorist of Skt. *bhárati* is *ábhārṣam* (suffix s plus lengthened grade), that of *sādhati* is *ásātsam* (suffix s with preservation of the root vowel).

A derivational process like *leiq^u > *liktó- may be analyzed as (I) *leiq^u → (II) *leik-tó- → (III) *lik-tó-. The absence of any semantic function at the stage (II) → (III) permits us to establish *an indirect definition of the morphoneme*. We call morphonemic a stage within a morphological (derivational) process or transformation, which is redundant from the morphological (semantic, syntactical) standpoint, but significant from the phonemic (diacritic) point of view. Therefore a plural like **Bander* from (*das*) *Band*, formed like *Bretter* from *Brett*, would be a phonemic, but not a morphological blunder. Lacking is only the last stage (II) → (III), which is phonemic, not morphological.

The stages (I) → (II) and (II) → (III) correspond to the Hjelmslevian terms *rection* (see the ending of the plural *-er*) and *dominance* (see the umlaut). Rection or government exists between *two morphemes*: see the root *Band* with its meaning 'ribbon, band' and *-er* as the ending of the plural, not as the ending of the masculine nominative singular of the adjective. On the other hand, dominance exists between a *morpheme* (for example the ending *-er* of the plural) and a *morph* (in our example the phonemic form of the root *Band,* containing a back vowel).

4.   Analysis of the Germanic strong verb offers a more complicated picture. Besides special endings (Gothic zero, *-t,* zero, *-um, -uþ, -un*), which have morphological functions, we find, as redundant morphs, ablaut, and reduplication, in a few cases even their cumulation. Compare Goth. *laí-lot-um* versus *haí-hait-um, bit-um, ber-um.* The morpheme common to all forms of the strong preterite is the specific ending, whereas the morphonemes ablaut and reduplication show complementary distribution.

Another type of morphoneme is represented by the so-called union-vowels and union-consonants. Compare the union-vowel *i* of Sanskrit. In Sanskrit future forms like *kar-i-ṣyáti, han-i-ṣyáti, stav-i-ṣyáti* (but *sat-ṣyáti, vak-ṣyati,* and so on) the presence of *i* depends on root structure. It appears after sonorant (*r, n, m*) or glide (*y, v*). Therefore the correct analysis of such forms will be *kar* > **kar-ṣyati* > *kar-i-ṣyáti.* But in the infinitive in *-tu*(*m*) the appearance of *i* is a phonological (diacritic) property of the root; see *hán-tum* as against *bhavi-tum* continuing the difference between the so-called aniṭ and seṭ roots.

The original difference between the Greek passive aorists in *-ην* and in *-θην* was presumably formal, *-θ-* being a union-consonant appearing after vowel (whatever the origin of *θ*): (ποιέω>) ποιε- > **ἐποιή-ην* > ἐποιή-θ-ην like *kariṣyá-* = *kar* > **kar-ṣyá* > *kar-i-ṣyá-* (and not *kar* > **kar-i-* > *kar-i-ṣyá-*). The penetration of *-θην* for *-ην* after consonant seems to be secondary.

From the descriptive point of view Slavic -*x*- of the sigmatic aorist is also a union-consonant. For -*s*- appears both before consonantal and vocalic endings, for example, *jęsъ, jęste,* but -*x*- only before vowels. Therefore *x* is to be regarded as a replacement of antevocalic *s* in certain forms only. Since in a form like *rěxъ* an *s* would be admissible (cf. *věsъ < vedǫ*), this form is to be analyzed as follows: *rě-s ъ > *rě- ъ > rě-x-ъ. That is, the replacement of *s* by *x* is to be considered as a subtraction of *s* followed by an insertion of *x*. Hence the role of *x* as a union-consonant serving to eliminate a hiatus. This fact has important consequences in word formation, as shown in *Onomastica* (X, 1–2 [1965], 180–185).

A further, more complicated, example of both union-consonant and of other morphologically conditioned modifications is the Celtic (Old Irish) *sandhi*. Lenition or nasalization of the following word often depends on *double morphological* conditioning, for example:

(a) on the syntactical function of the case form, for example, *tuaith*, when accusative, nasalizes, *tuaith*, when dative, lenites;

(b) at the same time, on the syntactical relation of the affected word to the preceding case form (attribute, genitive, apposition).

Lenition and nasalization after prepositions depend on the preposition as morpheme (phonetic structure *plus* meaning), for example, *fo* 'under,' *air* 'to, for,' *i* 'in' lenite or nasalize the following noun *as prepositions*.

The redundancy of the Irish sandhi results from the fact that within certain morphological conditions it can be *only partly* actualized: no lenition takes place in the case of a vocalic word-initial, and nasalization does not affect word-initial *r, l, n, m, s* (since *n + r, l, n, m, s* is phonologically identical with nonlenited initial *r, l, n, m, s*).

5. Let us now take an example of a morphoprosodeme, that is, the superposition of a redundant *prosodic* feature (accent, intonation) upon a morphological structure. When comparing a Lithuanian paradigm like acc. sing. *bóbą*, gen. sing. *bóbos*, gen. plur. *bóbų* with a paradigm like *nãgą, nagõs, nagų̃* we do not have the right to consider the apparent shift of accent in *nagõs, nagų̃* as a (redundant) morphoprosodeme. The oxytone accentuation in *nagõs, nagų̃* is a diacritic feature characterizing the feminine *ō*-stem *nag*-. In the instr. sing. *rankà* or

acc. plur. *rankàs*, however, the state of affairs is different. Here the accentuation depends on the *structure of the root* (shift of accent from a circumflexed or short syllable to certain endings, Saussure's law), whereas in the former case both the *phonemic structure and the meaning* of the root are relevant, for example, gen. plur. *gerų* adjective, *gėrų* substantive. The nominal stems of Lithuanian have either mobile or immobile accentuation and this accentuation is a diacritic component of the prosodic stem structure. The accentual alternation *nãgą:nagõs* is therefore a primary prosodic fact, whereas the change *rãnką:rankàs* is a morphoprosodic phenomenon, conditioned by the intonation of the stem provided with the ending of the accusative plural. From the purely phonemic standpoint **rañkas* would also be admissible; compare the nom. sing. *lañkas* and so on.

6.   In order to explain the phenomenon of dominance *historically*, take as example the Spanish and Italian subjunctive in *-ga*. In both languages there are a number of subjunctives in *-a* showing an inorganic (not original nor phonetically developed) *-g-* before the subjunctive ending proper *-a*. Thus Italian *salga (salire), valga (valere), tenga (tenere), venga (venire)*; Spanish *salga (salir), valga (valer), tenga (tener), venga (venir)*. We find such an inorganic *g* also in western French dialects and northern dialects of Old French.

In a remote epoch a structural law with the following content must have acted in these languages: palatal *l', ń* at the end of a verbal root were replaced by the groups *lg, ng* before the suffix of the subj. (*-a-*). That is, the ideal forms **sal'a, *val'a, *teńa, *veńa* (Lat. *saliat, valeat, teneat, veniat*) were realized as *salga, tenga,* and so on. Obviously this dominance is the result of certain sound changes. Yet, more important, it is not their *immediate* result, but so to speak the projection of the sound changes onto the morphological plane. The palatalization of the Latin groups *lg, ng* giving Romance *l', n'* before front vowels was a phonemic change; compare *colgit* (for *colligit*) >Ital. *coglie, pingit*> Ital. *pegne*. In a number of verbs that change must have been reflected on the morphological plane as a specific relation of the indicative to the subjunctive (*colga, pinga*). Thus *col'-e > *col'-a > col-g-a*. The relation between *col'-e* and *col-g-a* is perceived as the replacement of the expected *l', ń* at the end of the verbal root by *lg, ng* before the subjunctive suffix -*a*, that is, as an insertion of a redundant morph *g* (entailing the depalatalization of the preceding *l'*, *ń*). Hence this morphoneme is consistently applied to all verbs having palatal *l'* or *ń* before the *a* of the subjunctive, **sal'a* > *salga*, *teńa > *tenga*.

The above example shows us the tendency of redundant morphs to spread in derived or founded forms. The addition of a redundant morph *enlarges* the distance between the basic and the derived (founded) form and renders the latter expressive.

7. But morphologically redundant morphonemes appear also in basic forms; compare the -*s* of the nominative singular or the -*t* of the third person singular in Indo-European. Endings like the -*s* of the nominative and the -*m* of the corresponding accusative are not on an equal footing; they do not belong to the same level, neither do the verbal endings -*t* of the third person and -*m*, -*s* of the first and second persons. The nominative singular is the neutral member of the case-number system and so is the third person singular within the verbal paradigm. Therefore the -*m* of the accusative, the verbal endings -*m*, -*s* have to be regarded as *morphemes*, whereas the -*s* of the nominative singular as well as the -*t* of the third person singular are only *morphonemes*, subordinate to the *zero-morpheme* of these inflectional forms. Hence an important corollary regarding morphological proportions.

Linguistic proportions are the chief implement for creating new linguistic forms and simultaneously their most abundant source. Loan words and onomatopoeic creations play only a secondary role. The importance of linguistic proportions consists in the fact that they enable us to imitate external reality not in its concrete details, but in its relations. Thus, for example, the linguistic relation *count:countess, baron: baroness, lion:lioness, tiger:tigress,* and so on, repeats, always under the same form, the sex relation, identical in each pair of the denoted animate beings. Bühler called it *relationstreue Abbildung* of the external reality.

Proportions function within the morphophonemic as well as the morphological plane.

In morphological proportions the relation between the first and the second member, and similarly between the third and the fourth member, concerns both the phonological structure and the function (meaning). Such proportions reflect the relation between the basic and the founded form, whether it is derivational or inflectional, and constitute the nucleus of the linguistic system, the regular relations between the structure and the function of linguistic forms. For example, German *Bild:Bildchen = Brett:Brettchen = Bein:Beinchen*, establishing the category of diminutiveness. Within this category we find a morphophonemic proportion, which is obligatory (or at least has been obligatory, cf. the exception *Kuh:Kuhchen*) and represents a superposition of the redundant umlaut on the semantically pertinent suffixation, thus **Kappchen:Käppchen = *Wortchen:Wörtchen = *Hutchen: Hütchen.*

Since the umlaut is predictable, the proportion *Brett:Brettchen = Wort:Wörtchen* is morphologically (though not phonemically) in order. It shows us that morphophonemic elements, which are not carriers of semantic values, are simply to be disregarded without bearing prejudice about the correctness of the morphological proportion. Thus in derivations like *nominative singular:other case forms, present: other tenses, indicative:other moods, third person singular:other persons,* the formal surplus of the basic form may be ignored—and the same holds true for the so-called primary derivatives of Indo-European. Examples are as follows:

The sigmatic aorist of Indo-European, which expressed perfectivity, was in semantic contrast with the present-imperfect stem. Now the structure of the Indo-European present was manifold: thematic or athematic, reduplicated, with *-ie/io-* or *-ske/sko-* suffix, with nasal infix. Confronted with the (sigmatic) aorist all these presents were semantically neutral-negative (nonperfective, imperfective), although they may have served to express different kinds of imperfectivity (simply durative, iterative, inchoative, terminative). Therefore the formation of the aorist consists first in the elimination of these semantically redundant morphs, that is, in the reduction of the present stem to the simple root, then in the addition of the sigmatic suffix (entailing itself the redundant feature of lengthened grade). Thus *riṇákti > *rek-ṣ- > raik-ṣ-*. Hence the well-known rule of comparative grammar: the sigmatic aorist is built upon the root, not upon the stem of the present. But the latter possibility is not excluded once the suffix of the present blends with the root so as to constitute a new verbal root.

A form like Skt. *bhárati* is justly regarded by the Hindu grammari-
ans as the basic form of the whole conjugational system, since it is
neutral in all respects, as regards person, number, tense, and mood.
This choice of the basic form envisages the semantic relations in the
first instance. But it also meets to a high degree (though not absolutely)
the criterion of predictability, since the rest of the verbal forms (perfect, future, partially also the aorist) may be predicted on the basis of
the form of the present. Incidentally, this is not the case everywhere.
In Slavic the perfective form is semantically based on the imperfective
(the latter being semantically unmarked), whereas predictability
generally goes in the opposite direction: it is the form of the imperfective in *-ajǫ* (plus the redundant change of the root vowel) which is
predictable on the basis of the perfective form. See *sypljǫ:-sypajǫ*,
sъxnǫ:-syxajǫ. The same holds for the French adjective in cases like
laide:laid, forte:fort, épaisse:épais.

We therefore have the right to consider a proportion like Skt.
bhárati:aorist *ábhārṣit* = *riṇakti:áraikṣīt* as correct. The characteristic
features of the present form (thematic with stress on the root in *bhárati*,
with nasal infix in *riṇákti*) are redundant morphs, that is, morphonemes with zero value, once the present is confronted with the perfective value of the sigmatic aorist (whose form itself contains the redundant lengthened grade). Similarly, a proportion like Lat. *bonus*:
gen. *bon-ī* = *bona*:gen. *bona-ī*, hence *bonae*, may be considered as
being in order, since the ending *-us* of the masculine, unmarked as
against fem. *-a*, is to be disregarded. Morphologically this proportion,
explaining the innovation *bonae* for *bonās*, has to be rewritten under
the form *bon:bon-i* = *bona:bona-i*. This is the latent form underlying
the apparently inaccurate proportion *bonus:boni* ≠ *bona:bonae*.

The original secondary ending of the third person singular of the
Indo-European mediopassive is *-o*: see Vedic *-a* enlarged to *-at* in Vedic
áduhat, áśayat and Hittite *-*a* (third person singular preterite of the
ḫ-conjugation). As a rule this archaic *-o* is replaced by *-to* (Indo-Ir.*-ta*,
Gk. *-to*). The pertinent proportions are:

(I) *-t*(active):*-o*(mediopassive) = *-nt*(active):*-nto*(mediopassive),
the correct *morphological* proportion being
zero(zero number, zero voice):*-o*(zero number, voice) = *-nt*(number,
zero voice):*-nto*(number, voice)

(II) -*nt*:-*t* = -*nto*:-*to* (*t* negative, not neutral as in I).

Another example illustrating the importance of morphological proportions is the much discussed problem of the Greek desinences -εις and -ει of the second and third person singular of the thematic present.

According to Brugmann we get phonetically *λέγεσι > λέγει, hence λέγεις owing to the secondary addition of -*s*-; finally, on the model of (ἐ)λεγες:(ἐ)λεγε, a secondary form of the third person singular λέγει (replacing *λέγετι) was created.[1]

Later Brugmann modified his opinion about the second person singular, assuming its ending to have been inherited and identical with that of Lith. *sukì:sukíe-s*.[2]

But there is no need to postulate anything different from an original *λέγεσι or *λέγετι, with -*esi*, -*eti* as in the majority of the Indo-European languages.

The correct analysis of these forms is the following:
unmarked (fundamental)

series: 3rd. p. sing. *λέγετ → 2nd. p. sing. λέγες
marked (enlarged)   ↓   ↓
series: 3rd. p. sing. *λέγετι → 2nd. p. sing. *λέγεσι

Two phonemic changes take place: the final dental -*t* and the intervocalic -*s* are dropped. The latter change is probably older. In the second person the marked ending is formed from the unmarked one by subtraction of -*s* and addition of -*i*. Hence, once the final -*t* of the third person has disappeared, we get proportionally:

(I) λέγες (nonindicative) [> *λέγε]:*λέγει = λέγε (nonindicative) : λέγει

(II) λέγε (zero person) : λέγες = λέγει (zero person) : λέγεις

It is clear that such a solution would not have satisfied Brugmann or his successors since proportion (I) would not have been, from the *phonetic* point of view, admissible.

In the so-called primary word formation of Indo-European the basic

---

[1] *Griechische Grammatik*, p. 347 (3d ed. München: C. H. Beck, 1900). *Grundriss* II, 3, 582 (Strassburg: Trübner, 1916).

[2] "Zur griechischen u. germanischen Präsensflexion," *Indogermanische Forschungen*, 15 (1903), 126–128. "Zur Bildung der 2. Pers. Sing. in den idg. insbesondere den baltischen Sprachen," *Indogermanische Forschungen*, 17 (1904), 177–185. Followed by Meillet, *Introduction*, p. 228 (8th ed. Paris: Hachette, 1937).

form is reduced to the simple root before being provided with the necessary derivational suffix. See the derivational types in *-o* (Gk. τόμος and τομός), for example, Skt. *-bhará-* < *bhárati* but also *-kará-* < *kṛnóti*. Contrasting with the derived forms the affixes of the basic forms become semantically neutral and are disregarded in the morphological proportions:

  bhárati:-*bhará-* = *kṛnóti*:-*kará-*

In morphological proportions morphophonemes (i.e. redundant morphs) are disregarded, just as in phonological proportions allophones (i.e. phonemic variants) are disregarded. A relation like *Gut*: *Güter, Buch*:*Bücher* is phonemically, though not phonetically correct; see the *ach*-Laut in *Buch,* and the *ich*-Laut in *Bücher.*

Confusion between the morphological and the morphophonemic approach would make us reject, for example, Saussure's explanation of the rise of mobile accentuation in the Baltic (Lithuanian) vocalic stems. According to Saussure this mobility is to be accounted for by the pressure exerted by the consonantal stems in *-er, -en,* where the inherited alternation acc. *-ér-m, -én-m*: gen. *-r-és, -n-és,* transformed into *initial versus desinential accentuation,* has been imposed upon the different classes of the vocalic stems. The objection would be of a morphological order, namely, that such an explanation is in contradiction with the fact that the consonantal stems were almost unproductive as against the well-attested productiveness of *-o-, -a-, -i-* stems. But this semantic factor does not play a role in Saussure's explanation, which belongs to the *morphophonemic* level and is in the last instance based on the overt distinction of inflectional suffix and desinence in the consonantal stems versus their fusion into a portmanteau morph in the vocalic stems. This is a fact of *dominance* comparable to that stated in the example *Blatt*:*Blätter,* where the morphophonemic umlaut is imposed by the plural morpheme, that is, the marginal morpheme, upon the central morpheme (the root).

In a similar way the fact that verbs with preverbs are derived from simples (this being a derivational, i.e., semanticomorphological fact) does not prevent the recessive accent of compounds from influencing the accentuation of the simples (cf. *L'accentuation,* p. 152). It is the opposition of compound versus simple *morphs,* not *morphemes,* which is envisaged here.

8. The semantic zero value of morphonemes is a counterpart of the semantic function of morphological zero. Thus the ending of a form like Russian *slov* has the value of the genitive as opposed to the nominative plural *slová*. The stressed *-á* of *slová* is *positive* or *neuter* according to whether we envisage the contrast *slóvo:slová* or *slová:slov*. Morphoneme with zero function on the one hand, and zero with morphological function on the other hand, depend on actual opposition. The contrast Russian *slóvo* (nom. sing.):*slová* (nom. plur.) has to be reduced to *-o* with zero value:sign *-á* of the plural, whereas *within the plural* the relation *slová* (nom.):*slov* (gen.) must be regarded as *-á* with zero value:sign *zero* (gen.).

The difference between morpheme and morphoneme is also important for syntax. For example, the relation between subject and predicate is often analyzed from a twofold point of view: government of (verbal) person by the subject, government of the nominative of the subject by the verb. But both the exponent of the third person of the verb and the ending of the nominative are morphonemes with semantic zero function. Government, occurring only between meaningful elements, is therefore out of the question. As regards number (sometimes also gender) there is agreement of the verb with the subject; see the syncretism of number within the verb, but not within the noun, in constructions like accusative + infinitive.

It would not do to consider morphonemes as a kind of accessory or subordinate morphemes. Morphemes have a semantic or syntactical function, totally absent in morphonemes. Morphonemes serve as a supplementary phonemic characterization of *word forms already provided with morphemes*. They are not, however, a subject of phonology proper. The latter has to do with phonemes, their features and structures (like stress units, syllables, consonant clusters, and so on), but not with morphs. Morphonology or morphophonemics, on the other hand, is interested in phonemes, phonemic features and structures dominated by morphological, not phonological, factors, and therefore belongs to *morphology*.

9. In the history of a language morphonemes may become semanticized and raised to the rank of morphemes. This is a well-attested phenomenon. See the umlaut of OHG indicative *feris* versus subjunctive

farês. After the weakening of unstressed vowels (MHG *fer[e]st*: *far[e]st*) the back vowel of the subjunctive, contrasting with the front vowel of the indicative, becomes a full-fledged morpheme. The vowel change in English *feet, geese, teeth* versus *foot, goose, tooth* is likewise a morpheme.

The change of morphemes into morphonemes is also easily illustrated; see the rise of various union-consonants or union-vowels or the fate of the Indo-European -*t*- suffix mechanically attached to root nouns in sonorant or semivowel: Skt. *kr̥-t-, ci-t-, cyu-t-*.

We have seen that morphemes can under circumstances become morphonemes, that is, they can lose their semantic or syntactical function: if a morpheme stands in opposition as a neutral member to a positive one (*slová:slov*). This occasional zero value of the morpheme is to be distinguished from the zero value of the morphoneme, the latter being a phonological phenomenon dominated by the morphological structure of the word. *Within a given morphological category* there is a certain phonological dependence between a morpheme and a morphoneme (for example, between a suffix and ablaut or umlaut).

10. To sum up: The morphological analysis of a word yields morphs in the first instance. Some of them are carriers of morphological functions (semantic or syntactic), others are semantically void. The former are the only ones to deserve the name of *morphemes*. The latter, the *morphonemes,* may be represented not only by phonemes or phonemic features, but also by phonemic complexes (e.g., Lat. -*us* of the nominative singular). A morphoneme is therefore not necessarily an elementary phoneme. Taken as an *elementary unit* the morphoneme is a subject of morphonology, which belongs to morphology. Its phonemic structure is as irrelevant as is the phonemic structure of a simple morpheme. The analysis of the morphoneme into phonemes, that is into diacritic elements, is another matter. But from the point of view of phonemics, which undertakes such an analysis, the difference between morphemes and morphonemes is of no consequence.

The morphonemes of a language can be established only on the basis of morphological transformational processes (in derivation and inflection).

The distinction between morphemes and morphonemes is of primary importance also in historical linguistics. The superposition of morphonemes upon the morphological word form, the fact that they represent a superficial layer in the structure of the word, favors the proportional spread of these redundant elements. Phonemically obligatory, they are semantically void. Their function lies in an expressive swelling of the derived and founded word forms, increasing their external difference from the basic forms. In purely morphological proportions, established to account for morphological innovations, morphonemes may be disregarded, just as are allophones in phonemic proportions. This new appreciation of the morphological proportion may open a new vista in historical morphology.

Mutations of Linguistic Categories

ÉMILE BENVENISTE

Collège de France

The evolution of a language taken as a sign system consists in the mutations undergone by its categories. We define categories as those form classes which are distinctively characterized and capable of grammatical function.

Not all categories change in identical fashion, still less simultaneously. But since all are to some extent interconnected, even those which seem permanent are bound to be affected by the mutations involving those which are less so, whether in form, in function, or in both.

We shall find it useful to define more accurately the concept of mutation as a diachronic process observable in linguistic categories by distinguishing two types of mutations, inherently different, with different causes and effects in the evolution of languages:

(1) INNOVATING mutations result from the loss or emergence of formal classes, processes which thus modify the total stock of available categories. For the disappearance of categories, instances familiar to the Indo-Europeanist would be (a) the partial or complete loss of gender distinctions—elimination of the neuter, leaving only the opposition masculine/feminine, or elimination of the feminine, creating an opposition animate/inanimate; (b) the reduction of number distinctions through abolishment of the dual; and (c) the reduction, in varying degrees, of systems of nominal classes and—sometimes concomitantly —of the deictic system. We can illustrate the creation of categories with the genesis of the definite article, or of new classes of adverbs sprouting from compounds (Eng. -ly; Fr. -ment).

These curtailments and accretions modify the stock of formal categories of the given language; moreover, they entail a reorganization and redistribution of all forms represented in those oppositions whose structure has been affected—witness the redistribution of the three number classes into two residual classes; the absorption of the Latin neuter plural by the Romance feminine; the reorganization of demonstratives coincident with the specialization of the article.

(2) CONSERVATIVE mutations serve to replace a morphemic category by a periphrastic category with the same function—thus, the morphological (or synthetic) comparative yields to the sequence adverb + adjective; case endings give way to the combination preposition + noun. Let us focus our attention on mutations of this sort, to underline the fundamental importance of the concept of periphrasis in the very process of mutation.

The mutations of special interest to us in this context are those which are both productive of and realized by a new class of signs, to be known as signs of auxiliation. To illustrate this process of "auxiliation" we may select the periphrastic development of two verbal categories, the perfectum and the future, in the Romance domain. We are here confronted with a privileged situation, as regards both the abundance of data and the number of theoretical observations which they invite.

The formal characteristic of this mutation is its operation through the rise of a "syntagm," which stands as its essential condition, whatever the further course taken by this syntagm (kept separate in the perfectum, welded into a unit in the future). The auxiliation syntagm may be defined as the alliance of an inflected auxiliary with an uninflected element, the "auxiliate." To these two components we must add a third, which consists in the coalescence of the two, a combination productive of a new shape, distinct from either component, and a new function as well. We have elsewhere furnished a descriptive analysis of the structure of French auxiliation syntagms.

At this point we shall consider how these periphrases can be defined for the perfectum and the future in their Latin garb, viewed in their formal and functional relations.

I

The typical periphrasis for the Latin perfectum is based on *habēre* + past participle. This would seem to be a clear, readily intelligible, and pervasive structure, whether in Latin or at some more advanced stage, since it recurs in just this shape in Romance and in several other languages. On more careful inspection the delineation of the syntagm is controlled by a set of strict conditions, and presupposes certain basic theoretical distinctions. Neither the conditions nor the distinctions seem to have been clearly identified so far.

Two separate conditions are required for the forms of *habēre* and the past participle to combine into a single syntagm. Each of these conditions involves a choice between two possibilities.

Habeō in predicative construction displays two meanings, 'hold' and 'have.' This preliminary condition is of capital importance; it dominates the available pattern of choices. The difference between 'hold' and 'have' has by and large been misjudged in the many scholarly treatments of the perfectum. In most cases the question has not even been properly raised. Hence the widespread confusion that surrounds the analysis of this construction.

This first distinction is essential; depending on whether *habeō* is interpreted as 'hold' or 'have,' the avenue to the comprehension of the periphrasis is thrown open or is blocked. The primary distinction, bearing on the meaning of the auxiliary *habeō*, is linked to a complementary distinction bearing on the function of the auxiliate: the latter may be taken either as an adjective (as in the case of *promptus* 'presently visible, ready at hand,' *lectus* 'choice (adj.), excellent,' *ratus* 'valid, legal,' *tacitus* 'secret, silent,' *clausus* 'inaccessible,' *subitus* 'sudden'), or as a verbal participle *sensu stricto*. Each of these functions matches a single sense of *habeō* and gives rise to a distinct syntagm. Of these two syntagms one never serves to realize the perfectum, namely the sequence *habēre* 'hold' + adjectival participle. The other invariably realizes the perfectum—the combination of *habēre* 'have' with a verbal participle.

A third condition is required for the form of the syntagm to bring about the perfectum relation; it hinges on the semantic nature of the verb. In principle, the verb must denote a "sensory-intellective" process inherent in the subject, rather than an "operational" process brought to bear on an object external to the subject. Typical of this category are the verbs 'understand, discover, realize, notice, see,' which were the first to favor the rise of the periphrasis at issue.

These are the three conditions which govern the periphrastic perfectum. One can observe their interplay and yet discern their separate agencies in such a sequence as *hoc compertum habet* 'he has learned this,' where clearly (a) *habēre* means 'have, possess,' (b) *compertum* is the participle denoting the state in which the object has been left, and (c) the verb *comperīre* 'learn, discover' denotes a mental process.

Through the conjunction of these three factors the agent of *comperīre* and the grammatical subject of *habēre* inevitably coincide. In consequence, the agent of the process emerges, in and through this syntagm, as the possessor of the result, which is his PROPERTY. This feature is characteristic of a novel relationship between agent and process, one quite different from that which the simple temporal form asserts.

A second reverberation is the equally novel temporal situation which this group confers on the process. Because it is stated as accomplished, yet at the same time connected with the present, the process is carried back to a stage of anteriority vis-à-vis the moment of utterance. In the phrase *hoc compertum habet* the present tense of *habet* marks the lasting relation with the present moment, while the p. ptc. *compertum* characterizes the state of the object as past, hence logically preceding the moment of speech. Such is the twofold distinctive nature of the perfectum: the process is viewed as present, but conceptually classed as accomplished. No other verbal form rivals it in this function.

Starting from this point, speakers generalize the syntagmatic model, extending it to other verbs, until they reach *episcopum invitatum habes* 'You have invited the bishop' (Gregory of Tours). At this juncture the syntagm becomes a single bipartite form, the perfectum; the two parts fulfill distinct and mutually complementary intrasyntagmatic functions: *habēre* becomes the auxiliary charged with the syntactic relations proper to the utterance; the participle in turn serves as the auxiliate, conveying the semantic kernel of the verb. It is the alliance of the two parts which realizes the perfectum.

In the Latin verbal paradigm a reorganization of the original perfectum is effected, a change which leads through a split to two different forms. The value inherent in the synthetic perfectum (*audīvī*) is passed on to the periphrastic perfectum (*audītum habeō*), which restricts the value of *audīvī* to that of an aorist. Furthermore, the very fact that the auxiliary *habeō* retains the inflectional status of a free verb helps to establish a complete periphrastic conjugation which reshapes the paradigm of the perfectum.

Thus the periphrastic form is heir to the original perfectum, not only by virtue of a historical sequence of events, but also because it brings to light its inherent value.

We can here only hint at this unique relation, which would require major elaboration. The structural mutation results in a functional preservation.

None of this comes to light so long as one remains satisfied with repeating, as do so many textbooks, that *il a une lettre écrite; il a ses vêtements déchirés* is quite close, almost to the point of synonymy, to *il a écrit une lettre; il a déchiré ses vêtements,* an analysis triply in error, from the points of view of description, of history, and of general theory, and one which, worse, bars its correct formulation by creating confusion at the heart of the problem.

II

The transmutation of the Latin into the Romance future was effected, as is well known, through the medium of the periphrasis *habeō* + infinitive. The manuals are unanimous in representing this with the formula *cantāre habeō* > Fr. *je chanterai*.

This way of symbolizing the passage from one stage to another must be termed erroneous both as concerns the historical process it aims at representing, and as a theoretical model providing the clue to it. *Cantabō* was never replaced by *cantāre habeō* (except, at most, in the late Romance period, when all futures had become periphrastic) and it never could have been. This dual error, historical and theoretical, flows from an inaccurate interpretation of the sequence *habēre* + infinitive, which is indeed the transitional stage between the Latin and the Romance future.

Let us begin by laying down the precise conditions under which the periphrasis emerged. It is traceable to the Christian writers and theologians starting with Tertullian (early third century A.D.). The overwhelming majority of examples show that: (1) the periphrasis began with *habēre* and the PASSIVE infinitive; (2) it was initially used with

the IMPERFECT tense of *habēre*; and (3) it was restricted to SUBORDI-
NATE, chiefly relative, clauses. It was thus at the start a highly specific
construction. The underlying model was: ". . . in nationibus *a quibus
magis suscipi habebat*" 'among the nations by whom it had most to be
accepted.' In no way did it rival the conventional future, which the
same writers continued to use regularly and with neither qualification
nor hesitancy. This is the first significant ensemble of circumstances.

A second conditioning feature connected with the one just described
is the MEANING of *habēre*. It follows from this construction that *habēre*
did not mean 'have to,' as in Fr. *j'ai à travailler*, Eng. *I have to work*,
a meaning which would never have yielded the future *je travaillerai*
and which in fact clashes so sharply with it that, now as before, *j'ai à
travailler* is never confused with *je travaillerai*, nor *j'ai à dire* with *je
dirai*. In the Latin syntagm as it actually crystallized, *habēre* + infinitive
served to indicate the predestination of the object to follow a certain
course of events. This is a novel and distinctive semantic hue, totally
divorced from the purposive value often associated with the future
tense.

This periphrasis, when it arises, displays, I repeat, an idiosyncratic
syntactic structure. Is it then a substitute for the future? By no means.
It appears, at the outset, not in independent clauses but in subordinated,
typically relative clauses. Its function must then be defined as that of a
verbal adjective or a participle. In fact this periphrasis acts as the
equivalent of a future passive participle, indicating not obligation (as
does the -*ndus* form) but predestination. No nominal form of the Latin
verbal paradigm was available for this concept, which was both new in
regard to the classical "tenses" and vital in the conceptual frame in
which it developed.

Once this periphrasis had entrenched itself, it extended its hold. It
spread first to the independent clause: *Nazaraeus vocari habebat secun-
dum prophetiam*; next, it admitted the combination of *habēre* with the
infinitive of a deponential or intransitive verb: *quia nasci habebat*;
quod in omnem terram exire habebat praedicatio apostolorum; finally
habēre joined the infinitive of all verbs. But this generalization was
completed quite late (6th–7th C.). Only then did the syntagm actually
enter into rivalry with the traditional future and succeed in evicting it.
Two separate processes have to be distinguished in this context:

(1) The syntagm *habēre* + infinitive had long coexisted with the original future without crossing its path, because it rendered a distinct meaning. There were thus available two expressions of the future: one suggesting intention (the simple form in *-bō, -am*), the other pre-destination (the syntagm: 'what is to happen' > 'what will happen'). The two modes of expression inevitably had to clash at some point and, in various uses, to become confused. In this struggle, the simple shape of the original future, already weakened by its formal cleavage and by the phonic coincidences with the perfectum (*amābit ∼ amāvit*), was to be the loser.

(2) At the same time a formal shrinkage of the syntagm gradually takes place as the sequential order infinitive + *habēre* becomes fixed and as the two members coalesce: Between the final vowel of the infinitives and the first vowel of the attached *habēre* forms, the *h-* is lost; henceforth, *abere* carries the inflection: *essere abetis* 'you (pl.) will be' (6th C.), followed by *venire (h)abes, videre (h)abe*, and thus paving the way for *salverai, prinderai* of the Strasbourg Oaths. This eventual mutation of the syntagm into an indissoluble unit enabled it to replace the original future in the total verb paradigm.

We have here before us an example of a locution born out of a specific, clearly delimited need, embedded in a narrow syntactic frame, a locution which develops its innate potentialities, and then, through an unforeseeable semantic twist, takes over a certain expression of the future. Little by little the speakers exploit this device to establish a new set of temporal forms, which supplant the older set.

Another periphrastic mutation of a traditional future occurred in Greek, in a way curiously reminiscent of the preceding example. The inherited form of the future was replaced in Middle Greek by two rival periphrases which disclose a conflict between two distinct expressions: the one involving *ékhō* 'I have' + infinitive, the other *thélō* 'I want' + infinitive. Over the same domain there occurred a simultaneous extension of the modal form of the subjunctive aorist involving *na* (modal particle): *nà idô* 'I shall see.' This rivalry gave rise to a new form, periphrastic at first: *thélo nà (grapsō)*, later reduced to *thé nà* ... (13th C.), *thà nà*, finally *thà (gràpso)*, the demotic future. The Modern Greek future is thus the present or the aorist with a prefixed

particle *tha*. From the original periphrasis the element expressing intention is no longer recognizable as a meaningful form, since the second element (matching the infinitive in the Latin counterpart) was in
Greek a finite clause, obligatorily comprising a personal verb form.
The auxiliary *thélō* had thus become redundant as an inflected form and
could dwindle to a particle.

A third instance of mutation is supplied by Sogdian, an East Iranian
dialect. The original future, based on *-sya-*, as in Avest. *būšyati* 'he
will be,' here yields ground to a locution involving the present followed by the particle *kām* (initially, 'desire') : *but kām* 'he will be.'
At more advanced stages the particle coalesces with the verb form and
is ultimately reduced to *-kā,* no longer a free nor a meaningful form:
butqā 'he will be.'

It would seem that, through some inner necessity, the periphrasis of
the future is bound to eliminate the auxiliary, whether through fusion
with the auxiliate (as in Romance), or through demotion to the rank
of a particle (as in Modern Greek and in Sogdian).

III

These examples tend to show the similarity, in the mutation of formal categories, of the verbs used to produce rather disparate syntagmatic combinations, which follow different trajectories in the same
language.

The new perfectum and future were built on the same auxiliary,
habēre. If one were to study the mutation of the old synthetic passive
in the Romance languages, one would have to analyze the rôle of the
verbal periphrases with *esse* in Late Latin. In the process of periphrastic reorganization of the Latin tenses in Western Romance, with few
exceptions—*il est venu,* say—only *esse* and *habēre* (and its variant
tenēre; cf. Portuguese) were used.

Other mutations are on record, making use of other auxiliaries. One
of the most familiar is the shift of modal verb forms to syntagms based
on auxiliaries such as 'be able.' One also encounters instances of the
replacement of simple aspectual forms by syntagms containing an
aspectually slanted auxiliary.

But whatever function it serves, auxiliation is a syntactic process generously used in the widest range of languages. A syntagm involving an auxiliary universally exhibits certain common traits, which it is tempting to exemplify with two separate American Indian languages.

Wherever the phenomenon in question is observed, one notes that the auxiliary verb is endowed with special properties and pertains to the same series, transcending differences of linguistic structure. The verb at issue is semantically very broad, often defective and irregular, frequently suppletive.

Mary R. Haas distinguishes, in Tunica, three verbal classes: active and stative verbs beside auxiliaries. The auxiliaries are the following: *ʔúhki* 'he is, exists'; *ʔúra* 'he lies, is in a lying position'; *ʔúna* 'he sits, dwells'; *ʔúsa* 'he comes'; *ʔúwa* 'he goes'; -*ʔúta* 'he causes,' and, separately, *láka* 'they live' (anomalous 3d pl.).

Each can be used freely or as an auxiliary in construction with other verbs. They differ from the two other verb classes by virtue of the following characteristics: (1) certain auxiliaries are irregularly inflected: some forms in part resemble stative verbs, others active verbs, still others are unanalyzable; (2) they—and they alone—are suppletive; (3) they are also unique in using reduplication in the repetitive paradigms; and (4) they all occur in the periphrastic inflection of active verbs, even though (with one exception) they all likewise enjoy free use.

Aztec also recognizes auxiliary verbs. These verbs—Whorf counted ten of them—lead an independent existence. As auxiliaries, they are suffixed to the verb and, in the classical language, endow the verbal form with a certain aspectual force.

The auxiliaries at issue are: (1) *ka* 'be' (= continuative); (2) *nemi* 'walk, travel' (= goes along doing it); (3) *wi·c* 'come' (= comes doing it) (4) *mani* 'extend, lie' (= goes around doing it, does it over an area: *kiyawtimani* 'rains around'); (5) *ikak* 'stand' (= remains erect); (6) *ewa* 'lift' (= nondurative 'enters into the action' or simply inceptive: *kon-anatewa* 'starts forward to get it'); (7) *momana* and (8) *mote·ka*, both 'settle down,' the first having the idea of spreading, in idiomatic use; (9) *kisa* 'go forth,' and (10) *weci* 'fall,' nondurative and vigorous "launching-forward" inceptives: -*kʷitiweci* 'dashes upon and takes.'

The auxiliary is suffixed to the present *-ti-;* for example, with the auxiliary *ka* 'be' + *mo-λalia* 'sits' one arrives at *o·mo-λalitikatka* 'he was sitting,' *mo-λalitiyes* 'he will be sitting.'

The technique of auxiliation is especially clear and instructive in the Altaic languages. In Old Turkish (Gabain) the auxiliary construction encompasses an inflected auxiliary verb and a fixed "coverb" in *-u* or *-p.* The rather broad spectrum of auxiliaries includes verbs of general meaning which, as auxiliaries, produce periphrases descriptively or modally slanted: from *tur-* 'stand' one extracts *altayu tur* 'be in the habit of deceiving'; from *tut-* 'hold': *küyü tut-* 'protect continuously'; from *alq-* 'exhaust': *qïlu alq-* 'carry out to the end'; from *tart-* 'pull': *qutu tart-* 'die out slowly.'

Numerous other parallels which come to mind attest to both the wide applicability of the procedure and the striking mutual resemblance of its various realizations.

These insights enable us to place the auxiliary constructions of the Indo-European languages in a broader descriptive frame, which accounts for them more effectively. Conversely, where languages without recorded history exhibit auxiliary structures comparable to those of the Indo-European languages, we should feel free to make use of the Indo-European model in genetic explanations.

(Translated by YAKOV MALKIEL and MARILYN MAY VIHMAN) *

* To avoid possible ambiguities in the English, the following terminological equations were introduced here: Fr. *transformation* = *mutation; parfait* = *perfectum*; *auxiliant* = *auxiliary*; *auxilié* = *auxiliate*; *auxiliation* was rendered, for lack of any satisfactory English equivalent, by the cognate neologism *auxiliation.*

The American Indian examples in the text are drawn from H. Hoijer (ed.), *Linguistic Structures of Native America* (New York: Viking Fund VI, 1946): Mary R. Haas, "A Grammatical Sketch of Tunica" (p. 349) and Benjamin Lee .Whorf, "The Milpa Alta Dialect of Aztec . . ." (p. 386). All the Tunica forms are glossed as both present and past tense in Haas' article.

Empirical Foundations
for a
Theory of Language Change

URIEL WEINREICH, WILLIAM LABOV,
and MARVIN I. HERZOG

Columbia University

URIEL WEINREICH

Uriel Weinreich died on March 30, 1967. Those who knew him, friends and colleagues in many fields of research, find it difficult to contain their grief. He was not yet forty-one years old. In the last weeks of his life he devoted his major effort to the final revision of this paper, and worked actively on it until two days before his death.

This paper emerged when, after several years of research and discussion on problems dealing with language change, the three authors felt it opportune to attempt a joint formulation of certain ideas on which their thinking had been converging. It was Weinreich who prepared the original draft incorporating appropriate materials submitted to him by the second- and third-named authors. He was, at the time, an NSF Senior Postdoctoral Fellow at the Center for Advanced Studies in the Behavioral Sciences; the first draft, for presentation to the Symposium in April, 1966, was produced across a geographic distance, and under a schedule which ruled out the possibility of full discussion. Thereafter, some conclusions remained to be hammered into more mutually agreeable form. This process of revision began after Weinreich's return to New York in the fall of 1966, and proceeded actively despite his illness.

Weinreich's personal editing of the final draft comes to an end with Section 2.4. The final formulation of the remainder, from 2.41 on, is the work of the second-named author. The third section of the paper was sketched out only lightly in the draft presented at the Texas conference. Though many of Weinreich's formulations and evaluations appear here, and the overall framework is a product of our joint thinking in the early months of 1967, there are undoubtedly many details which would have taken a different form if he had shared in the final editing.

Whatever revisions have been introduced, the basic orientation of the paper remains unchanged. It thus largely reflects Weinreich's conception. The historical perspective, especially the sections on Paul and Saussure, are exclusively his. The Introduction is also Weinreich's work: it emerged after our frequent meetings during the last few weeks of his life. In this final version, after many revisions, Weinreich fused the several themes of the paper into a single statement. His coauthors are honored that he deliberately chose this means of preparing a final statement of his views on the structure of language and the nature of linguistic change.

0. INTRODUCTION

The present paper[1] is based on the observation that structural theories of language, so fruitful in synchronic investigation, have saddled historical linguistics with a cluster of paradoxes which have not been fully overcome. Ferdinand de Saussure, in laying the foundations of synchronic study, was aware of the corresponding intractability of language change, and was apparently resigned to it. But with the majority of linguists after Saussure, the choice between studying either the structure or the history of languages did not sit well. It would not be unfair to say that the bulk of theoretical writing in historical linguistics of the past few decades has been an effort to span the Saussurean dilemma, to elaborate a discipline which would be structural and historical at the same time.

We would like here to depict the origins of the structure-history antinomy in Neogrammarian theory; we will dwell particularly on Hermann Paul, who apparently was the first to isolate the language of the individual as the most legitimate object of linguistic study. We

[1] The research on which the paper is based has enjoyed support from several sources. The Language and Culture Atlas of Ashkenazic Jewry, of which the first author was director until his death, is currently being compiled under the direction of the third author with aid of Public Health Service Research Grant MH 08106 from the National Institutes of Health to Columbia University. Research on New York City English is being continued by the second-named author as Project 3288 of the Cooperative Research Branch, U.S. Office of Education.

will trace the hardening of the paradox in the Saussurean period, when homogeneity of language—assumed to be found in the idiolect—was drawn upon as a prerequisite for analysis. We will show the fresh opportunities for explaining language change that came with the efflorescence of linguistic description after World War II, and comment also on the limitations that developed in viewing language states as determinants of their own further development. We will review a number of attempts that were made to see the language of a community as a differentiated system and to reconcile the observed facts of linguistic heterogeneity with the theoretical desiderata of finding order and structure. We will, finally, suggest that a model of language which accommodates the facts of variable usage and its social and stylistic determinants not only leads to more adequate descriptions of linguistic competence, but also naturally yields a theory of language change that bypasses the fruitless paradoxes with which historical linguistics has been struggling for over half a century.

In referring to *theory* in the title of the paper, we have been conscious of the new connotation which this term has acquired in the discourse of linguists of the past decade. When Chomsky in 1957 proposed to view the grammar of a language as (1) a *theory* of its sentences, and linguistics as (2) a *theory* of correct grammars, he gave a new seriousness to linguistic investigation and reached out for a fresh alliance between linguistics and the exact sciences. To be sure, Chomsky's second use of *theory* has turned out to be more utopian than it seemed originally. But the first application of the term has already brought about such significant advances that it is worth considering the bearing which this strong sense of theory may have on language change.

A "theory" of language change in the rigorous sense can be visualized in a relatively strong form and in a weak form. In its strong form, the theory would predict, from a description of a language state at some moment in time, the course of development which that language would undergo within a specified interval. Few practicing historians of language would be rash enough to claim that such a theory is possible.[2] In a more modest version, a theory of language change would

[2] Coseriu (1958), in his monograph on structuralist theories of language change and their philosophical foundations, distinguishes between the "ra-

merely assert that every language constantly undergoes alteration, and it would formulate constraints on the transition from one state of a language to an immediately succeeding state. It might predict further that no language will assume a form in violation of such formal principles as are postulated to be universal in human languages. Without predicting positively what will happen (except that the language will somehow change), such a theory would at least assert that some changes will *not* take place.

Our own view is that neither the strong nor the modest version of such theories of language change, as they proceed from current generative grammar, will have much relevance to the study of language history. We will argue that the generative model for the description of language as a homogeneous object (see §2.1) is itself needlessly unrealistic and represents a backward step from structural theories capable of accommodating the facts of orderly heterogeneity. It seems to us quite pointless to construct a theory of change which accepts as its input unnecessarily idealized and counterfactual descriptions of language states. Long before predictive theories of language change can be attempted, it will be necessary to learn to see language—whether from a diachronic *or* a synchronic vantage—as an object possessing orderly heterogeneity.

The facts of heterogeneity have not so far jibed well with the structural approach to language. We will see the seeds of this conflict in Saussure (§1.21) and its deepening in the works of descriptivists struggling with the phenomena of change. For the more linguists became impressed with the existence of structure of language, and the more they bolstered this observation with deductive arguments about the functional advantages of structure, the more mysterious became the transition of a language from state to state. After all, if a language has to be structured in order to function efficiently, how do people continue to talk while the language changes, that is, while it passes through periods of lessened systematicity? Alternatively, if overriding

---

tional" problem of why languages change of necessity, the "general" problem of conditions under which particular changes usually appear in languages, and the "historical" problem of accounting for concrete changes that have taken place. He finds linguistics widely plagued by the mistake of confusing the three levels of the question (p. 37).

pressures do force a language to change, and if communication is less efficient in the interim (as would deductively follow from the theory), why have such inefficiencies not been observed in practice?[3]

This, it seems to us, is the fundamental question with which a theory of language change must cope. The solution, we will argue, lies in the direction of breaking down the identification of structuredness with homogeneity. The key to a rational conception of language change —indeed, of language itself—is the possibility of describing orderly differentiation in a language serving a community. We will argue that nativelike command of heterogeneous structures is not a matter of multidialectalism or "mere" performance, but is part of unilingual linguistic competence. One of the corollaries of our approach is that in a language serving a complex (i.e., real) community, it is *absence* of structured heterogeneity that would be dysfunctional.

The problem of constraints on immediately succeeding language states, to which we alluded above, is in our view subsumed under the broader theoretical question. Of course, we too want to inquire into the set of possible changes and possible conditions for changes which can take place in a structure of a given type. Nor do we want to dismiss the *transition* problem: it remains entirely relevant to ask about intervening stages which can be observed, or which must be posited, between any two forms of a language defined for a language community at different times. But if the theory is to be illuminating with respect to recorded histories of languages, we must ask two further questions: How are the observed changes *embedded* in the matrix of linguistic and extralinguistic concomitants of the forms in question? (That is, what other changes are associated with the given changes in a manner that cannot be attributed to chance?) And how can the observed changes be *evaluated*—in terms of their effects upon linguistic structure, upon communicative efficiency (as related, e.g., to functional load), and on the wide range of nonrepresentational factors involved in speaking?

We will refer to these four questions and their associated problems

---

[3] We are aware, of course, of Gilliéronian examples of "pathology" in language, which have been adopted by Martinet as explanations of push-chains in phonology (1955:54 ff. and *passim*). However, we will try to show below that only a small fraction of well-documented language changes seems at present explicable by such causality.

as those of *constraints, transition, embedding,* and *evaluation.*[4] Evidently the problems are partially ordered: a solution to the constraints question provides a set of changes within which the other questions can be put. In the light of answers to these, we can approach a fifth question, perhaps the most basic: What factors can account for the actuation of changes? Why do changes in a structural feature take place in a particular language at a given time, but not in other languages with the same feature, or in the same language at other times? This *actuation problem* can be regarded as the very heart of the matter. It is thus apparent that we want a theory of language change to deal with nothing less than the manner in which the linguistic structure of a complex community is transformed in the course of time so that, in some sense, both the language and the community remain the same, but the language acquires a different form.[5]

We will not be presenting a fully worked-out theory of linguistic change in this paper; it is doubtful whether any linguist has enough relevant facts at his disposal to attempt anything so ambitious, and we are not sure that with the facts available to us, the three coauthors would agree on the detailed outlines of such a theory. But, as our title suggests, we do feel in a position to make concrete proposals concerning the *empirical foundations* for a theory of change. By this we mean (1) the empirical findings which have significance for the theory, which the theory must account for, and which indicate directions for fruitful research; (2) certain conclusions drawn from these findings as to the minimal complexity of linguistic structure and domains for

---

[4] The transition, embedding, and evaluation problems were discussed by Labov (1965) under the heading of *mechanism* of a change. However, it seems difficult to give a precise meaning to the term *mechanism of a change,* and here we do not distinguish between explanation of a change and the analysis of the mechanism itself.

[5] The community has also changed, of course: it will be important for the purposes of this paper to note that the structure of the community, as well as the individuals who fill various functional slots in the structure, will normally show changes. In many cases, then, it will be difficult to establish that the community and the language are the same as they were, since both are changing; the changes may be so rapid that it is not easy to assert that the new members are the simultaneous inheritors of the same language and the same community. The major empirical studies referred to in this paper deal with changes so rapid that it is impossible to trace the gradual transformation of one form into the other.

defining such structure; and (3) methods for relating the concepts and statements of a theory to empirical evidence—that is, evidence based on rules for intersubjective agreement among investigators. We feel it important to dwell explicitly on empirical foundations, in view of the conscious or unconscious disregard of empirical principles which pervades some of the most influential work in linguistics today. We will, in what follows, try to document and account for this state of affairs.

We think of a theory of language change as part of a larger theoretical inquiry into linguistic evolution as a whole. A theory of linguistic evolution would have to show how forms of communication characteristic of other biological genera evolved (with whatever mutations) into a proto-language distinctively human, and then into languages with the structures and complexity of the speech forms we observe today. It would have to indicate how present-day languages evolved from the earliest attested (or inferred) forms for which we have evidence; and finally it would determine if the present course of linguistic evolution is following the same direction, and is governed by the same factors, as those which have operated in the past.[6]

It is the third general area of investigation which is the focus of the present paper: the description and explanation of linguistic change over the past four or five millennia. But even this limited area would be too large for a theory of change today. We might consider different temporal ranges separately: long-term changes with similar effects over millennia; completed changes which cover a century or two at the most; ongoing processes that can be observed in the course of one or two generations; or even purely synchronic sections in which we identify inferentially the directions of change of certain variable elements. In this discussion we will be concerned primarily with the second and the third of these ranges, although some comments will be made on the first problem and some data drawn from studies of the last.

---

[6] Investigations of the long-range effects of language planning, of mass literacy and mass media, have therefore a special relevance to the over-all study of linguistic evolution, though these factors, whose effect is recent at best, may be set aside for certain limited studies of language change. On language from an evolutionary point of view, see Greenberg 1954: chap. V; Greenberg 1959; Hymes 1961.

1. THE ISOLATION OF THE IDIOLECT

1.1. THE THEORIES OF HERMANN PAUL

Long before the nineteenth century it was widely realized that languages change,[7] but it is that century which is distinguished as the most vigorous period of historical linguistics. The theoreticians of the period were at pains to show that consistency of linguistic behavior, and in particular the regularity of sound changes, could be derived from more general, preferably psychological, principles. The culmination of this search was achieved by Hermann Paul (1880),[8] who developed the view that the language of the individual speaker-hearer encompassed the structured nature of language, the consistency of speech performance, and the regularity of change. In isolating the language of the individual from the language custom of the group, Paul developed a dichotomy which was adopted by generations of succeeding linguists and which lies, as we will try to show, at the bottom of the twentieth-century paradoxes concerning language change.

Idiolect and Language Custom. The task of the historian of language, according to Paul, is to state the sequence of particular language states (*Sprachzustände*; p. 29). The primary datum in this procedure is an object which he calls *psychischer Organismus.* This organ-

---

[7] For obvious reasons, awareness and discussion of language change developed first in the Romance world. The interest of Dante in this question is well known, that of his compatriot Tolomei less so (Claudio Tolomei, *Il Cesano,* ca. 1530). J. Chr. Kraus (1787) was already sophisticated enough to stress the opportunities offered to culture history by the greater conservatism of grammar over vocabulary. Many other examples could be cited. Therefore, Hockett (1965:185), like the authorities on which he bases himself, oversimplifies the matter in attributing the "genetic hypothesis" to Jones, Gyármathi, Rask, Grimm, and Bopp. The plain enumeration of these names is an oversimplification in another sense, too: the writers named differed greatly in their ability to draw inferences from the fact of change. For Grimm, temporal seriation of attested stages of Germanic languages was fundamental, but then he set himself no reconstructive tasks; Rask, on the other hand—although perhaps the boldest and most clear-headed thinker of the group—was slow in coming to terms with the facts of change; in his 1818 masterpiece he was still asking what *attested* languages Old Norse may have originated from.

[8] Our page references are to the more or less "standard" fifth edition (1920), which does not differ from the original on the points at issue here.

ism is conceived by Paul as a psychologically internalized grammar which generates the utterances of speakers.[9] "The true object of the linguist is the totality of manifestations of speech activity in all individuals in their mutual interaction" (p. 25). [This and succeeding translations are ours.]

The description of a language, in order for it to form a truly usable foundation for a historical view, must do more than fully enumerate the elements of which a language consists; "it must depict the relation of the elements to each other, their relative strengths, the connections into which they enter, the degree of closeness and strength of these connections" (p. 29). All these linguistically crucial relations can be found only in the language of the individual, in whose mind one will find the "interlocking image groups, with their multiple interlaced relations, which are relevant to speech activity" (p. 39). The image groups consist of "images" (*Vorstellungen*), that is, traces in the unconscious of physically and consciously perceived utterances.[10] Since the individual psyche is seen as the locus of the associations and connections between language components, we realize why Paul isolates the individual as the primary carrier of a language, and brings the argument to its logical conclusion by asserting that "we must distinguish as many languages as there are individuals."[11]

The isolation of the individual, Paul thought, had the advantage of

[9] Paul is specifically concerned with the generative power of an internalized totality of "image groups," as appears from his interest in kinesthetic and auditory self-monitoring of sound production and from his statement, in connection with (synchronic!) analogy, that speakers are able to form and understand sentences never before encountered. Paul expects a faithful description of an idiolect to reveal to us, "to put it in a popular way," nothing less than the speaker's *Sprachgefühl* (p. 29). As Paul sees it, it is impossible to infer the structure of the idiolect merely from the observation of utterances. "To relate [observed physical facts] to mental ones," Paul writes (p. 30), "is possible only through analogical inferences based on what we have observed in our own minds. Constantly renewed exact self-observation, meticulous analysis of one's own *Sprachgefühl*, is consequently a prerequisite for the training of the linguist."

[10] The "images" are by no means to be understood as pictorial representations, for example, of things nameable by concrete nouns; quite the contrary, every linguistic unit, every class of units, and every relation between classes is explicitly said to have a corresponding image as its mental representation. These images are related by "association" to form groups (pp. 26 ff.), thus yielding a full mental representation of the speaker's linguistic capacity.

[11] The ultimate individuality of language was of course already an important

attaching linguistics to a more general science of psychology. The price of such isolation, however, was the creation of an irreconcilable opposition between the individual and society. Paul then had to construct a theoretical bridge for passing from the unique, individual object of linguistics to a transindividual entity.

A comparison of individual languages (which we may, at the risk of terminological anachronism but with little fear of distortion, relabel "idiolects"[12]) yields a certain "average," which determines what is actually normal in the language—the Language Custom (*Sprachusus*; p. 29). For the purpose of later discussion, let us note the following features of Paul's "Language Custom." First, it is (unlike the idiolect) an artifact of the linguist—a product of his work of comparing idiolects; no independent "existence" is claimed for it.[13] Secondly, a Language Custom has no determinate bounds: every grouping of speakers into dialect groups is arbitrary, without theoretical motivation (p. 38). Clearly the Language Custom, or "average," resulting from a comparison of idiolects A and B would differ from that resulting from a comparison of idiolects A, B, and C—and there is no way to decide on the grounds of Paul's circumscribed theory whether C should be included or omitted from the comparison. Thirdly, if "Language Custom" were seriously to be interpreted as an "average," it would be meaningful only with reference to gradient phenomena; we might argue that $ü$ is the "average" of u and i, but there is no obvious meaning to an "average" of, say, *soda* and *pop* as two idiolectal designations of carbonated beverage. Fourthly, we must note that in postulating the absolute individuality of idiolects, Paul provides no clues for ranking differences among idiolects on any scale of importance. It follows, then, that for Paul the only object of theoretical significance is the idiolect: Language Custom is derivative, vague, unstructured; since on his terms

---

idea of romanticism; cf. Herder (1772:123–124), as quoted by Sapir (1907: 133–134).

[12] See § 1.22 below.

[13] Paul draws an analogy with the fictional conception of the species prevalent at the time: "Nothing has real existence except the particular individuals. . . . Species, genera, classes are nothing but arbitrary summaries and distinctions of the human mind" (p. 37).

structure and homogeneity imply one another, no structured object which is transindividual can be conceived.[14]

Change in Idiolect and in Language Custom. We are now ready to see how Paul treats language change. Changes in language can be understood in two senses: (1) as changes in an idiolect, and (2) as changes in Language Custom. Changes in Language Custom, in turn, can arise in two ways: (1) through changes within the idiolects over which a given Language Custom is defined; (2) through additions or subtractions of idiolects from the set of idiolects over which a Language Custom is defined. Suppose we define Language Custom LC_1 for the idiolects *A, B, C, D*. If idiolect *B* changes to *B'*, then there results a change in LC_1; alternatively, if idiolect *B* is removed from the set (e.g., through the death of its speaker), or an idiolect *E* is added (through the birth or immigration of its speaker), or both, there is also a change in the Language Custom LC_1, for in principle every idiolect contributes something different to the Language Custom as a whole. Since the boundaries of the set of idiolects over which a Language Custom is defined have no theoretical foundation, and since changes in Language Custom are completely derivative (p. 18), it is change within idiolects which, for Paul, has exclusive theoretical interest. (What saves the investigation from being an absolute sociological fantasy is the fact, duly noted by Paul, that sets of idiolects of course often do have *natural* boundaries in the sense of communication breaks among speakers or communities of speakers; cf. p. 40).

What causes changes in an idiolect? There are two mechanisms involved: spontaneous change, and adaptation to the idiolects of other speakers (p. 34). On the intraindividual, spontaneous mechanism Paul has little else to say; he refers just once more to the role of an

[14] Beginning with this view of things one might yet think of salvaging, for study as a transindividual phenomenon, the *common core* of a group of idiolects—that is, not the "average," but that fragment of the Language Custom which is shared by all idiolects. However, Paul wants no part of this, and excoriates "descriptive grammar" for its procedure of recording "which out of a set of grammatical forms and relations are current in a speech community at a particular time, what can be used by everyone without being misunderstood and without striking one's interlocutors as strange" (p. 24). The cardinal sin of such an approach is its concern with "abstractions."

individual's "personal particularities and the peculiar stimulations (*Erregungen*) of his own mental and bodily make-up" (p. 38), but it does not occur to him to instantiate any such peculiarities, so that a serious proposal of correlations between individual traits and idiolect change is out of the question. The other mechanism of idiolect change, as we have said, is the selective adoption of features from the idiolect of one's interlocutors. One suspects that for Paul this, the social mechanism, is the more important one; thus he says summarily in another passage that it is "solely through intercourse (*Verkehr*) that the language of the individual is created" (p. 39).

In view of the relation between idiolects and Language Custom, which we have already discussed, we can see that Language Custom changes "through the summation of a series of . . . shifts in idiolects moving in the same direction"; a new Language Custom is formed from an accumulation of parallel changes in the idiolects for which it is defined. Now it is clear that this theory says nothing about two other kinds of change which can be conceived of with equal reasonableness: (1) qualitative, nongradual changes in idiolects, and (2) nonparallel behavior of idiolects. If the changes are nongradual, they can hardly yield to a "summation"; and if the idiolects are not changing in parallel, what will be the result in the overall Language Custom? But it would be meaningless to press the question in the context of Paul's theory, because for him Language Custom with respect to nongradient phenomena (i.e., in effect, with respect to the bulk of language) is not a construct to be taken seriously.

Childhood and Adulthood. Given the two mechanisms of idiolect change (and, by extension, of Language Custom change), we may stop to consider whether an individual is equally liable to idiolect changes throughout his life. In principle, says Paul, yes: "it is impossible to designate a point in the life of an individual at which it could be said that language learning has ceased." On the other hand, the great bulk of language learning (idiolect changing) takes place in childhood, and the difference in degree is enormous (p. 34). As a result, Paul feels justified in concluding "that the processes of language learning are of supreme importance for the explanation of changes in Language Custom, that they represent the most important cause of these changes" (*ibid.*).

Unfortunately Paul does not develop this idea into any concrete hypotheses, and a number of questions remain unanswered. For example, if the mechanism of language learning works efficiently and uniformly, we would expect the set of young children's deviant idiolects to make the same small, stable contribution to every Language Custom; it would then be *untrue* that language learning explains changes in Language Custom. If, on the other hand, the learning mechanism works inefficiently, then we are entitled to know why children's mislearning does not have random, mutually canceling effects. In other words, invoking children's incomplete language learning as an explanation of language change is vacuous unless it suggests at the same time a *pattern* of learning failures. This Paul has failed to offer.

Unawareness. We may now go over to the discussion of a puzzle which arises from a combination of basic tenets in Paul's theory. If the significant locus of language change is in the idiolect, and if the idiolect is a psychological representation (the speaker's *Sprachgefühl*), why is it that speakers are not aware of changing their idiolects?[15] For an answer, Paul looks to the supposition that idiolect change takes place by infinitesimal steps (p. 19). But how can there be infinitesimal steps among discrete, quantized phenomena? How could one, let us say, move from *dived* to *dove*, or from *pop* to *soda* by infinitesimal steps? Possible solutions come to mind, and we will see below how other theorists have dealt with the question. Paul's own way out was arbitrarily to narrow the discussion from language in general to such aspects of language as are continuous (rather than discrete) in their design. He thus simply avoided the *general* question, which must of necessity deal with noncontinuous aspects of language as well.

The continuous side of language design with which Paul deals[16] is

---

[15] That change is in fact unconscious is for Paul an empirical finding, though he admits that it is "not so generally acknowledged and must still be demonstrated in detail" (p. 18). He is thinking, of course, of the "natural" development of language, not intentional regulatory intervention which may be observed in standardized languages and which is nothing if not conscious.

[16] His main concern is with sound. In his account of semantic change (Chap. IV), where he distinguishes between customary meanings (idiolectally coded) and occasional meanings ("dispersed" acts of reference), Paul also deals with a continuum. Had Paul been interested in the problem of discreteness versus continuity as a feature of language design, he might have both enlarged on the parallelisms between phonetic and semantic change, and realized that they are

now elaborated by a further feature: variable performance. A speaker's phonetic performance, we are told, varies around an (idiolectally coded) goal in the way a marksman's shots scatter around a bull's-eye (p. 54). The mental representations of the speech sound involve both a kinesthesis (*Bewegungsgefühl*; p. 49) and a sound image (*Lautbild*) for audio-monitoring (*Kontrolle*; pp. 53, 58). It is an empirical fact for Paul that these representations are insufficiently precise to guarantee absolutely consistent performance; for example, what is coded as a single kinesthesis and sound image (today we would say: a single phoneme) is manifested as the physiologically discriminable pair of sounds [n] and [ŋ] in German *Land, Anger*; similarly, a single psychologically coded unit appears as [d] in *Feldes* and as [t] in *Feld*. Hence, where we can conceive of continuous dimensions of phonetic space, "there is always a *continuous series of infinitely numerous sounds*" (pp. 51–52).

This, then, explains fluctuation in performance which is not coded in the idiolect and is not even perceived by the bearer of the idiolect.

Causes of Change. From here we move to the real crux: why does the mean of the scattered performances shift? That it *can* shift without being noticed by the performer is due, says Paul, to the fact that the sound image for monitoring moves in parallel with the kinesthesis that controls production (p. 61). But, granting that they shift together, why do they shift at all? On this crucial question Paul's answer has a general and a specific part. In general, language develops subject to constraints of utility:

In the development of Language Custom, purposiveness (*der Zweck*) plays the same role as that which Darwin attributed to it in organic nature: the greater or lesser usefulness (*Zweckmässigkeit*) of the resulting patterns (*Gebilde*) is decisive for their preservation or extinction. (p. 32)

---

jointly not representative of the rest of language change. In characterizing Paul's diachronic phonology as a study of continuous phenomena, we realize, of course, that subsequent linguistic theory imposed a quantization where Paul still saw a continuum. However, as should be apparent from the discussion, Paul's views are not at all obsolete insofar as those phonetic phenomena are concerned which form a residual continuum even after the discrete structure has been "extracted" by phonemics.

Now, since an explanation by natural selection is vacuous unless an independent criterion for survival is postulated, Paul invokes, as a specifically linguistic factor, the principle of greater comfort:

It is hardly possible to detect any other cause for the inclination to deviate more to one side than to the other than the fact that deviation in one direction in some respect *suits* the organs of the speaker *better* [*bequemer* ist]. (p. 56)

In cases such as assimilation in consonant clusters (*octō* > It. *otto*), the factor of ease[17] is obvious. Sometimes length and accent may also be involved. Even the fact that "all languages display a certain harmony of their sound systems" (presumably related to different rest positions of the organs among their speakers) is an explanation. Of course, there are many additional kinds of change, especially of the "unconditioned" kind, and Paul seems to realize that the more transparent instances do not yet yield a *general explanation*. But he feels that further psychophysical research is the key; "the investigation of the essence of this greater or lesser comfort is a task for physiology" (p. 57). That the pursuit of comfort by infinitesimal shifts in phonetic performance is indeed the explanation—of that Paul is certain.

Correlations of sound change with climate, soil conditions, way of life, and other environmental factors are unproven, and those involving differences in the anatomy of speech organs are often incorrect and, in any case, indecisive (p. 60). Ease, admittedly, "depends on a variety of circumstances which may be different for each individual," but they "can also affect larger groups" (p. 57). When they do, a sound shift takes place (p. 59).[18]

But if the pursuit of ease is the cause of sound change in idiolects, the fundamental questions arise: why do not speakers go about it more quickly, and why do Language Customs split in that some speakers set out on a particular ease-seeking path whereas others retain their less comfortable pattern? This fundamental question will arise repeatedly in our discussion; we have already alluded to it as the actuation prob-

---

[17] The German *bequem* means both 'convenient' and 'comfortable.' As a noun, though, 'ease' seems preferable to 'comfort.'

[18] Elsewhere (p. 227), Paul also cites the elimination of morph alternation as a general tendency; presumably this, too, could be interpreted as a pursuit of ease.

lem. For even when the course of a language change has been fully described and its ability explained, the question always remains as to why the change was not actuated sooner, or why it was not simultaneously actuated wherever identical functional conditions prevailed. The unsolved actuation riddle is the price paid by any facile and individualistic explanation of language change. It creates the opposite problem—of explaining why language fails to change.

Let us see how Paul copes with the actuation riddle.

Conformity. At all times, he says, the performance of a speaker is under the pressure of different forces to change in different directions. During stable periods of an idiolect, these forces are in exact balance and cause the spontaneous deviations from the target to cancel each other. For example, during a stable period of an idiolect, the scatter of performances of the sound *a* may be under equal pressure to shift toward *i* and toward *u*.

Yet it is very improbable that this should be the case at all points and at all times. Chance alone can easily bring it about that in an area held together by particularly intensive intercourse one tendency should achieve preponderance over another. This may happen even if the consensus of the majority is not conditioned by any particular inner coherence *vis-à-vis* the individuals remaining outside the group, and even if the causes which impel the shift into a particular direction are perhaps altogether different for different individuals. The preponderance of a tendency in a limited circle of this type is enough to overcome the contrary tendencies. (p. 61)

In this passage Paul seems to attribute the actuation of a change to chance. However, if the beginnings of changes were random processes, occasional losses of balance would alternate with restorations of balance, and beginnings of infinitesimal change would alternate with cessations of infinitesimal change. Thus, chance is here invoked illegitimately, since we are out to explain a specific, not a random process. The substantive theoretical principle which Paul has covertly slipped in is different—it is what we might call the "avalanche mechanism." But in the case of avalanches, the stickiness of snow explains why a rolling mass attracts additional snow; and in explaining avalanches, we may indeed attribute their actuation to chance (or to some uninteresting event, such as a skier telemarking in a particular location: cf. Martinet

1955:36). In the case of sound changes as described by Paul, however, no independent reason for believing in an avalanche mechanism is suggested.

There is, in fact, one more hypothesis covertly involved in Paul's theory: the hypothesis that speakers like to conform to the idiolects of their interlocutors. But whether or not this is a true belief, let us establish that it contributes nothing whatever to the explanation of sound change. This is because it is invoked *ad hoc* to explain both initial resistance to change and subsequent yielding to change. As we saw earlier, Paul holds that speakers adapt features from the idiolects of others *selectively,* but he offers no account whatever of their selectivity.

In describing the diffusion of a change from idiolect to idiolect, Paul makes free use of his conformity hypothesis:

Once a definitive shift in the kinesthesis [or any other idiolect feature[19]] has taken place through the elimination of the inhibitions exercised by communication [i.e., speakers' desire to conform to their interlocutors' idiolects], a further small shift is made possible by the continuing effect of the tendency. Meanwhile, however, a whole minority is swept by the movement. The very factors which prevent the minority from getting too far ahead of the general custom also prevent it from remaining significantly behind the progress of the majority . . . The movement proceeds in such small distances that a salient opposition never arises among individuals standing in close intercourse with each other. (p. 62)

Two important empirical claims are introduced here: (1) that the progress of a language change through a community follows a lawful course, an S-curve[20] from minority to majority to totality; (2) that frequency of a form guarantees its exemplariness for a speech community. We will have occasion later to discuss these claims further.

[19] Though Paul's discussion centers around sound change, everything he says here about the diffusion of changes (as distinct from their origin) could equally well apply to discrete domains of language, and his discussion from this point on could be generalized from sound change to language change without distortion.

[20] Compare Osgood and Sebeok (1954:155): "The rate of change would probably be slow at first, appearing in the speech of innovators, or more likely young children; become relatively rapid as these young people become the agents of differential reinforcement; and taper off as fewer and fewer older and more marginal individuals remain to continue the old forms."

The S-curved social trajectory of a change may in principle be located anywhere in a community. But it acquires special interest if it can be correlated with the universal differentiation of speech communities by age. According to Paul, we must distinguish between intra-generational and cross-generational changes. S-curved changes within a generation, he feels, are possible but necessarily minute. They reach major proportions only when the S-curve coincides with a shift in generations. If the change has already engulfed the majority, then the young people will "naturally" follow suit (i.e., they become the tail end of the S-curve). But even if a majority is still holding out, it will eventually die out. Moreover,

the same reasons which drive the older generation to deviate from kinestheses already formed must act on the formation of fresh kinestheses among the younger generation. It may therefore be said that the main cause [*Veranlassung*] of sound change is the transmission of sounds to new individuals. For this process, then, the term "change" is not appropriate, if one wants to be completely accurate; it is rather a deviant new formation [*Neuerzeugung*]. (p. 63)

In other words: what for mature speakers is a performance that deviates from the coding of the idiolect becomes, for the children, an idiolect-controlled (nondeviant) performance.

It is easy to see why the notion of generations appealed to Paul, and to many other scholars, as a safe haven in a dangerous theoretical sea. If chronological changes in language can be superimposed on the turnover of population, the need for a theory of change as such is canceled, since one can then simply think of the speakers of one dialect replacing those of another. (In geographic terms, diffusion of language material by speaker migration offers a similar, atypically easy case.) But a full-fledged theory must be accountable also for changes at different rates and in different directions, other than the replacement of fathers by sons (see § 2.41 below). Moreover, Paul's theory appears to take comfort from an unrealistic idea that the difference between generations is discontinuous. To be sure, generations are discrete within a family, but in the community they form a continuum. A solid theory that is based on age differences must be prepared to treat them as an uninterrupted gradient.

Regularity of Change. When we come, next, to the question of regularity of sound change, we find Paul following not the extreme position of the Neogrammarian manifesto,[21] but a moderate point of view illuminated by the criticisms of Kruszewski. Since the history of this matter is usually presented inaccurately,[22] a slight digression is necessary.

The postulate of completely regular sound laws (i.e., without exceptions that are themselves accountable by non-*ad hoc* phonetic contexts) received its main momentum from Osthoff and Brugmann's reading of Winteler's 1876 monograph on the German dialect of Kerenzen, Switzerland. In the descriptive part of his monograph— which we honor today as a pioneering effort in phonemic analysis— Winteler stated the distribution of allophones in item-and-process terms. (As a Sanskritist—the Sanskritist, in fact, who put the term *sandhi* into European circulation—Winteler had of course studied Pāṇini, so that item-and-process phonology was a natural model for him.) Now, in looking for the most impressive instance of a sound law without exceptions, Osthoff and Brugmann resorted to Winteler's phonology: look at Kerenzen German, they said, where every *n* for example changes to *ŋ* before *k, g*—without any exception whatever. Historicists that they were, Osthoff and Brugmann did not notice that they were extrapolating from a synchronic process to a diachronic one.[23] The difference between the two, and the vastly lesser lawfulness of dia-

---

[21] Osthoff and Brugmann (1878).

[22] The standard treatments of the history of this period were written by scholars who were themselves Neogrammarians in spirit—notably Pedersen, but also Bloomfield. To seek a balanced view in these accounts is like basing the history of war on autobiographies of the victorious generals. Jakobson (1960) has performed a most valuable service by his study of the anti-Neogrammarian Kazan school; unfortunately, his article is as yet available only in Polish. A still broader treatment of the Neogrammarian controversy would consider the dialectological along with the synchronistic-analytical arguments against the doctrine of exceptionless sound laws.

[23] Leskien (1876), who is usually cited as the originator of the Neogrammarian hypothesis, could not possibly find support for it in his indeterminate material. Because historians of this period overlooked the strongest evidence available to Osthoff and Brugmann (viz., Winteler's monograph), they have tended, somewhat apologetically, to downgrade the postulate of exceptionless sound laws to a "hypothesis," and to attribute Osthoff and Brugmann's self-confidence to the exuberance of their youth. A less psychologizing, more strictly scholarly explanation of their self-confidence, however, is the fact that

chronic shifts, was soon afterwards pointed out by Kruszewski (1881); the difference was lost, however, on the more orthodox Neogrammarians; it was not understood by Pedersen, and unfortunately also went unheeded by Bloomfield, for whom synchronic process did not exist.

Paul *did* understand Kruszewski's point (cf. his references to Kruszewski's papers in Techmer's *Zeitschrift* [vols. 1, 2, 3, 5], p. 49), and as he had no item-and-arrangement prejudices in phonology, he assimilated the distinction easily. He thus distinguishes between sound "shifts" (*Lautwandel*) and "alternations" (*Lautwechsel*). The former are shifts in terms of *synchronic* process only, and are taken as completely regular. The latter are remnants of earlier synchronic processes which (may) have ceased to function and which have left irregular residues that must be learned as lists (p. 69). To avoid confusion, we will hereinafter render Paul's *Lautwandel* by "phonetic rule," roughly in the sense of Halle (1959). The problem for Paul, then, is not the absolute regularity of phonetic rules, but the irregular redistribution of sounds among lexical elements. In other words, how does a productive phonetic rule of an idiolect get snagged? Can this result from intercourse with other speakers? Here is Paul's answer:

The only way in which this could be visualized is that an individual would simultaneously stand under the influence of several groups of persons which had become differentiated by different sound development [i.e., different synchronic phonetic rules], and that he would learn some words from one group, others from the other. But this presupposes a thoroughly exceptional relationship. Normally there are not [interidiolectal] differences of this kind in a communication community within which an individual grows up and with which he stands in much more intimate ties than with the broader environment. . . . Within the same dialect, therefore, no inconsistencies develop, only in consequence of dialect mixture, or, as we shall have occasion to put it more precisely, in consequence of the borrowing of a word from a foreign dialect. . . . In the formulation of sound laws [i.e., synchronic phonetic rules], we need not of course reckon with such inconsistencies. (pp. 71–72)

The weakest link in this argument is the notion "single dialect," be-

---

in the synchronic phonetic rules of Kerenzen German the Neogrammarians did indeed have verified, nonhypothetical examples of exceptionless sound laws.

cause, as we have seen, it has no theoretical standing in Paul's thinking. Indeed, Paul shows some concern about this weakness, for he promises to consider later "the extent to which, and the conditions under which" word borrowing from other dialects takes place (p. 72). Actually, however, in the chapter on language mixture, only a short section is devoted to dialect interference (pp. 402–403), and the question of "conditions" for word borrowing is not even raised.

Phonology and Idiolect Grouping. We took note above of the manner in which Paul slipped from a theory of language change in general to a theory of sound change in particular. We may now examine the paradox that emerges as a consequence of this unmarked narrowing of discussion. Insofar as language change *in general* is concerned, we have learned, idiolects are subject to random development. To be sure, intercourse may cause parallel shifts in group idiolects, but they need not, and as Paul knew from dialectological research, do not in fact result in a hierarchically structured subdivision of the community (pp. 37–42). Idiolect *A* may form a dialectal grouping with idiolect *B* with respect to Feature 1, a grouping with idiolect *C* with respect to Feature 2. There is for Paul no end and no organization to these mutually intersecting principles because (1) the linguist knows of no grounds for a hierarchy of linguistic features, and (2) he has no explanation for the selective diffusion of idiolect features (i.e., no scale of diffusibility). Paul realizes that if there are breaks in the intercourse network —especially absolute breaks caused by migration—a dialect split will emerge; but this is completely "external" to the language, and we might add that it is in any case a highly unusual phenomenon (even if in the history of the ancient Indo-European languages it may have played an important role). Not so in the case of sound change; here there is a *linguistic* basis for grouping two idiolects into a dialect, namely, their sharing of a (complete?) set of phonetic rules. Idiolects *A* and *B* would be assigned to the same dialect if they shared the same phonetic rules, and a word adopted by *A* from *B* would be automatically submitted to the same phonetic treatment.

It would appear, then, that if our goal were a classification of idiolectal phonologies, Paul's theory would offer us a reasoned linguistic criterion for it—at least for a single-level, all-same-or-all-different clas-

sification of idiolects. But if we are seeking a classification not of idiolectal phonologies, but of idiolects in their entirety, Paul's theory is of
no use, because it does not guarantee (and could do so only contrary
to factual evidence) that nonphonological differentiation goes hand in
hand with phonological differentiation. It would be perfectly natural,
for example, to find a set of idiolects A, B, and C such that A and B
share phonologies while jointly differing in their phonologies from C;
but A and B may have numerous lexical and grammatical differences
in points on which B agrees fully with C.

Paul writes: "The truly characteristic factor in the dialectal articulation of a continuous area is always the phonetic conditions." The reason for this, thinks Paul, is that it is in the formation of phonetic conditions that everything depends on direct personal intercourse. "In
vocabulary and in word meanings, in morphology and in syntax, mediated transmission offers no difficulties." By contrast, according to Paul,
phonetic influence (i.e., diffusion of phonological rules) depends on
intimate and intensive intercourse. Thus, he continues,

much greater differences develop in phonetics than in vocabulary, morphology, or syntax, and the former last more uniformly through long
periods than the latter. . . . Least typical of all is the vocabulary and its use.
Here transmissions from one dialect to another mostly take place [in the
same way] as from one language to another. Here there are more individual differences than in any other domain. Here there may also be differences [e.g., in professional vocabularies] which have nothing to do with
dialect differences, and which intersect them. (p. 47)

In this passage we face the conceptual difficulty of counting and weight-
ing phonological against other innovations. Are there not perhaps
more lexical innovations simply because there are more words? And
what is the theoretical basis for disregarding highly stable dialectal
differentiations in vocabulary and grammar? One suspects that Paul was
really deceiving himself. The priority he was giving to phonological
criteria of idiolect classification was based, not on the empirically demonstrated manner of their transmission (for this he had no evidence),
nor on their stability (for this the evidence was quite inconclusive),
but simply because phonology, in the sense of a consistently applied
set of phonetic rules, was the *only* domain of language which gave any

hope of quantizing (=imposing discreteness upon) the continuum of the speech community.

To base motivated idiolect classifications on phonology may be a counsel of despair; it may also be justified by further argument, for example, as to the primacy of phonology within language as a whole. While we would disagree with both procedures, we would consider them as legitimate proposals meriting discussion. What makes Paul's approach illegitimate, on the other hand, is its use of a theoretical assumption in the disguise of a factual claim—and, to make it worse, on a factual claim which is incorrect.

Summary. Let us now attempt to restate critically Paul's position on the essential points:

The sole theoretically grounded object of linguistic study is the idiolect, and within the idiolect, the only domain in which change is related to stable performance is phonology (in view of its nondiscrete nature). An individual's usage is in principle consistent, and conforms to his mental representation of it, except that phonetic performances are scattered randomly as about a target. An individual may, by infinitesimal unconscious steps, skew the distribution of his (phonetic) performances as he seeks more comfortable behavior patterns. (No explanation is offered for the slowness with which allegedly more "comfortable" behavior is achieved; i.e., the actuation riddle stands unsolved and even unformulated.) Dialects are conceived as groups of (phonologically) identical idiolects; consequently, dialect change is simply idiolects changing in parallel, and dialect splitting is no more than idiolects changing diversely.

An idiolect or dialect may also change by "borrowing" forms from other idiolects or dialects. Such borrowing is selective, but no explanation is offered for particular selections. Opportunity to borrow from other idiolects depends on exposure to them; however, both borrowing and nonborrowing are attributed to conformity—either with the innovators or the conservers.

1.2. The Neogrammarian Heritage

Paul's *Prinzipien* may be said to reflect the best achievements of Neogrammarian linguistics. With his Neogrammarian predecessors and contemporaries Paul shared the virtues of maximum rigor of formulation, an intensive interest in recurrent regularities, a feeling for the atypicality of standardized languages among the totality of languages, a concern with phonetic detail, and a desire to view language in the setting of its functioning in order to understand its development, to "portray as many-sidedly as possible the conditions of the life of language [*Sprachleben*]" (p. 6). Written and revised after the dust had settled over the sound-law controversy, Paul's book has the further merit of recognizing the dialectological point of view on language change. It is therefore not surprising that it became enormously influential, and though it eventually may have served as a target of anti-Neogrammarian opposition it functioned as the basic text for more than a generation of linguists.

1.21. SAUSSURE

The revolutionary effect of Saussure's thought is not belittled if we assert that in the question of the individuality of language, he owes a great deal to the Neogrammarian doctrine. For Saussure, the systematicity of language (see § 2.0) depends on the existence, within the individual, of a faculty of association and one of co-ordination (p. 29). The relations between elements of a language are located in the consciousness of speakers. The following quotation is typical:

Synchrony knows only one perspective, that of the speakers, and its whole method consists in gathering their testimony; in order to know the extent to which a thing is a reality, it will be necessary and sufficient to investigate the degree to which it exists in the consciousness of the speakers. (p. 128)

Indeed, it is the psychological unreality of diachronic and dialectological relations that leads Saussure to assign historical phenomena to a totally different domain of investigation. "The synchronic 'phenomenon'," he writes, "has nothing in common with the diachronic . . .; one is the connection between simultaneous elements, the other is the substitution of one element for another in time—an event" (p. 129). As a consequence,

diachronic linguistics, in contrast to [synchronic linguistics], will study the relations connecting successive items that are not perceived by a single collective consciousness, items which are *substituted for one another* but which *do not form a system among themselves.* (p. 140; italics supplied)

To guarantee the psychological reality of the object of synchronic investigation, Saussure further requires that such an object be homogeneous. The object of synchronic linguistics, he argues, is not everything which is simultaneous, but only those simultaneous facts which belong to a single language. The separation of legitimate, that is, homogeneous, objects of study must proceed, "to the extent that this may be necessary, all the way down to dialects and subdialects" (pp. 128–129). Indeed, linguists are put on notice that there are no natural dialects—"there are as many dialects as there are localities" (p. 276). And Saussure adds: "Basically the term *synchronic* is not precise enough; it should be replaced by the (admittedly longish) *idiosynchronic*. On the other hand, diachronic linguistics does not require, but repels, such a breakdown."

It has often been stressed that by distinguishing speech from language, Saussure broke away from the psychologism characteristic of Neogrammarian thinking: he saw language as social and speech as individual. However, let us note that Saussure has nothing concrete to say about the community as the matrix of individual speech performance. In particular, there is nothing in his theory which could accommodate a heterogeneous language while saving it as a legitimate object of synchronic investigation. "A language . . . is of homogeneous nature" (p. 32). And Saussure echoes Paul when he writes: "Among all the individuals thus linked by the use of language [*langage*], a kind of average will be established: everybody will reproduce—not exactly, to be sure, but approximately—the same signs joined to the same concepts" (p. 29). Clearly, Saussure here views heterogeneity within the language custom of a community not as a subject of systematic description, but as a kind of tolerable imprecision of performance. His view is thus again in full conformity with Paul's, who had said that the "great uniformity of all language processes in the most diverse individuals is the essential basis for an exact scientific knowledge of such processes" (Paul, p. 19). We see no evidence that Saussure progressed beyond Paul in his ability to deal with language as a social fact; for him the precondition of dealing with language as a social phenomenon was still its complete homogeneity.

In broaching the cause of sound change, Saussure rejected all explanations which had been advanced (pp. 202–208). Although he was convinced that all changes originate in speech, he nevertheless had no suggestions for distinguishing, other than a posteriori, between individual innovations which enter the language and those which do not (pp. 138–139). Although he posited two conflicting forces—that of intercourse and that of provincialism (*clocher*)—to describe an individual's imitation and nonimitation, respectively, of the speech of others, the balance of these forces remained a vacuous explanation, since Saussure could not show (pp. 284–285) that the prevalence of one force over the other covaried with anything else.

We can today easily assent to Saussure's argument that Old High German *gesti* 'guests' did not coexist in the consciousness of any speaker with the Modern German counterpart, *Gäste*, with the result that these items have therefore never been linguistically opposed. What is missing in his conception, however, is the possibility of a moment in time when a more archaic *gasti* and a more innovating variant, *gesti*, did coexist in the minds of some very real speakers of the language. Similarly, when Saussure cautions against gathering spatially remote dialects under the heading of a single synchronic description, we can agree with him easily, but he regrettably omits from consideration the crucially important case of *neighboring* dialects, whose systems are very much "in the consciousness" of the same speakers.[24] Saussure's error, it seems to us, was to equate the juxtaposition of remote stages of a language with the juxtaposition of stages in general.[25] It is this unjustified generalization which lay at the basis of his antinomy between the structural and the historical, an antinomy which has been accepted by the fundamentalists of the Geneva School[26] but which virtually all other linguists have been trying to overcome.

1.22. BLOOMFIELDIAN DESCRIPTIVE LINGUISTICS

In the works of American descriptive linguists we find a varying

---

[24] Saussure fails to consider this possibility despite devoting a special section (pp. 265ff.) to the "coexistence of several dialects at the same [geographic] point" (where else, then, but in the minds of the same speakers?) and another to the mutual influences of dialects coexisting with literary languages (pp. 267ff.).

[25] Paul was perhaps more farsighted in claiming that the portrayal of processes from a comparison of language states will be more successful if the compared states lie as close to each other as possible (pp. 31–32).

[26] Compare Sechehaye 1940:30ff.; Frei 1944.

level of interest in language diversity within a speech community; what unites this group with that of its Neogrammarian teachers is the lack of interest in the systematic character of the heterogeneous language of a community.

Bloomfield writes:

A speech community is a group of people who interact by means of speech. . . . If we observed closely enough, we should find that no two persons—or rather, perhaps, no one person at different times—spoke exactly alike. . . . These differences play a very important part in the history of languages; the linguist is forced to consider them very carefully, even though in some of his work he is forced provisionally to ignore them. When he does this, he is merely employing the method of abstraction, a method essential to scientific investigation, but the results so obtained have to be corrected before they can be used in most kinds of further work. (1933:42–45)

As a preliminary set of guidelines, this statement would be unobjectionable; what is important, however, is that Bloomfield has no suggestions to make as to the way in which the "abstraction" is to be derived from the description of individual usages, or how it is to be "corrected."[27] Reflecting Saussure's emphasis on *langue* as a social phenomenon, Bloomfield concedes that

we are concerned not so much with each individual as with the whole community. We do not inquire into the minute nervous processes of a person who utters, say, the word *apple*, but content ourselves rather with determining that, by and large, for all the members of the community, the word *apple* means a certain kind of fruit. . . . However [he immediately concedes], as soon as we try to deal accurately with this matter, we find that the agreement of the community is far from perfect, and that every person uses speech-forms in a unique way. (p. 75)

Writing before the major developments in diachronic phonemics, Bloomfield did not yet respond to the possibility that the state of a language may itself function as a determinant of changes within it. Like Paul he therefore puts the whole burden of explaining change on the mechanism of imitating the speech habits of one's fellows. The direction of imitation, Bloomfield believes, is determined entirely by the

[27] Furthermore, the same questions as those which were raised by Paul's conception of "averaging" could be asked regarding Bloomfield's notion of abstraction.

"prestige" of the model (p. 476). Although this is now known to be factually incorrect, it is at least a step beyond Paul's and Saussure's vacuous balance and imbalance of contrary forces. Like Paul, Bloomfield distinguishes true phonetic and analogic-semantic changes, which take place in the speech of individuals, from the diffusion of such changes by the mechanism of dialect borrowing. "The processes themselves rarely escape our observation" (p. 481). "It is useless to ask what person or set of persons first favored [certain] variants. . . . By the time a sound-change becomes observable, its effect has been distributed by the leveling process that goes on within each community" (pp. 480–481). The distinction between the origin of a language change and its diffusion, and the pessimism about observing the origins of language change, steered Bloomfieldian thinking about language change into an antiempirical direction.

An important milestone in the isolation of the individual's language as the legitimate object of linguistic description par excellence was Bloch's "Set of Postulates for Phonemic Analysis," in which the term *idiolect* was first introduced. (Whether his recourse to the prefix *idio-* actually echoes Saussure's *idiosynchronic* is at this moment difficult to determine.) Bloch writes:

The totality of the possible utterances of one speaker at one time in using a language to interact with one other speaker is an *idiolect* . . . As for the words "at one time," their interpretation may safely vary within wide limits: they may mean "at one particular moment" or "on one particular day" or "during one particular year" . . . The phrase "with one other speaker" is intended to exclude the possibility that an idiolect might embrace more than one STYLE of speaking: it is at least unlikely that a given speaker will use two or more styles in addressing a single person. . . . Phonological analysis of a given idiolect does not reveal the phonological system of any idiolect belonging to a different dialect. (1948:7–9)

We see Bloch here executing Paul's and Saussure's atomistic principle of reducing the language of a community to its ultimate homogeneous parts. But we cannot refrain from noting that even this reduction *ad absurdum* is based on a counterfactual assumption that a pair of speakers always stick to the same style. (For evidence to the contrary, see, e.g., Labov 1966:90–135.)

The logic of the Neogrammarian theory, as inherited through Saussure and Bloomfield, was developed most fully by some of Bloomfield's students. We will return to their analysis below (§ 2.1), after discussing the isolation of structure as a factor in language functioning.

1.23. THE PRACTICE OF GENERATIVE GRAMMARIANS

Although generative linguistics has so far touched on historical problems in only a marginal fashion, there are several theoretical pronouncements on record suggesting that the Neogrammarian-descriptivist conception of a homogeneous system as the sole legitimate object of analysis has been adopted by this school of thought. Thus Chomsky writes:

Linguistic theory is concerned with an ideal speaker-listener, *in a completely homogeneous speech-community,* who knows its language perfectly and is unaffected by such grammatically irrelevant conditions as memory limitations, distractions, shifts of attention and interest, and errors (random or characteristic) in applying his knowledge of the language in actual performance. (1965:3–4; italics supplied)

The requirement of homogeneity is here made central: the linguistic competence which is the object of linguistic analysis is the possession of an individual; linguistic theory concerns the community only insofar as the community is homogeneous and insofar as the individual informant is a perfect representative of it. Procedures for overcoming the actual observed diversity of speech behavior are not suggested any more than in the work of Paul or Bloomfield; in harmony with Saussure, but more explicitly, Chomsky declares such diversity to be theoretically irrelevant. Thus he is quite right in saying: "This seems to me to have been the position of the founders of modern general linguistics"; but we cannot agree with his further statement that "no cogent reason for modifying it has been offered." As we will show below, we find cogent reasons for modifying this position in the confirmed facts that deviations from a homogeneous system are not all errorlike vagaries of performance, but are to a high degree coded and part of a realistic description of the competence of a member of a speech community.

2. PROBLEMS OF CHANGING STRUCTURE

2.0. TYPES OF RELEVANT THEORY

For Paul, the theory of language (*Prinzipienwissenschaft*) was, at least officially, coterminous with the theory of language change. After the development of the Saussurean antinomy between the diachronic and the synchronic, however, there arose a place for *two* bodies of principle—theories of language change and theories of language structure. The refinements achieved in the latter area, it turns out from our point of view, had inevitable and important implications for the history of language even where the original motivation of the conceptual advance was other than historical.

In relation to language change, each refinement in the theory of language structure (and the same could be said about refinements in the theory of speech communities) had the following potential effects:

(a) a *reclassification* of observed changes according to new principles;

(b) proposal of fresh *constraints* on change; and

(c) proposal of new *causes* of change.

Effect (a) is easiest to visualize. For example, when a separation between distinctive and redundant features was introduced into phonological analysis, all sound changes could be divided according to whether they did or did not involve distinctive features. Similarly, the distinction between prestigious and prestigeless dialects yielded a fresh classification of innovations depending on whether they moved up or down the prestige "slope." In the wake of most new theories of language, we indeed find papers setting forth the implications of the new ideas for history. However, in offering mere reclassifications of changes previously observed or observable, this type of advance is of limited interest for a *theory of language change* as such.

Far more significant is the possibility that a refinement in linguistic or sociolinguistic theory may allow (b) the hypothecation of *constraints* on change. Thus, a crude theory of speech sounds does not make it possible to assert very much about the actual phonological make-up of languages, but as the theory becomes more refined, the possible generalizations about how languages are constituted become richer and richer. Even in a completely inductive spirit, it becomes possible to make highly specific statistical generalizations about existing languages; it becomes possible, accordingly, to show whether a given change produces a language state that violates or, more significantly, conforms with the statistical norms. If one's observations of languages are, in addition, tied together by a broader theoretical structure, still greater significance can be attached to interconnected series of changes, and all the more challenging and meaningful becomes the search for "optimization" tendencies in language change.

Of maximum importance is (c) the proposal of new causes of change, based on a theory of language states so firmly established that one change in a language state necessarily implies another change *ex hypothesi*, so that event A can be designated a cause of change B. In its stronger form, a theory of change would identify A as the *sufficient* cause of B; in a weaker form, event A would appear at least as the *necessary* cause of B. It is only rarely that historical linguistics has had glimpses of such causal theories, even of the weaker (necessary cause) variety; but from such achievements as are on record we may draw hope of further advances.

The balance of our discussion is organized as follows: In the present chapter we consider the implications for language change of the structural theory that views language as a system of oppositional relations. The phonological problems here receive special prominence, since this is an area where contrastive and noncontrastive functions of the same substance have been distinguished with considerable success. We then turn (§ 2.4) to the historical implications of the factorial analysis which synchronic theory has applied to linguistic systems. The notion of distinctive features in phonology here receives the bulk of our attention. The theories discussed in Sections 2.1–4 represent important advances over Paul, but they share with him and his successors in American descriptive and generative linguistics the approach to language as a homogeneous, undifferentiated object; such subsystems as are posited within a language are viewed as noncompeting, but jointly necessary and complementary (phonology, grammar, lexicon). In Section 3 we turn to work that breaks with the homogeneity postulate and grapples with language as a systematically differentiated system.

2.1. CONTRASTIVE FUNCTION OF PHONEMES

As we saw above, Paul, the Neogrammarian, had no particular pre-dilection for atomism in linguistics; we noted the structured way in which he thought of a *Sprachgefühl* as a generative device. But it was Saussure who came to stress the psychological reality of contrastive rela-tions in a language and thus was required, in the interest of consistency, to relegate historical correspondences to another domain, one of the psychologically unreal. Using a chess game as his well-known analogy Saussure insisted on disassociating the mutually determined functions of the pieces (a synchronic fact) from the Persian origins of the game. (What we miss in his program is an investigation into the changing rules of chess.)

Soon after the contrast idea came to be applied to the study of sound systems, mainly in Prague, descriptive linguists found occasion for a predictable reclassification of observed changes. The required infer-ences were first drawn by Jakobson (1931), who showed how sound changes may be grouped into phonemic mergers (dephonologization of variants) and splits (phonologization of variants).[28] A very similar analysis was independently provided in America by Hill (1936).[29]

According to our scheme, these classifications in themselves consti-tute only the lowest-level historical consequences of a new theory of language. But before we examine their explanatory capabilities, let us

---

[28] It is also Jakobson (1928) who must be credited with the bold attempt to salvage Kruszewski's insights by proclaiming outright what escaped the more Neogrammarian-minded Bloomfield—that the only sound laws operating with-out exception in a given language are in fact the laws governing the distribu-tions of contextual variants of a phoneme in a synchronic system.

[29] Bloomfield himself in 1933 had not yet quite assimilated his prephonemic outlook on language history to his latterly acquired phonemic approach to de-scription. Thus, in Sections 20.1–10 of his chapter on phonetic change, the ques-tion of distinctiveness does not even arise; the presentation follows Paulian lines quite closely. It is only in the last Section (20.11), which adheres to Paul's doctrine about intimate contact as a condition for the borrowing of sound-variant distributions (i.e. phonetic rules), that Bloomfield labels the sound variants "non-distinctive," or "sub-phonemic." The key structuralist formula-tion, incidentally, seems stronger than is warranted: "We can speak of sound change only when the displacement of habit has led to some alteration in the structure of the language" (p. 367). Granted that structure-altering changes are more important by some descriptive criterion, why should they be claimed as the only ones?

note that they also led to formal difficulties. The straightforward application of phonemic quantization to the continuum of language change soon turned up a dialectic puzzle: how do gradual, nondistinctive changes suddenly make the leap into a new distinctive category? Consider Hockett's eloquently baffled account:

Sound change itself is constant and slow. A phonemic restructuring, on the other hand, must in a sense be absolutely sudden. No matter how gradual was the approach of early M[iddle] E[nglish] /æ/ and /ɔ/ towards each other, we cannot imagine the actual coalescence of the two other than as a sudden event: on such-and-such a day, for such-and-such a speaker or tiny group of speakers, the two fell together as /á/ and the whole system of stressed nuclei, for the particular idiolect or idiolects, was restructured. Yet there is no reason to believe that we would ever be able to detect this kind of sudden event by direct observation . . . (1958:456–457)

Reflected in Hockett's discussion is the synthesis of the Neogrammarian and Saussurean positions that the language of the idiolect serves as the locus of structural, that is, linguistically relevant, and legitimate facts. But the net result of this consistent synthesis is that a theory of language change becomes removed from empirical foundations almost entirely. It is difficult to accept an explanation through phenomena which are not only unobserved, but unobservable.

Elsewhere we have discussed the consequences of the claim that sound changes in progress cannot be observed (Weinreich 1960; Labov 1963, 1965). In our view, this self-defeating dilemma proceeds from an untenable distinction between the origin of a change and the propagation of the change which Saussure and Bloomfield adopted from Paul.[30] It stands to reason that the transition problem cannot be solved unless intervening stages in the propagation of a change are studied. In the quotation given above, Hockett focuses on the obverse problem: the unobservability of infinitesimal sound change is coupled with the unobservability of instantaneous structural change.

For scholars who feel uncomfortable with such an approach, several alternative solutions come to mind. One is to deny that change takes place within a system and to assert instead that the system (e.g., the dialect) has borrowed the new phenomenon from another dialect (e.g.,

---

[30] We earlier discussed the place of this distinction in Paul's thinking. The distinction was adopted virtually intact by Saussure (*Cours*, p. 283).

Hoenigswald 1960:72–73). If this formulation still contains dangers of a conceptual mystery (e.g., at which precise moment does the borrowing of the new phenomenon become "total"?), it can be revised further to envisage two coexisting dialects—one with the opposition in question, the other without (cf. Bloomfield 1933:328)—and speakers who fluctuate between the two styles of speech, favoring the "coalescent" dialect in increasing measure.[31] We reconsider this possibility in Section 3.2 as one approach to a more adequate view of linguistic structure.

Another solution is to assert that continuous variation exists within each dialect as a structural element, correlated with some other linguistic or nonlinguistic factor, and that the steady movement of tokens from one categorial class to another is part of the underlying structure (Labov 1966). Thus change would normally occur as one variable moved from a position *within* a given phoneme, to a position *across* phoneme boundaries, to a position *within* a second phoneme, and such a variable would be strictly defined by covariation with other features. (See §3.31 below.)

A second problem which arose in grafting phonemic theory onto the Neogrammarian theory of sound change was the temptation to identify the new analytic distinction, subphonemic/phonemic, with the historical (mutually coterminous) distinctions infinitesimal/discrete, fluctuating/stable, irregular/regular, and unconscious/conscious. Bloomfield, for example (1933:365ff.), thought that nondistinctive changes are observable only by the phonetician who has at his disposal "an enormous mass of mechanical records, reaching through several generations of speakers." But the identification of the dichotomies raises at least two theoretical difficulties:

(a) Granting (for the moment) that nondistinctive changes are not observed by naïve language users, why must the linguist necessarily have "an enormous mass of mechanical records" to determine, let us say, that subgroups of a speech community differ consistently in the use of allophones such as [x] versus [h] or [r] versus [R]? In other words, what deductive reasons are there to believe that nondistinctive variation is necessarily inconsistent or infinitesimal, so that phonetic

---

[31] Weinreich (1960:332). Corresponding reformulations could be worked out to cover phonemic split.

measurements of enormous masses of recordings are required for its detection?[32]

(b) If the explanation of changes in phonemic structure rests on the distinction between continuous phonetic behavior and discontinuous phonemes, how can we envisage a unified theory which would also encompass grammar, where the nondistinctive elements (morphs) are not continuous?[33]

But regardless of whether or not these theoretical difficulties can be ironed out, we are obliged to take note of empirical evidence which disconfirms the identification of the analytically distinctive with the historically discrete and the psychologically conscious. Thus the largely subphonemic replacement of lingual by uvular *r* in many European languages must have taken place by discrete steps (Hoenigswald 1960: 73); moreover, the distribution of the two variants is by no means the unstable one that their nondistinctiveness would imply. As to awareness, we find that speakers in many parts of the United States are extremely sensitive to subphonemic variants of /θ/ and /ð/, and quick to stigmatize the nonstandard usage of others. Similarly, the subphonemic raising of the vowels of *off, lost* in New York City is a matter of extreme sensitivity and a subject of much overt comment and correction in formal styles. On the contrary, the sweeping change in the repertory of phonemes which resulted from this process—the loss of distinction between *sure~shore, lure~lore*—is quite unnoticed and seems to evoke no social evaluation (Labov 1965, 1966). When we see a comparable absence of social awareness of the coalescence of phonemes illustrated by the massive merger of *cot~caught, hock~*

---

[32] The same objections could have been made against Paul. Non-distinctive variation has, in fact, been observed by Labov (1963, 1966) through far from "enormous" samples. Some scholars, incidentally, have been far more cautious than Bloomfield and Hockett. Lehmann, for example (1962:148), does not hold that subphonemic changes are unobservable, only that they are not taken into account by scribes rendering their language in phonemic terms. It is for this far-better-formulated reason that linguists have little information about nondistinctive changes of the past; and there is nothing in Lehmann's view to discourage us from phonetically observing nondistinctive changes in process.

[33] It is understandable why Hoenigswald (1960), at work on an over-all theory of language change, speaks of the "alleged" gradual character of phonetic alteration; to unify the conception of morphological and phonological change, he explains even the latter by resort to "dialect borrowing"—a discrete process by definition.

hawk throughout large sections of the United States, we are forced to conclude that there is no correlation between social perception and structural status.

A serious weakness in the empirical foundations of the various theories of linguistic change considered here stems from their automatic reliance upon cognitive function as the prime determinant of linguistic behavior. The assumption that perception was determined only by contrastive (morph-distinguishing) units was never based upon a sound empirical foundation, but rather upon a large number of uncontrolled (anecdotal) observations of cases where perception did match phonemic categories. A growing body of evidence from controlled sociolinguistic studies indicates that perception is indeed controlled by linguistic structure; but it is a structure which includes not only units defined by contrastive function but also units defined by their stylistic role, and their power to identify the speaker's membership in a specific subgroup of the community (Hymes 1962; Labov 1966).

Let us see next what *explanatory* possibilities were found by historical linguists in the contrastive function of phonemes which contribute to the solution of the *evaluation problem*. This function made it clear, for one thing, why phonemes should be rendered as far apart as possible (de Groot 1931), and this in turn suggested why a shifting phoneme should "repel" its neighbors in the system if mergers were to be prevented (Hill 1936). In this matter, Paul had argued the opposite:

Nowhere is any effort exerted for the prevention of a sound change. For those involved are not even aware that there is anything of the kind to prevent; after all, they continue in their faith that they speak today as they spoke years ago, and that they will speak the same way till the end of their days. (p. 58)

To the extent that Paul was doubting the likelihood of anyone changing a synchronic phonetic rule, one may go along with him; but of course in his conceptual framework the assertion automatically carried over to historical processes as well, and in so doing it became too sweeping. Other observers were beginning to see matters differently. Gilliéron understood the clash of homonyms as a dysfunctional phenomenon for which language users had "therapeutic" correctives available to them. Martinet[34] integrated the views of other forerunners with a systematic functionalism in phonetics, and broadened the pathology-therapy conception from individual words to whole sets of words distinguished by a particular phonemic opposition. Our nineteenth-century predecessors would have been horrified at this teleological way of thinking; Martinet's statement of "prophylactic" aversion to phonemic mergers appeared more plausible to structural linguists, since he utilized the concept of the morph-distinguishing function of the phoneme rather than speakers' conscious efforts to avoid misunderstandings (1955:41–44).

For all the dysfunctionality of homonym clashes and mass word mergers, the coalescence of phonemes is plentifully attested in the history of languages. To prevent the preservation-of-contrast mechanism from explaining too much, Martinet adapted Mathesius' concept (1931) of "functional yield" as a kind of variable contrastiveness (1955:54–59). It was hoped that the theory would then permit oppositions from low-functional yield to collapse while still explaining the preservation of high-yield oppositions.

Thus, Martinet put forward one persuasive explanation for the fact that many changes occurred in groups or sequences—a fact that fascinated every linguist from Rask and Grimm on, but which was squinted at by the best of them out of a sound mistrust of "abstractions" or of mysticism in history. Martinet, moreover, solved a large part of the puzzle of "unconditioned" sound changes: the principle of syntagmatic context now found a paradigmatic counterpart, and syntagmatic "ease" (in Paul's terms) could now be matched by a thoroughly plausible notion of "paradigmatic ease" (Martinet 1955:59–62).

But it would be unfortunate if Martinet's achievements were to be accepted as defining the over-all framework for the explanation of linguistic change. The work of Moulton (1961, 1962) and some findings of Labov (1966) have provided empirical foundations for many of Martinet's conclusions which strengthen the less detailed evidence given by Martinet himself and his students. But, even within Martinet's framework, there is a need for detailed analysis to make important

[34] For simplicity we base our references to Martinet's work on his synthesizing book of 1955.

concepts more precise and reliable. Thus, the concept of functional yield needs a great deal of refinement. There are few quantitative studies bearing on it, and they suffer from a rather narrow conception of the frame in which contrasts important for communication must be maintained. They take a rather simplified approach to language by calculating the yield of oppositions among minimal pairs uttered as isolated lexical items. Other studies of functional yield have also erred by setting too narrow an environmental frame (following and preceding element), making it impossible to deal with such phenomena as "breaking," vowel harmony, umlaut, or "preconsonantal *r*." We have every reason to expect that transitional probabilities among phonemes and the syntactic context (let alone the situational one) furnish vast amounts of redundancy which variously diminish the value of a contrast, and we feel that more complex measures of functional load will have to be worked out and evaluated before this highly attractive notion is abandoned.[35]

Ferguson (1959) has suggested that the grammatical structure of the lower-status member of two languages in the "diglossia" relation, that is, the variety of language used in less formal situations, will regularly show fewer distinctions. As far as phonology is concerned, he indicates that the lower-status system is the basic one, while the higher-status system is best understood as a sub- or parasystem of the lower. We now have empirical evidence to show that in one speech community the most highly systematic phonology, which shows the processes of linguistic evolution most clearly, is the one used in casual speech with the minimum number of distinctions and the maximum contextual support. In the long and ingliding system of vowels in New York City *r*-less speech, one can find examples to support a seven-membered series of contrasts—in the most formal speech. Thus we have:

beard	/ih/			moored	/uh/
bared	/eh/	stirred	/əh/		
bad	/æh/	barred	/ah/	bored	/ɔh/

but the forms to support this system are produced in a most irregular

---

[35] See Hockett (1966) and Wang (1967) for critical approaches to this problem. King (1965) explores the role of functional yield empirically with negative results, but his environments are unfortunately limited to the immediately preceding and following segments as discussed above.

and unreliable manner. On the other hand, the most spontaneous speech (among lower-middle-class speakers) will yield a very regular system of the form:

> bear, bared, bad /ih/   moored, bored /uh/
> stirred /ʌh/
> barred /ah/

and this system is the product of a regular and rational process of linguistic evolution (Labov 1966: 559–565). Apparently there are motivating forces in linguistic change which can ride roughshod over any tendency to preserve cognitive distinctions.

The consequences of these findings must be built into the functional-yield concept and into a contrast-preserving explanation of serial language change.

Another example: the ancestor of the Yiddish dialects of Central and Eastern Europe distinguished long and short high-front and high-back vowels: *ū, ŭ, ī, ĭ*. In Southern Yiddish the back series was fronted to merge with the front vowels; in Northeastern Yiddish the long vowels merged with their corresponding short ones. We thus have:

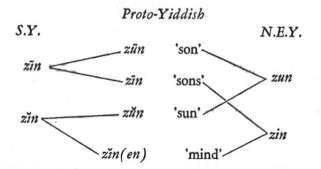

Now, it could have been argued (in an admittedly circular manner) that the functional yield permitted each two-way merger, but not a four-way merger (Weinreich 1958). Even this circular "explanation," however, is now invalidated by fresh empirical evidence. The most recent research (Herzog 1965:211 ff., 1968) has turned up two areas in which all vowels have merged into a uniform *i* (see Fig. 1): one in North Central Poland, the other in the Northern Ukraine. It turns out, further, that in the region surrounding the second area a shift

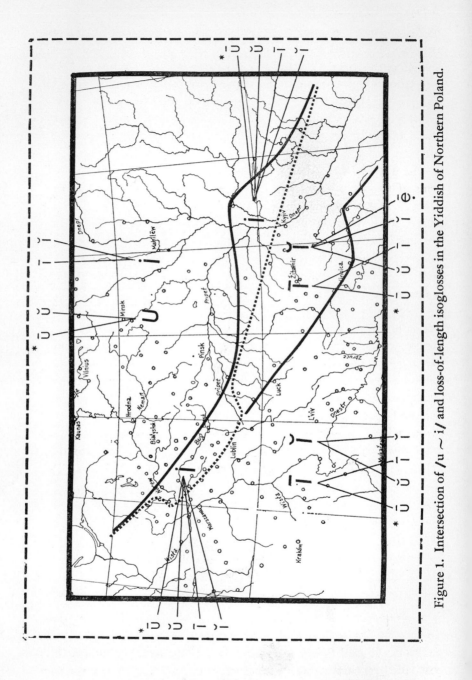

Figure 1. Intersection of /u ~ i/ and loss-of-length isoglosses in the Yiddish of Northern Poland.

of $*\bar{\rlap{.}e} > i$ is in geographic complementary distribution with the full collapse of u's and i's. It would appear that still a fifth source of i vowels (producing, e.g., further homonymy with *zin* 'to see' $< *z\bar{\rlap{.}e}n$) would have been too much. In the theory of functional yield as so far formulated, we find no basis for predicting that the merger seen in Northern Polish Yiddish was possible, or that the merger of Ukrainian Yiddish was possible only on condition that $*\bar{\rlap{.}e} > i$ did not also take place.

The Yiddish Atlas, designed from the beginning to bear on problems of this kind, is turning up large amounts of relevant materials from phonology as well as grammar and lexical semantics.

It is also worth noting that the homonymy-prevention theory contributes little to the solution of the "actuation riddle." It is, of course, entirely proper to leave room for "further research," and one is entitled to hope that in some (privileged) cases, deep study of language states will explain not only why a change took place at a certain time in a certain direction, but also why it did not take place sooner. Martinet is certainly right in saying (1955:62) that a linguist should not be diverted from his search for causes by the complexity of the problems; but it is not clear that a theory based upon the functional yield of cognitive contrasts can provide the machinery for assessing the full complexity of causal relations within phonological structure. We note that the mechanism of ordered rules developed within a generative framework, which is not dependent upon a set of contrasting units at any level lower than the lexical level, does offer a rich field for searching out such deep-seated relations between superficially unconnected phenomena. But it seems to us unlikely that the actuation problem will readily yield to purely structural investigations, and we expect that their contribution will be confined to the task of stating limitations and elucidating—in part—the mechanism of language change. Solutions to the actuation problem must be expected from other directions.

2.2 GRAMMATICAL STRUCTURE

Revisions of analytical grammatical theory have, again expectedly, led to a reclassification of historical events on record. To take as an example the best-defined post-Paulian system of grammatical analysis—Bloomfieldian morphemics—we find the historical consequences of the etic/emic distinctions developed systematically by Hoenigswald (1960). We may expect similar extensions of generative grammar to the description of historical events. Among investigations aiming at explanation rather than simple description, two lines of theoretical work, at least, may be cited. The first is connected with the formulation of grammatical universals; the second, with the study of conflicting productive patterns.

Underlying the search for universals is the Humboldtian vision that the languages of the world, in all their morphological variety, are designed to perform the same syntactic goals. This insight gives a theoretical foundation to such findings as the one that the loss of case systems in ancient Indo-European languages has been compensated for by the development of stricter word-order and prepositional systems.

A remarkably rich list of grammatical universals has been proposed by Greenberg (1963b); they are mostly concerned with word order. Recently (1966), he has turned to the examination of the diachronic implications of such universals, with promising results. Furthermore, he has taken a major step in testing certain synchronic universals which fail the test of absolute synchronic application, by examining their role as determinants of the directions of change. For example, he has investigated the claim that semantically unmarked categories (nominative) will tend to be morphologically unmarked, and semantically marked categories morphologically marked. Although there are many obvious counterexamples in Slavic noun declensions, his review of historical developments in Czech shows that any changes which did take place in the last few centuries were in the direction predicted by this rule. Two important modes of investigation are indicated by Greenberg's work: (1) the clarification through empirical means of the abstract claim that synchronic systems have "dynamic" tendencies (see Matthesius 1911), and (2) the use of quantitative methods to replace anecdotal evidence and persuasive argument. Though Greenberg has not presented any over-all theory of language structure or language change, his work is nonetheless extremely important for the empirical foundations of such a theory.

We are encouraged by Greenberg's use of quantitative methods and his ability to isolate significant trends in structure. At the same time, one must admit that he is necessarily confined to surface structure at the lowest level of reliability which is common to the descriptions of languages available to him. It is sometimes argued that one must have a comprehensive theory of language, or a theory of language change as a whole, before one can begin to investigate language or language change seriously. If one holds to this doctrine, one would have to be extremely critical of Greenberg's workmanlike procedures. But one might argue that some of the more lasting contributions to linguistics have been in the form of partial explanations of limited areas of language, while comprehensive theories which attempted to account for everything have not shown the same longevity. We might ask in turn whether any all-embracing theory can be erected at this time without the rigidity which rejects new data and new methods. For the historian, a set of validated universals becomes a constraint on possible changes in a language. However, it must be admitted that so far grammatical universals have provided language with an overlong historical tether that is observed to stretch all too rarely; that is, the universals, especially those envisaged by Chomsky, are so broad that we are unlikely to find cases of changing languages which are approaching a possible "violation." But, of course, this type of linguistic investigation is only in its infancy, and the future possibilities are quite unsurveyable.

The second line of work referred to above stems from a desire to escape the vacuities of the Neogrammarian doctrine of analogy. In the domain of irregular morphophonemic alternation, Paul and his contemporaries observed much unpredictable change, which they classified as "analogical." But as the critics of Neogrammarianism were quick to point out, "analogy" as an alternative to exceptionless sound laws not only was itself an *ad hoc* explanation, but also converted the sound law itself into an *ad hoc* concept. (It is amusing and instructive to find Osthoff, in the very volume whose preface became the Neogrammarian manifesto, "explain" some changes in Greek numerals with the most fanciful and arbitrary appeals to analogy.) Paul was well aware that "since a form can, by virtue of its shape, belong to several classes, it is possible to derive the remaining associated forms from it according to different proportions" (p. 114). Of the various possible developments, Paul therefore surmised, a form follows that proportion which has the greater "power" (*Macht*). But since he suggested no criteria for independently testing the "power" of a proportion, the argument is completely circular: the cause, itself unmotivated, can be known only through its effects. Bloomfield, despite the benefit of decades of additional research, in his discussion of analogical change could report no progress over Paul.

Fresh attempts to systematize linguists' experience with analogy were made after World War II by Kuryłowicz (1949) and Mańczak (1958); they are conveniently summarized by Lehmann (1962:188–192). The general rules formulated by these scholars, with a considerable body of documented evidence, provide new frameworks where previously there was mostly disorder.

Another way out of the free-for-all of analogy was sought by Frei (1929) and Bally (e.g., 1944). In the patterning of mistakes committed against normative French grammar, the Geneva scholars looked for evidence of dysfunctional aspects in the system against which the waves of change had begun to lap. This material would be particularly worthy of reconsideration if it could be extended to cover a variety of dialects in actual use by a given population.

2.3. ARGUMENTS RELATED TO LONG-TERM TRENDS

We have seen that a particular historical datum changes its status when it is viewed in the framework of different theories of language. Thus, the fronting of *u* (as in German umlaut) constitutes a significant change as soon as it happens—in a theory innocent of phonemics. From a phonemic point of view, this fronting is overridden in importance by the loss of the contextual condition (high-front vowels in the following syllable). Examples could be multiplied and ramified at will.

A given datum may also acquire fresh significance if viewed, not through a different theory of language structure, but as part of a different long-range trend. As Meillet put it:

Language changes get their meaning only if one considers the whole of the development of which they are parts; the same change has an absolutely different significance depending on the process which it manifests, and it is never legitimate to try to explain a detail outside of a consideration of the general system of the language in which it appears. (1906a:11)

The concept of *drift* endows the story of language with a meaningful "plot" that plays much the same role as a trend introduced by a historian into the retelling of a sequence of sociopolitical happenings. Considered by itself, for instance, the fluctuation between clause-initial objective *who* and *whom* in English is but another case of allomorph alternation; but seen, as Sapir saw it (1921), as a conflict between two trends—movement of interrogatives to initial position versus specialized word order for the several noun phrases of a sentence—this fluctuation is converted into the last act of a long drama and endows it with enormous suspense.

As a rule, long-range trends have been formulated for one language or language group at a time. An example of a richly documented exploration of this type is Malkiel's paper "Diachronic Hypercharacterization in Romance" (1957–1958), in which polysemous entities are shown to have split up again and again into pairs of signs with separate signifiants (e.g., Lat. *leō* 'lion, lioness' into French *lion/lionne*). Malkiel seems to us to be quite right when he concludes that the study of a trend such as hypercharacterization "endows with rich meaning processes which, viewed in isolation, have traditionally been dismissed as insignificant" (p. 36), and that there is nothing incompatible between the documentation of such a trend and any accepted principles of linguistic theory. On similar grounds, we can appreciate Žirmunskij's work on long-term trends in German and in Germanic (1958). One wonders, however, whether the trends thus studied would not gain in theoretical significance if they were drawn from some independently motivated "schedule" of *possible* trends, rather than detected separately for each group of languages whose data happen to be within the grasp of a given historian (no matter how inspired). That is to say, despite the systematizing value of these long-range trends studied within their separate fields, one has the feeling that they will remain marginal to a comprehensive theory of language unless we can formulate a better *system* of trends.

2.4. DISTINCTIVE FEATURES AND PHONOLOGICAL CHANGE

The imposition of a purely functional conception of the phoneme onto the history of sound change often led to strange results; a radical change like

$$
\left| \begin{matrix} t & d \\ & \\ & \theta \end{matrix} \right| \quad > \quad \left| \begin{matrix} d & ð \\ & \\ & h \end{matrix} \right|
$$

fails to qualify as a linguistic change because the repertory of phonemes (i.e., the "structure") had not been affected; after the change,
there were still three phonemes, in one-one correspondence with the
three before the change (cf. Hill 1936:15; Hockett 1958:380). Such
a purely functional view contended that the phonetic realization of the
contrastive units was irrelevant to structure; and it thereby obscured the
structural character of the most systematic large-scale sound shifts. The
difficulty can be avoided, however, if we follow instead the Prague
tradition of understanding the phoneme not only in terms of its morph-
distinguishing function, but also in terms of its distinctive-feature
structure (Weinreich 1960:330).

Applied to the history of languages, the structural understanding
of phonemes again had, as its first consequence, a reclassification of
certain changes. In the paper already referred to, Jakobson (1931)
formulated a third type of change in addition to phoneme merger and
phoneme split—reinterpretation of phonemes (rephonologization). It
became possible to show how an opposition remained invariant while
the means of its implementation changed: for example, the shift of
Indo-European aspirates and nonaspirates to a corresponding pair of
series of voiced and voiceless consonants. The very formulation of such
a change was beyond the capability not only of Paul's theory, but also
of a purely contrastive phonemics represented by Hockett (1958),
where the phonetic realization of the units carried no structural significance.

More substantial advances in the diachronic application of distinctive-feature theory were made, again, by Martinet. First, he enriched
the concept of "rephonologization" by a more fully developed and
amply illustrated doctrine of the preservation of useful features (e.g.,
1955:186–187, 199–211). Even more important was his development
of what had long fascinated and puzzled linguists—the symmetry of
sound systems. The Neogrammarians were mistrustful of it—again
they saw dangers of mystification—and could not quite come to terms
with the fact that "all languages display a certain harmony of the sound
system" (Paul, p. 57), until Sievers offered a physiological explanation: a different rest position of the organs in speakers of different
languages. Sievers' contemporaries welcomed this empirical basis for

the puzzling symmetries—but empirical evidence has not sustained the claim, nor has anyone been able to explain why such a rest position should control the functional realization of sound segments. It was the Prague phonologists who proceeded to a systematic description of these harmonies; and it was Martinet who attempted a major *explanatory* step by arguing that the conflict between the asymmetrical geometry of the speech organs and the (presumably) psychophysical economy of symmetrical utilization of distinctive features guarantees a permanent instability of sound systems. Martinet's illustrations of actual oscillations of systems between symmetry and asymmetry (1955:88 ff.) provide solid arguments for his theory, which must be included in any explanation of linguistic change, even if it still leaves the actuation riddle untouched.

The development of distinctive-feature theory also made it possible for the first time not merely to characterize sound systems in terms of presence or lack of certain sounds (or sound classes), but also to suggest necessary implications; for example, if a language has affricates, it will also have homorganic fricatives. The most ambitious attempt along these lines is Jakobson's (1941), and in the atmosphere of a reviving interest in universals of language, the search for implications seemed to be the most promising line of work in phonology (e.g., Ferguson 1963). Of course, the list of valid implications is still extremely shaky, so that attempts to use alleged universals as constraints on reconstruction (e.g., Jakobson 1958) remain highly controversial (cf. S. W. Allen's discussion, *ibid.*). But the possibilities along these lines are surely still far from exhausted.

2.41. GENERATIVE PHONOLOGY AND THE ECONOMY OF GRAMMARS

As in all the cases previously cited, the development of a new format of linguistic description—"generative phonology" (Halle 1959, 1962)—implies a restatement and reclassification of changes long on record. In particular, the formulation of phonetic redundancies in terms of ordered rules makes it possible to describe the differences between some phonological systems in terms of the same rules differently ordered (Halle 1962; Keyser 1963; Saporta 1965). Correspondingly and predictably, some changes can now be described as reversals of order among existing rules. There was a time when sound changes were being reclassified under the headings of "*additions* of phonemes to the inventory, *deletion* of phonemes, *substitution* of phonemes, *transposition* of phonemes." We presume that a repetition of this simplistic exercise in relation to *rules* (addition, deletion) is not to be taken as the chief contribution of generative theory to historical linguistics. For regardless of the merits of generative phonology in the description of language changes, it is far more important to see whether it offers any new perspectives in the *explanation* of changes.

The most general statement of the application of generative phonology to historical explanation is still that of Halle (1962); it has served as the point of departure for a number of recent discussions of historical change(e.g., Closs 1965 on syntax). Many of the issues raised by Halle are both constructive and penetrating; yet consideration of the empirical foundations of Halle's viewpoint reveals serious causes for concern. We argue (§1.23 and elsewhere) that the generative model for the description of language as a homogeneous object is needlessly unrealistic, and we contend that it is quite pointless to construct a theory of change which accepts as input descriptions of language states that are contrary to fact and unnecessarily idealized. We will now take up three aspects of Halle's argument which illustrate these limitations most clearly: (1) the isolation of the individual parent-to-child relationship from the speech community, and the use of this relationship as a model of linguistic change; (2) the isolation of specific historical developments from their social context; and (3) the application of distinctive features to concrete examples of change in phonological space.

(1) *The parent-to-child model of linguistic change.* Halle's approach to what we have called the transition problem (see §3.1 and ff.) postulates "discontinuities in the grammars of successive generations" (1962:65) and cites Meillet's parallel views on this point. Halle's conception necessarily isolates the individual speaker-learner and the individual parent-model from the speech community. The mechanism he proposed for linguistic change might be diagrammed as follows:

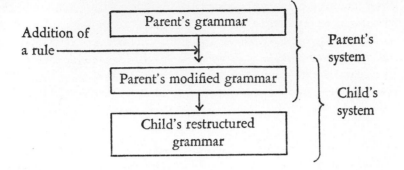

The image of the parent-to-child relationship as a model for language change is a plausible one, in the context of a structural model based on the study of individuals (or of a "homogeneous community," which is simply an individual under a group label). Furthermore, it seems clear that children do restructure their grammars not once, but many times, as they mature (Miller and Ervin 1964; Bellugi 1967). But the model depends upon the unexamined assumption that the children's grammars are formed upon the data provided by their parents' speech. Yet there is a mounting body of evidence that the language of each child is continually being restructured during his preadolescent years on the model of his peer group. Current studies of preadolescent peer groups show that the child normally acquires his particular dialect pattern, including recent changes, from children only slightly older than himself.[36]

In the light of this consideration, it is apparent that Halle's model

[36] In the various empirical studies of speech communities referred to in this paper, it has been found regularly that children of "first generation" parents do not differ in their dialect characteristics from children of families that have lived in the same area for many generations, even when the parents' dialect is markedly different from the local one. Thus the majority of the Lower East Side native speakers in the New York City study were second generation users of English—that is, English was not their parents' native language—but this fact was not inconsistent with a uniform and regular evolution of the basic vernacular of New York City (Labov 1966). There are two situations where parents' language may indeed be taken as the definitive model for children's language. One is in the isolated household—rural or urban—where the child cannot or may not play with other children. The other is in the direct transfer of a prestige feature from parent to child in the variety of careful speech used for scolding and correction (see Labov 1966b).

leaves many questions unanswered. Does the added rule originate within the community? Do all parents in the community add the rule? If not, what happens when a child from a family that has added the rule speaks to a child from a family without it? The alternative situations implied here would undoubtedly affect the course of linguistic change in different ways, which cannot be anticipated within Halle's framework. He, like Paul, posits a discreteness of generations which cannot be supported unless one ignores the fact that children derive their language input from many sources. If we now suppose that the preadolescent child can construct and reconstruct a simplest grammar as his experience grows, it is apparent that structural changes produced by his parents' late rule addition may never appear in the child's final adolescent grammar. The very fact that the child can restructure his grammar means that there is little point in looking at the parents' language as the model for change in the child's grammar. Radical differences between parent and child are then not evidence of the discontinuity of language change, but rather of the social distance between the generations.

A further weakness of Halle's model is the implication that a change is completed within a generation, the product of a specific relation between parents' and children's grammars. But this implication is not borne out by the empirical evidence of change in progress (cf. Gauchat 1905; Hermann 1929; Reichstein 1960; Labov 1963, 1966). These investigations have described changes that continue in the same direction over several generations. Persistence in the direction of change suggests that these changes are variables which have been evaluated in the same way by the speech community over a considerable period of time (see §3.3). A continuous process of transfer within the peer group, from children slightly older to children slightly younger, is consistent with such middle-range developments; but proposals for the automatic restructuring of the parents' data by the child do not show us any reason why the process would be repeated in successive generations.[37]

---

[37] Finally, it is worth noting that the problems presented here are not irrelevant to the historical status of the switching rules suggested in recent generative treatments of the Great Vowel Shift. If we consider that switching rules are in any way parallel to the changes that did take place, there would be some

(2) *Application to historical examples.* When Halle deals with an actual historical example, the isolating character of his basic model emerges even more prominently. Having separated the individual speaker from his group, Halle devises structural arguments to relate several individuals (= idiolects), without regard for the historical evidence available on the process of change within the speech community. He discusses the case of Early Modern English ę̄ in *meat, sea, beat* as an example of a mutation in the order of the rules which operate upon an underlying structure preserved from earlier stages of the language.

It is true that students of English have been puzzled for some time by the apparent reversal of a completed merger: in early sixteenth-century London, the word classes of *mate* and *meat* had apparently merged and were opposed to the class of *meet*; but in the seventeenth century the system emerged in its modern form with *mate* opposed to *meat* and *meet*:

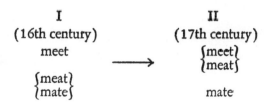

I	II
(16th century)	(17th century)
meet	{meet}
	{meat}
{meat}	
{mate}	mate

Halle uses this example to argue that merger at the (contrastive or bi-unique) phonemic level is not irreversible. But his example—no matter how hypothetical—loses its force in the light of the rich evidence brought forward by Wyld (1936) and Kökeritz (1953), which shows that the Systems I and II alternated in London for a considerable period, and that the social significance of the conservative and innovating rules must have been well known to most Londoners. In Shakes-

---

obvious problems of communication between speakers who pronounced *sigh* as [siʲ] and *see* as [seⁱ], and speakers who reversed these two pronunciations. One might argue that switching is possible between two successive and discontinuous generations, although this hardly seems consistent with Halle's restriction on mutual intelligibility as a constraint upon change (1965:66). But if we think of successive age levels transmitting linguistic tradition in a continuous pattern, then switching rules seem even more remote from processes which can occur in the actual process of linguistic change.

peare's texts, for example, Kökeritz finds ample support for the notion that the conservative system was identified with refined and aristocratic speech—as well known to the London commoner, no doubt, as Received Pronunciation of the BBC is to Londoners today. Such speakers must master both the old and the new systems, at least in their perception. Whether we view the process as prolonged bidialectalism or as inherent structural variability (see §3.3 below), we must assume that some speakers of all ages were competent in the phonology of both I and II (Halle's rules [14] and [22–23]). Surely an empirical solution to the transition problem must take precedence over arguments based on the manipulation of isolated structures; to ignore empirical evidence, even in a hypothetical example, represents a step backward in the explanation of change (in effect, to the position of Saussure; see §1.21 above).

(3) *Application of distinctive-feature theory to sound shifts observed in progress.* Studies of phonological changes in progress suggest that Halle's proposals are inadequate in not being able to account for frequently observed modes of transition. We have considerable quantitative evidence to show that there is close covariation between the movement of low vowels in a front-and-back direction and mid vowels moving to a higher or lower position. Moulton (1962) showed that the position of the low-center vowel in Swiss dialects was a function of the structure of mid- and low-mid-vowels in the front and back series. Labov (1966:529–535) established that in a single speech community the position of /ah/ was narrowly determined by the relative heights of mid-vowels /eh/ and /oh/. These quantitative relations imply the steady movement of a vowel along one dimension in coordination with other vowels moving along other dimensions—over several generations. Qualitative evidence of many recently completed changes suggests the same pattern; in Yiddish dialects, the shifts $u > y$ [$> i$] and $\bar{o} > u$ are systematically related (Herzog 1965:170); in many American dialects, we find similar on-going processes of the fronting of /ah/ with accompanying raising of /æh/ toward /eh/.[38]

---

[38] This development is especially advanced in such Northern cities as Buffalo, Detroit, and Chicago. A fifteen-year-old Detroit speaker, for example, was amused to find that New Yorkers say "[bɑṭl] for [baṭl] ('bottle') and [bæṭl]

This evidence shows that the mechanism of change is not a sudden substitution or addition of higher-level rules, but rather the application of a continuous function to phonological space at a level where continuous values are possible. Furthermore, it shows that the two-dimensional model of the vowel quadrangle, based on articulatory positions of the tongue, provides the framework within which such changes operate, and that direct measurements of distance between low and mid-vowels are a factor in the rules operating (see §3.3 below). However, the distinctive-feature framework in which Halle is operating resolves the phonological space into independent dimensions. None of the definitions of gravity and compactness provided so far will give us a theoretical motivation for the covariation of gravity and compactness among consonants, and no such evidence has appeared. Thus if the historian of language should accept the distinctive-feature matrix, he loses the possibility of describing in a coherent way a series of shifts moving around the periphery of the vowel trapezoid.

Despite the three limitations discussed above, there remains a strong intuitive appeal in Halle's view of the role of children's rule-forming behavior in language change. We cannot ignore the obvious point that preadolescent children do construct grammars independently and may restructure them many times. But the parent-child hypothesis obscures rather than clarifies the empirical question as to whether change is continuous or discontinuous. The critical point for examination is whether we can locate any linguistic discontinuity in the succession of age groups in a given community.

Such a realistic investigation of discontinuity can proceed from a theoretical model which constructs grammars for heterogeneous speech communities. We argue that while linguistic change is in progress, an archaic and an innovating form coexist within the grammar: this grammar differs from an earlier grammar by the addition of a rule, or perhaps by the conversion of an invariant rule to a variable rule (see §3.3 below). If we adopt a view similar to Sturtevant's (1947: Chap. VIII), we would expect social significance to be eventually attributed to the opposition of the two forms. At some point the social and linguistic issues are resolved together; when the opposition is no

---

for [biᵊt̬l] ('battle'). In one group of working-class Chicago boys, we find *John* realized as [jæn], *locks* as [læks] and *that* as [ðeᵊt].

longer maintained, the receding variant disappears. This view of change fits the general observation that change is more regular in the outcome than in process. We can expect that abrupt change or discontinuity will occur at the point of resolution. It is at this point that we might expect a sudden restructuring of the grammar: a search for linguistic discontinuities in the succession of age groups would therefore be a necessary first step if Halle's suggestion is to receive firm empirical support.

3. LANGUAGE AS A DIFFERENTIATED SYSTEM

3.0 A SYSTEMATIC APPROACH TO HETEROGENEOUS STRUCTURES

We now return to the fundamental question raised in Section 0: if a language must be structured in order to function efficiently, how does it function as the structure changes? We will propose a model of language that avoids the fruitless paradoxes with which theories of homogeneous structure have encumbered historical linguistics.

We have seen that for Paul as well as for Saussure, variability and systematicity excluded each other. Their successors, who continued to postulate more and more systematicity in language, became ever more deeply committed to a simplistic conception of the homogeneous idiolect. They provided no effective means for constituting a speech community out of several such idiolects, nor even of representing the behavior of a single speaker with several idiolects at his disposal. Neither did they offer an effective method for constituting a single language out of chronologically disparate homogeneous stages. Yet most linguists acknowledge the evidence which demonstrates that language change is a continuous process and the inevitable by-product of linguistic interaction.

The paradoxes have been deeply felt. Hockett, for example, exhibits a painful sensitivity to the difficulty of reconciling the fact of change with the categorial nature of homogeneous structure. On the one hand, he asserts that the process of sound change is too slow and too gradual to be observed except by its effects; on the other hand, he maintains that the process of structural change is instantaneous and hence equally unobservable by its effects. One can follow, as we have done, the historical developments that led to these extreme positions, but few linguists can rest content with an explanation of change which depends upon the joint unobservability of all the processes involved.

We have suggested (§0) that the solution to the fundamental question lies in the direction of breaking down the identification of structuredness with homogeneity. We have proposed, instead, that a reasonable account of change will depend upon the possibility of describing orderly differentiation within language. In this section we will present such a model of language structure, together with some of the data which support it; we will then outline a strategy for a study of language change which rests upon these empirical foundations.

3.1. THE TESTIMONY OF LINGUISTIC GEOGRAPHY

From the beginning, the findings of linguistic geography have been used by historical linguists to bolster their theoretical viewpoints, but seldom has the evidence provided the proof that was desired.[39] If the isoglosses for each word involved in a sound change should coincide, the Neogrammarian hypothesis would receive strong support. But the painful fact is that they rarely coincide, even when they do aggregate to form loose bundles. The contention that each word has its own history reflects our inability to predict or even account for the ways in which one word precedes another across the dialect geographer's maps. Nevertheless, this evidence is presented in the standard Neogrammarian texts alongside unqualified pronouncements of the unexceptionable nature of sound laws (Bloomfield 1933:341, 361).[40]

Historical linguists also hoped that isoglosses would support the firm division of linguistic territories into hierarchically ordered sets of languages, dialects, and subdialects. Here again the evidence has been disappointing: an unselected set of isoglosses does not divide a territory into clear-cut areas, but rather into a crosshatched continuum of finely subdivided fragments. Bloomfield reviews this problem (1933: 341), but his own criteria for selecting the most significant isoglosses

---

[39] Compare Osthoff and Brugmann's reading of Winteler.

[40] One approach to reconciling the facts of dialect geography with the uniformity of sound laws is to argue that the attested fluctuations are the results of borrowing and reborrowing from one regular dialect to another. The process of sound change then drops out of the class of observable phenomena. (Cf. Weinreich 1960:330 for a critique of Hockett's development of this theme.)

for dialect classification have not proved successful in empirical research (Weinreich 1968).

It was also hoped that dialect geography would provide support for the notion that there is a negative correlation between "structuredness" and communicability of linguistic phenomena. For Paul, for example, everything in language was infinitely communicable by social intercourse, and everything in a language responded freely, without resistance, to outside influence—*except* phonological rules. In quite a similar vein, Saussure felt that the wave model enlightens us about the primordial laws of all the phenomena of differentiation (p. 287), although we must presume that for purposes of reconstruction, that is, again in phonology, Saussure would retain the *Stammbaum* which postulates the mutual dependence of particular innovations.

The negative correlation between structuredness and communicability was a perfectly natural extrapolation for a socially agnostic theory of language. However, the correlation was never more than hypothetical and it now appears that it was factually incorrect. Evidence was given above that phonemic mergers expand outward, and this tendency seems to be very general indeed.[41] It might be argued that the spread of mergers represents the loss of structure, rather than the transmission of structure. Yet evidence for the communication of structural features is broader than this. The studies growing from the Yiddish Atlas, for example, are turning up such interesting examples as the transmis-

[41] One can observe the expansion of mergers in a great many areas of the United States on the basis of the Linguistic Atlas records completed a generation ago. The merger of the low-back vowels in *hock* and *hawk*, *Don* and *dawn* is expanding beyond the core areas of Eastern New England and Western Pennsylvania. Systematic observations of the same merger in the Western United States indicate rapid expansion and solidification. The merger of /i/ and /e/ before nasals is expanding outside of the South, and has been observed as far north as Gary, Indiana. Many distinctions before *r* are being lost in areas where they were quite firm a generation ago: /or∼ɔr/ in *hoarse* vs. *horse*, *pork* vs. *storm*, is one of the most striking examples, in the South as well as the North. The distinction of /hw ∼ w/ in *which* vs. *witch*, *whale* vs. *wale* displays a comparable instability, despite the fact that it is supported by spelling. The chief exception to this tendency is the advance of *r*-pronunciation into previously *r*-less areas, restoring in some regions the distinction between *god* and *guard*, *sauce* and *source*. The advance of this prestige pattern, supported by mass media, is discussed below (§3.3). Note that in the great majority of *r*-less areas, most of these distinctions have been maintained by vowel quality.

sion of a reoriented gender system from Northeastern to Central Yiddish (Herzog 1965:101–118). While the over-all advance of the Northeastern pattern manifests the loss of the neuter category, we also observe the importation of a new "intermediate" category which is the result of the borrowing of abstract concord relations rather than direct borrowing of lexical items. Moreover, this transition area shows the communication of a new constraint upon gender assignment involving the mass-noun:count-noun opposition which did not exist in the borrowing dialect (p. 103).

We do not mean to deny that a synchronic structural dialectology is possible: as an analytic exercise there is nothing wrong with it; but as the facts come in, such a mechanical extension of structuralism is becoming increasingly unilluminating as an account of the way languages develop.

We are not claiming, of course, that all innovations are equally communicable; if they were, there would be no intersecting isoglosses and no enduring dialect differentiation. We are merely denying that the synchronic structure of language furnishes us with the principal criteria for differential communicability.

The network of isoglosses which proceeds from a study of dialect geography often represents the synchronic equivalent of the *transition* problem—that is, the route by which a linguistic change is proceeding to completion. An understanding of the relation of these isoglosses to linguistic change frequently depends upon a solution to the *embedding* problem—that is, their relation to the linguistic systems and histories of the speech communities involved. It is more probable that a given isogloss represents a linguistic change in progress if its location cannot be accounted for by the linguistic or historical context. We can distinguish four types of isoglosses in terms of such "accountability."

(1) The isogloss or bundle of isoglosses coincides with a social or political (or geographic) boundary, representing the limits of the pattern of communication which led to the diffusion of the linguistic feature. The major discontinuities in the Yiddish of Northern Poland show several such boundaries (Herzog 1965:246–252). The isogloss bundle separating North Central from Central Yiddish coincides with a number of well-known political boundaries of the sixteenth century. The linguistic boundary between Northeastern and North Central

Yiddish coincides with a social discontinuity which is less obvious: the line along which Lithuanian Jewish settlers from the North met Polish Jewish settlers from the South and Center when this area was opened to Jewish settlement in the sixteenth century. This bundle of isoglosses is also a major division in the area of nonverbal culture.

(2) The location of the isogloss is accounted for by its systematic relation to other isoglosses which bundle with it. The clearest cases are those of linguistic *incompatibility*: where the advancing change represents a feature that cannot be simply added or subtracted from the system of the neighboring dialect encountered across the isogloss bundle. We observe such an example in the spread of a monophthongization of *aj* from Central Yiddish into the southern Ukraine, so that *hajnt* 'today' became *ha:nt,* and *majlexl* 'little mouth' became *ma:lexl.* The diffusion of this changing feature ended abruptly at just that point where the distinction of length was lost in the Northern Ukraine. If the monophthongization had continued, the monophthong would have coincided with short *a* in that region, so that *hant* would have represented both 'today' and 'hand,' and *malexl* would have represented both 'little mouth' and 'little angel' (Herzog 1968: Fig. 7).[42]

(3) The location of the isogloss is not accountable by any linguistic or social factors, but the direction of movement is predictable on linguistic grounds. Figure 1 shows an example of two such "free" isoglosses: on the one hand, the merger of *i* and *u* moving from southwest to northeast, and on the other, the merger of *i:* and *i, u:* and *u* moving from northeast to southwest. A general constraint upon linguistic change discussed above, that mergers expand at the expense of distinctions, leads us to posit the directions of the changes from the synchronic facts alone. It has of course been observed that the direction of movement can be predicted in many cases from geographic and configurational factors of dialect maps.

(4) The location of the isogloss is not accountable by either linguistic or social factors, and the direction of movement is not predictable. Many individual lexical isoglosses have this character. It may

---

[42] Length was subsequently lost in the Southern Ukraine as well. Consequently, *a*($<a$:$<aj$) does occur in *hant* 'today' and *malexl* 'little mouth.' However, original short *a* has moved to short *o,* and 'hand' is *hont,* and 'little angel' is *molexl.*

prove true that in all these cases we are dealing with items carried by mobile individual speakers along lines of trade and transit, rather than a steady diffusion of the linguistic feature from one neighboring speech community to another by more frequent and predictable patterns of communication.

The problem of accounting for the geographical transition of dialects across a territory thus appears to be symmetrical with the problem of accounting for the transition of dialects through time in one community. In each case, there is a contact between speakers with different systems. If we are to solve the mysterious paradoxes of change outlined above, it will be necessary to analyze the processes which occur in such contact situations in terms of how a speaker can understand and accept as his own the structural elements in the speech of others.

3.2. LANGUAGES AND DIALECTS IN CONTACT

A close study of the transition problem inevitably leads us to consider the transference of a linguistic form or rule from one person to another—more specifically, from one linguistic system to another. The simplest mechanism was that proposed by Paul in which the transference takes place between two isolated, homogeneous idiolects. For Paul, "language mixture" (including dialect mixture; p. 402) arises when two individuals, each by definition speaking his own idiolect, communicate with each other. When this happens, "the speaker influences the language-relevant imaginations (*Vorstellungsmassen*) of the hearer" (p. 390). There thus takes place either intercourse of nonidentical idiolects, or modification of idiolects by mutual influence.

No matter how we consider this model of language change, it seems unworkable; it neither matches empirical observations nor does it provide a reasonable model to satisfy our native intuitions. The problem is seen at its clearest in the rapid transference characteristic of pre-adolescent verbal culture. In the Boston area, children claim a share of cake or candy from their friends by saying "Allies," "Cokes," or "Checks." If a child from Providence or New York City should move into the Boston area, and attempt to claim a share by using an alien claiming term, we would reasonably expect his attempt to be rejected. Yet by one means or another, the claiming term "Thumbs up" spread to Boston and other Northern cities in the late 1950's, and displaced the local terms. The direct influence of one speaker on another in the process of communication is clearly counter to the apparent self-interest of the recipient.

In Paul's account, command of two idiolects is considered only for historical purposes (as an explanation of the influence of one idiolect on another). No synchronic properties of bi-idiolectalism as such—neither analytic nor psychological nor social—are proposed for investigation. Thus Paul's theory allows *shifts* to other idiolects as well as interidiolectal *influences*, but not switching between idiolects.[43] If we abandon the individual homogeneous idiolect as a model of language we can suggest a more intelligible mechanism of transfer. It seems reasonable that the transfer takes place when Speaker A *learns* the form or rule used by Speaker B, and that the rule then coexists in A's linguistic competence along with his previous form or rule. Change then takes place *within* the complex linguistic repertoire of A: one type is the gradual disfavoring of the original form at the expense of the new one, so that it moves to the status of "archaic" or "obsolete."

Bloomfield's treatment of Dutch sound changes showed a clear advance over Paul in this respect:

Every speaker is constantly adapting his speech habits to those of his inter-locutors; he gives up forms he has been using, adopts new ones, and perhaps oftenest of all, changes the frequency of speech forms without entirely abandoning old ones or accepting any that are really new to him. (1933: 327–328)

The fact that Bloomfield was willing to entertain the possibility of a more complex model of transference indicates a general recognition of the importance of stylistic alternations in linguistic behavior. Studies of linguistic change in progress regularly uncover this type of alternation (Kökeritz 1953:194 ff; Labov 1963; Reichstein 1960). Every dialect atlas provides many examples of the archaic/innovating opposition within the competence of individual speakers. But we can also point to a distinctly different mechanism of change which can occur simultan-eously with this one. When Speaker A first learns a rule, q, from B, it is not to be expected that he will learn it perfectly. Influenced by his

---

[43] In the study of language contact, too, one distinguishes between back-and-forth switching and once-and-for-all shifting; cf. Weinreich 1953: 68–69.

own system, *P*, and without the full range of *B*'s experience which supports *B*'s system, *Q*, *A* acquires a rule, *q*′, of a somewhat different sort—a phonological rule with features altered, a lexical rule with different privileges of distribution, or a grammatical rule with some special conditions lost. Thus, in this initial transference, a second type of change has already taken place. But the more profound and systematic change is to be expected *after A* has acquired *B*'s rule. Within the single repertoire available to *A* (containing *p* in *P* and *q*′) we can anticipate an accommodation of *p* and *q*′—normally, an assimilation of *q*′ to the features characteristic of *p* so that eventual insertion of a modified *q*″ into the system *P* is possible. This process has been noted many times in the phonological adjustment of loan words. When *Trauma* was borrowed from German, the uvular *r* automatically became an American voiceless apical; but in the ensuing period of adjustment we can observe the /aw/ shifting to /ɔ/ in conformity with the general rule which restricts /aw/ before labial consonants. Yiddish *štik* 'piece, antic' was borrowed into New York City English in approximately the same phonetic form; but in the Negro community, where š does not occur in initial clusters,[44] the form shifts to [stɪk], homonymous with *stick*, with a number of semantic consequences.

When a traditional Negro speaker from the South migrates to the North he acquires the general term *common sense* which is only a partial match for his native term *mother-wit* or *mother-with*.[45] The two coexist as archaic *mother-wit* versus innovating *common sense*, but as the alternation between the two is resolved in favor of *common sense*, the modifier *mother-* shifts from its original meaning 'native, original' to the general 'female parent.' Thus some young Negro

[44] Thus *Schneider* appears as [snaɪdə], *shmuck* as [smʌk], and *shnook* as [snʊk].

[45] The term *mother-wit* is archaic or learned in the speech of whites, but is a matter of everyday use for Southern Negro speakers. Although it is equivalent to *common sense* in representing everyday, practical wisdom not learned from books, it differs in its firmer connection with the concept of native, innate intelligence; most white speakers do believe that one can acquire more common sense as one gets older. One of the remarkable facts about the *mother-wit* ~ *common sense* opposition is that whites are uniformly ignorant of the Negro use of *mother-wit*, and Negroes are uniformly ignorant that whites do not use the term. (Data proceed from semantic investigations associated with Labov 1963 and 1966.)

speakers, asked if men can have mother-wit, look puzzled and answer "No."

The study of languages in contact confirms the notion that stable long-term coexistence is largely an illusion, perhaps promoted by the existence of a relatively stable (or even dissimilating) lexicon and morphophonemics. Gumperz' investigation of the long-standing intimate contact of Marathi and Kannada in Kupwar (1967) shows the most radical adjustment of semantics, phrase structure, transformational component, and phonetics of the two systems. On the other hand, the vocabulary and grammatical morphemes are so patently differentiated that there can never be any doubt in a given sentence whether Marathi or Kannada is being spoken. Languages which are obviously different in surface structure have in fact become so similar that mechanical translation appears to be quite feasible through a simple dictionary look-up procedure.

Gumperz' findings were the products of a close study of bilingualism within its social context; his approach to the development of Marathi was a study not only of the transition problem, but also of the embedding problem. The objects which Gumperz analyzed were not the standard Marathi and Kannada described in textbooks but the coexistent systems which were in use within a specific social context. Part of the solution to the embedding problem for a particular language change is of course the study of its structural interrelations with the linguistic elements that surround it; but the solutions to these problems have often been artificial and unsatisfactory, since they compared structures which were not in actual contact in any real social situation. In principle, there is no difference between the problems of transference between two closely related dialects and between two distantly related languages.

In examining the linguistic changes which take place within the speech of bilingual or bidialectal individuals, we may look to purely structural factors; but the isolation of structure has failed signally to solve the problem of specifying bilingual interference. As Weinreich noted:

Of course, the linguist is entitled to abstract language from considerations of a psychological or sociological nature. As a matter of fact, he SHOULD pose purely linguistic problems about bilingualism . . . But the extent, direction and nature of interference of one language with another can be explained even more thoroughly in terms of the speech behavior of bilingual individuals, which in turn is conditioned by social relations in the community in which they live. (1953:4)

We can now turn to the more specific examination of the contact situation and the systematic nature of the style alternation which is posited here.

3.21. Coexistent Systems

It was suggested above that we find a certain amount of contact between any two regional dialects: some speakers who control both dialects actively, and a larger number who have passive knowledge of the neighboring dialect but active command of only one. We also find in most speech communities distinct forms of the same language which coexist in roughly the same proportion in all of the geographic subregions of the community. This is the case not only in urban areas such as New York City, London, or Paris, but also in rural communities such as Hemnes, Norway, or Martha's Vineyard, Massachusetts. These coexisting forms may be known as "styles" but also as "standards," "slang," "jargons," "old talk," "cultural levels" or "functional varieties." In terms of the model of a differentiated language system that we are developing, such forms share the following properties:

(1) They offer alternative means of saying "the same thing": that is, for each utterance in A there is a corresponding utterance in B which provides the same referential information (is synonymous) and cannot be differentiated except in terms of the over-all significance which marks the use of B as against A.

(2) They are jointly available to all (adult) members of the speech community. Some speakers may be unable to produce utterances in A and B with equal competence because of some restriction in their personal knowledge, practices, or privileges appropriate to their social status, but all speakers generally have the ability to interpret utterances in A and B and understand the significance of the choice of A or B by some other speaker.

Throughout the 1920's and 1930's, one can trace a general tendency for linguists in both Europe and America to draw away from the simple psychological unity of the idiolect as posited by Paul. Mathesius and his colleagues in Prague used a multilayer approach to characterize systems coexisting in the same community. Jakobson (1931) declared style switching to be a permanent fact which does not compromise the systematicity of each style as an object of linguistic description. In the United States we have seen that Bloomfield envisaged the coexistence of archaic and innovating forms in the same speaker. Furthermore, Bloomfield was fully capable of correcting his own earlier view that the complexities of "good" and "bad" speech styles are artifacts of literate cultures; when confronted with the Menomini situation, he recognized that hierarchically organized styles are the product of general social processes (1927). Confronted with this growing awareness of the heterogeneity of the language used by each individual, Bloch proceeded to develop a notion of the idiolect which represented only one of the possible systems within individual competence (1948:7).

Today it may seem naïve for Bloch to have imagined that he could avoid facing the facts of heterogeneity by limiting the idiolect to one speaker and one listener. If Bloch's idiolects were indeed to achieve homogeneity, then topic, situation, and even time would have to be rigidly controlled (Ervin-Tripp 1964; Labov 1966:90). As the awareness of the complexity of linguistic behavior grew, the domain of the idiolect shrank—eventually to the vanishing point.

Not every American linguist was devoted to the separation of the homogeneous linguistic objects from the heterogeneous life situations in which they were located. Some were not averse to discovering *within* the idiolect a multiplicity of layers. Fries and Pike, in their article "Coexistent Phonemic Systems" (1949), raised the possibility that systematicity and variability were not mutually exclusive. Although the writers restricted themselves to phonology, everything they said about coexistent systems could have been extended, *mutatis mutandis*, to the rest of language. Fries and Pike's paper did not deal with a really substantial example of competing subsystems; the Arabic elements in Swahili discussed by Harris (1951), for example, have much more internal coherence than the few Spanish elements labeled by Fries and Pike. But their paper marks a real advance because they did more than set these elements aside as extraneous: they saw that there could be a rich variety of systematic relations within such complex mixed systems. Nor was their innovation purely synchronistic: the implications for history were quite clear to the authors, even though they were cautious to state them as mere "assumptions":

In the process of change from one phonemic system to a different phonemic system of the same language, there may be a time during which parts of the two systems exist simultaneously and in conflict within the speech of single individuals. . . . It is impossible to give a purely synchronic description of a complex mixed system, at one point of time, which shows the pertinent facts of that system; direction of change is a pertinent characteristic of the system and must also be known if one wishes to have a complete description of the language as it is structurally constituted. (pp. 41–42)

Strange as it may seem, however, Fries and Pike's significant departure was hardly utilized in concrete historical work. True, their scheme did become a keystone for the study of bilingualism—specifically for "dialinguistic" descriptions serving as a kind of specification of the competence of bilingual speakers (e.g., Haugen 1954, 1957; Weinreich 1953, 1957b). However, even though contact theory was perfectly capable *in principle* of handling pairs of chronologically "marked" dialects as well as the contact between more dissimilar systems (Weinreich 1953:2, 94–95), it does not seem in fact to have occurred to anyone that the theory could serve as a socially realistic basis for the investigation of language change.[46] Nor was there any rush to test Jakobson's view that style switching was a permanent feature of language against the few existing studies of sound change in process (Gauchat 1905; Hermann 1929).

The most detailed and reliable descriptions of such coexisting forms have been provided by scholars working in the Near East and South Asia. A rich body of qualitative, descriptive data on social and stylistic levels was developed by Ferguson, Gumperz, Bright, McCormack, Kelley, Ramanujan, Levine, and others, and Ferguson and Gumperz succeeded in assembling this material into a coherent set of principles which have been supported by further studies (Ferguson and Gumperz 1960; see especially the "Introduction"). Bright and Ramanujan (1964) were the first to develop a specific hypothesis on differential directions of language change based on a multilayer model of socio-

[46] An outstanding exception is a paper by Pulgram (1961).

linguistic structure. Gumperz went considerably beyond simple description in his study of Hemnesberget: here, for the first time, we have controlled data on natural groups within the community which demonstrate conclusively the mechanism of switching between strata which are functionally available to all members of the community (1964). Friedrich (1966) has now provided the most detailed explication of parallel change in complex social and linguistic systems. These empirical studies have confirmed the model of an orderly heterogeneous system in which the choice between linguistic alternants carries out social and stylistic functions, a system which changes with accompanying changes in social structure.

In order to assure the sharpness of our orientation, let us note that history is not the only direction in which the coexistent-system approach to language can be bent; the motivating interest for its development actually lay elsewhere. Mathesius, whose views on the inherent variability of the component subsystems are considered below, provided a synchronic distinction between portions of a vocabulary having different historical origins (1934)—an application which coincided with Fries and Pike's stimulus. The multilayer conception can also be used for purely analytic purposes to represent a language as a "diasystem" composed of member dialects (Weinreich 1954). For the theory to be of significance to historical linguistics, on the other hand, we have specified that the layers which it encompasses, while functionally distinct, be nevertheless functionally available to a group of speakers.

We insist on *functional distinctness* for two reasons. First, the layers must be in competition, not in complementarity. The coexistent phonological subsystems discovered in English, Mazateco, or Czech vocabulary are complementary—there is not, as a rule, a choice of rendering the same word in either system. They do not, consequently, constitute the layers in which the observer of change is interested.[47] Secondly, it is necessary to provide a rigorous description of the conditions which govern the alternation of the two systems. Rules of this

---

[47] This is not to deny that occasional "spot" competitions arise between members of complementary systems, for example, *defendable—defensible*, *mustáche—mústache*. When they do, corresponding dynamic consequences may be drawn.

sort must include extralinguistic factors as governing environments (Geertz 1960; Martin 1964) since the parallel subsystems all satisfy the linguistic conditions. The rules themselves, exclusive of their external environmental elements, must provide a *linguistic* description of the relations governing units matched across layers. If the coexisting subsystems have internal consistency, as discussed, for example, by Gumperz (1964:140, with further references), then a set of rules will share the same over-all external environments.[48]

We wish also to insist on the availability of the layers to a real group of speakers. Any pair of dialects can be brought under the heading of a single "diasystem"; the operation may be carried out even on areally noncontiguous dialects, and may serve a useful purpose in reconstruction. But it is only when a pair of dialects are jointly available to a group that switches back and forth between them—even if some members of the group only *hear* one of the styles and never speak it— that the multilayer formulation is relevant to an understanding of language change.[49] In urban societies, we find typically that the many

[48] In his analysis of a historically stabilized type of bidialectalism ("diglossia") Ferguson (1959) made a start toward the linguistic characterization of variables. He thus went further than was to go Gumperz (1964), who also contributes extremely valuable data but—perhaps out of a hesitation to compromise the structural rigor of linguistics by extending it to multilayer objects—postulates a "verbal repertoire" whose structure "differs from ordinary [one-layered] descriptive grammars" (p. 137). The differences between the two dialects of Hindi and Norwegian are sampled by Gumperz through loose lists, without an attempt to show by some kind of "diasystemic" formulas the presence of familiar relations, such as two-to-one phoneme correspondences or case syncretisms across the layers. Note, however, that in more recent work on the Marathi–Kannada situation in Kupwar (1967), Gumperz has explored the systematic relations of the two systems much more deeply, and his concept of a single linguistic repertoire has taken on greater solidity. For further articulation of the *diglossia* concept, see Fishman (1967); note that there are diglossia situations where the layers are *not* jointly available.

[49] For a comparable distinction between bilingual societies (without necessary presence of bilingual individuals) and bilingual mother-tongue groups (with bilingual individuals present by definition), see Weinreich (1953:88–89). In his Preface to that book, Martinet laid down a blueprint for a theoretical unification of three topics of study: language contact, dialectology, and style shifting. Unfortunately this unification remained unimplemented all too long. Moulton (1962) has judiciously criticized the idea of diasystemic formulas on the grounds that they would in practice be unmanageably complex. However, under the socially realistic requirement of joint availability of layers, as set

strata *are* available to the population as a whole, at least in the passive sense: their competence includes the ability to decipher alternate versions of the code.

The multilayer conception of language, initiated by Mathesius and Jakobson in Prague, developed by Fries and Pike in America, and currently applied more systematically to sociolinguistic studies by Gumperz, has opened new horizons for the theory of language change. It replaced the concept of dialect borrowing—in principle a momentary and accidental event—with the concept of style switching—in principle a durative and recurrent phenomenon. It thus made unnecessary the abortive search (envisaged, e.g., by Paul and Bloomfield) after pure dialects undergoing change without interference. In short, it justified the study of language change *in vivo* and made it unnecessary to rely on the past, which—no matter how richly recorded and ingeniously studied[50]—can never replace the present as a laboratory for the linguist.

The Subjective Evaluation of Code-Switching. The great majority of the investigations of heterogeneous speech communities have been studies of linguistic behavior: the authors have aimed at separating the various levels and determining the conditions for the speakers' choice or alternation among them. Some predictions of the course of language change in multilingual communities have relied entirely upon a second source of data—demographic factors (Deutsch 1953)—but most discussions introduce a third source—social attitudes toward language (Kelley 1966; Rona 1966). A series of systematic investigations of such attitudes have been carried out with considerable ingenuity by Lambert and his colleagues (1960, 1967) with extremely regular re-

---

forth here, we would ordinarily be dealing with no more than two or three layers at a time; in such a case the complexity of the description would be less likely to get out of hand. It should be added that multilayer statements can be couched in any descriptive format; for a generative approach to a syntactic multilayer phenomenon, see Klima (1964).

[50] Among the works which we have most admired are Kökeritz (1953) for English and Fónagy (1956) for French. These brilliant studies are based on a conscious recognition that the well-documented, socially conditioned fluctuations which they trace belong to the central mechanisms of language change, not to some marginal process of "dialect mixture." Compared to these analyses, the schematicism of the Neogrammarians and of some modern structuralists, generative or otherwise, is surprisingly antihistorical.

sults: the subjective correlates of language alternation appear to be more uniform than behavior itself.

Lambert's basic technique employs "matched guises"—the same speaker is heard at different times speaking French and English, or Hebrew and Arabic, or English with and without a Jewish accent—and the subjects rate these voices for a series of personality traits, without being aware that they are rating the same person twice.[51] There can be no doubt that deep-seated sets of social attitudes are powerful factors in determining the course of language history in multilingual communities; the case of India (Kelley 1966; Weinreich 1957b) is sufficient witness. In a further series of investigations, Lambert found that English-Canadian students who participate in the set of negative attitudes toward French speakers have much greater difficulty in learning French than students in the United States (1967:101–102).

Thus the study of the *evaluation* problem in linguistic change is an essential aspect of research leading to an explanation of change. It is not difficult to see how personality features unconsciously attributed to speakers of a given subsystem would determine the social significance of alternation to that subsystem and so its development or obsolescence as a whole. But the effect of social values on the internal development of a linguistic system is a more difficult matter, which we will consider in the following section.

3.3. VARIABILITY WITHIN THE SYSTEM

The heterogeneous character of the linguistic systems discussed so far is the product of combinations, alternations, or mosaics of distinct, jointly available subsystems. Each of these subsystems is conceived as a coherent, integral body of rules of the categorial, Neogrammarian type: the only additional theoretical apparatus needed is a set of rules stating the conditions for alternation. While these rules may be quite complex (Geertz 1960; Martin 1964), they do not interfere with the isolation of one or the other subsystem—a procedure which is typical

---

[51] Thus the basic data consist of the *differences* between personality ratings given to the same person in two different guises (i.e., French-speaking vs. English-speaking). These reactions are thus evaluations of the use of a language or dialect as a whole. For subjective reactions to individual linguistic variables, see below.

of the traditional approach to nonstandard dialects. It has been assumed that the linguist can abstract one level or subsystem of such a complex without losing any information necessary for linguistic analysis, and many studies which isolate one of several such jointly available systems were carried out under the further assumption that the only possible basis for description is a homogeneous, invariant system. Thus we find that Sivertsen, in her excellent study of Cockney English (1960), abstracted from the actual data to provide a homogeneous account of a Cockney independent of any alternations with co-existing systems. Bailey did the same in her penetrating account of Jamaican Creole Syntax (1966). In both cases it was assumed that the variable elements in the data were the products of dialect mixture— irregular insertions of the standard language with which speakers were in contact. The consistent system of Cockney or Creole was identified as the set of variants which were *most different* from the standard language.

Although isolating studies of this sort may provide valuable starting points for linguistic analysis, in our opinion they offer no rational basis for the explanation of linguistic change. Such abstractions are no doubt more *consistent* than the actual data, and thus more amenable to the writing of rules without exceptions. On the other hand, if one attempted to describe how a speaker of Cockney or Jamaican English actually used the language, there would be many puzzling and uninterpretable inconsistencies in the data. Such inconsistencies would be interpretable within a more adequate model of a differentiated language applied to the entire speech community, which includes variable elements within the system itself.

3.31. LINGUISTIC VARIABLES WITHIN THE SYSTEM

There is no doubt that the differentiated model of a speech community presented so far is not entirely adequate to account for the complexity of observed structure. It is true that in many cases we find regular code-switching between two integrated structures, as in switching from Canadian French to English. Such switching implies strict *co-occurrence* between the linguistic elements and rules concerned. A *code* or *system* is conceived as a complex of interrelated rules or categories which cannot be mixed randomly with the rules or categories of another code or system. So, for example, one would normally say in Jamaican Creole *im tired a tired* or in standard English *he's tired, that's all*, but not *he's tired a tired*.

Strict co-occurrence is often claimed for the rules of a dialect, but proof is seldom provided. A minimum requirement would be for the analyst to state that over a sufficiently large population of sentences *A* and *A'* were associated in the same sentence, and *B* and *B'*, but that no instances of *A* and *B'* or *A'* and *B* were found; however, this type of statement is seldom supplied.

Since it often happens that the details of the alternating situation do not support such a claim, the analyst is forced to maintain that the speakers can switch codes in the middle of a sentence, a clause, or a phrase, not once but several times. For example, it is claimed that in the speech of young Negro children in Northern cities, the copula does not appear in the present tense, as in *You a swine!*[52] Yet for all speakers in this community the copula *is* will appear frequently in this portion. It is not uncommon to find in the most excited peer-group interaction, utterances such as *Make believe this is a team and this a team!* To claim that this and hundreds of other such examples are instances of code-switching would be an artifact of the theory and hardly an inescapable conclusion demanded by the data.

To account for such intimate variation, it is necessary to introduce another concept into the mode of orderly heterogeneity which we are developing here: *the linguistic variable*—a variable element within the system controlled by a single rule.

The inherent variability of linguistic phenomena was of considerable interest to members of the Prague Circle. In 1911 Mathesius demurred from Paul's requirement that languages necessarily be studied under the aspect of their homogeneity. Linguists have forgotten, Mathesius argued, that the homogeneity of language is not an "actual quality of the examined phenomena," but "a consequence of the employed method" (p. 2). In reality language is characterized by synchronic[53] oscillation in the speech of individuals. The systematic (coded) aspect of this oscillation Mathesius called "potentiality":

[52] Compare Stewart 1966. For an analysis of the syntactic arguments, and data on linguistic variables in Negro speech, see Labov and Cohen 1967.

[53] We follow the translator-editor, J. Vachek, in interpreting Mathesius' "static" as "synchronic."

If any dialect were absolutely constant from the phonetic viewpoint, this would imply the constancy of its inventory of sounds and of the phonetic make-up of each individual word; on the contrary, phonetic potentiality of a dialect implies potentiality of the inventory *and/or* of its distribution in words. (p. 23–24)[54]

Mathesius was careful to make clear that the potentiality which he discusses is primarily a *synchronic* phenomenon. There can, of course, also be dynamic (diachronic) oscillation, but

the dynamic [= diachronic] issues can only be solved after a more thorough research in individual languages has firmly established which phenomena can have been regarded in them, at the given time, as constant and which as potential. Only then will one be in a position to ask how long a potential phenomenon α can still have been regarded as basically the same phenomenon, only slightly affected by a shift of its potentiality, and when one must have already admitted the existence of a new phenomenon β, replacing α. The necessary investigations will be very difficult, but after they have been carried out we shall be better informed of the fundamentals of what is going on in language than we have [been] so far. (p. 31)

Mathesius' examples show a clear recognition of the transition problem that we have outlined above; however, they do not show that he had succeeded in the integration of his notion of "potentiality" into a systematic description of language. These examples show a near-random distribution of length or oscillation of grammatical options—variation without direction. The emphasis is on the variability of the individual rather than the regularities inherent in such variation.

Prague School writers have continued in the last two decades to develop their interest in variability and continuous change. We are particularly impressed by the papers of Neustupný (1961, 1966), reformulating the views of V. Skalička, which present penetrating criticisms of the rigid categorial framework normally employed by linguists. Neustupný insists on the recognition of the complex character of linguistic categories and the importance of marginal and

---

[54] Among Mathesius' antecedents, according to his own comment, special honors go to Daniel Jones, who had characterized different styles of English in phonetic terms.

peripheral elements; he does not fail to underline the importance of these concepts for the theory of language change:

Closed classes do not allow for the transition from one phoneme to an-other . . . It was not by accident that R. Jakobson . . . postulated for phono-logical change the character of absolute leaps. However, the described method can explain the change by the inner, gradual development within a phonological class or group of classes. (1961:6)

The studies of historical change carried out by Vachek (1964a) have contributed a great deal to our understanding of the role of peripheral elements and their lack of systematic integration, in terms thoroughly consistent with Martinet's views. But despite our profound theoretical sympathy for the position of the Prague School, it must be conceded that they have not presented their views with a formal precision ade-quate for the complexity of the linguistic data. Nor have they de-veloped empirical methods for work within the speech community which would allow them to investigate the processes of continuous change in a convincing manner.[55] It is therefore understandable that these writings have not had the impact upon the American scene which their theoretical importance would warrant. Certainly it is not enough to point out the existence or importance of variability: it is necessary to deal with the facts of variability with enough precision to allow us to incorporate them into our analyses of linguistic structure.

A linguistic variable must be defined under strict conditions if it is to be a part of a linguistic structure; otherwise, one would simply be opening the door wide to rules in which "frequently," "occasionally," or "sometimes" apply. Quantitative evidence for *covariation* between the variable in question and some other linguistic or extralinguistic element provides a necessary condition for admitting such a structural unit. *Covariation* may be opposed to *strict co-occurrence*, or co-occurrence may be conceived as the limiting case of covariation. Proof of strict co-occurrence relations may in fact emerge from a quantitative investigation of the type which provides proof of covariation. All rules may be considered to be of the form:

---

[55] Vachek, for example, relies upon a miscellaneous collection of phonetic observations in the literature to argue that [W] (voiceless [w]) has been and is now opposed to [hw] as a social and stylistic variable (1964a:29–46), and this proposal forms the basis of his analysis of the linguistic developments.

$$(1) \qquad A \rightarrow g[B] / X \begin{bmatrix} \underline{} \\ Z \end{bmatrix} Y$$

$$(2) \qquad g[B] = f(C, D, E \dots),$$

where B is one or more features of A, and C, D, and E are linguistic or extralinguistic variables. The expression g[B] is the *linguistic variable* defined by the rule, usually denoted (B). Thus the variability of r-pronunciation in New York City can be represented:

$$(3) \qquad /r/ \rightarrow g[r] / - \begin{Bmatrix} K \\ \# \end{Bmatrix}$$

$$(4) \qquad g[r] = f(\text{Style, Class, Age}).^{56}$$

In (3), the category /r/ is rewritten as the variable (r) in final and preconsonantal position, equivalent to the frequency of the constricted consonant [r], a function of style, class, and age level of the speaker.

The usual categorial rule has the value of g set at 1. When entire systems of variables covary together, then the value of the controlling function g is identical for each rule which differentiates the systems. The value of g may also be idiosyncratic for a particular variable, but related to other variables in a more or less regular manner. The heterogeneous system is then viewed as a set of subsystems which alternate according to one set of co-occurring rules, while within each of these subsystems we may find individual variables which covary but do not strictly co-occur. Each of these variables will ultimately be defined by functions of independent extralinguistic or internal linguistic variables but these functions need not be independent of one another. On the contrary, one would normally expect to find intimate covariation among the linguistic variables.

The Transition Problem. Any close study of the transition from one linguistic system to another will require the determination of the value of a linguistic variable. It is possible, of course, that a linguistic change might occur as a discrete step—a simultaneous mutation of grammars on the parts of great numbers of speakers, despite the difficulties set forth above (§ 2.41). However, the changes which have been studied closely (e.g., Gauchat 1905; Hermann 1929; Reichstein 1960; Labov

---

[56] A previous rule develops the /r/ in *bird, work, shirt* in a different direction and so (3) does not apply to this class (Labov 1966:337–342). A somewhat different set of formal conventions for variable rules, embodying the same general principles, is presented in Labov, Cohen, Robins, and Lewis (1968);

1963, 1966) show continuous transitions in the frequencies and modal values of forms. Thus we can write for Gauchat's community of Charmey:

(5) $\qquad\varepsilon \rightarrow g[\varepsilon^1]$

(6) $\qquad g = f(\text{time})$,

that is, the variable (ey) representing the diphthongization of $[\varepsilon]$ is a function of time. The independent variable of time is often inferred only from a study of distribution across age levels; this was indeed the case with Gauchat who actually showed only that:

(6') $\qquad g = f(\text{age})$.

Hermann's work, a generation later, gave the data needed to move from observations of age levels to statements about real time, for the diphthong $[\varepsilon^1]$ did in fact become quite general throughout the population. In other cases, detailed quantitative studies of distribution across age levels have served to supplement more fragmentary observations made a generation earlier to provide the necessary anchor point and distinguish age-grading from the process of linguistic change.

If the linguistic variable were a simple distribution across age levels, then the process of transfer from one group of speakers to another somewhat younger would be a mysterious fact, easier to note than to explain. We might posit an intricate series of borrowings (Bloomfield 1933:403) or argue with Halle that the grammars of younger speakers are reconstructed along simpler lines with consequent mutations in the rules (§ 2.41 above). However, the cases that have been studied most carefully show the variable as a function of style as well as age, even in the early stages. We find that uneducated speakers, who show little self-consciousness and no correction in formal styles, will still show a stylistic differentiation between archaic and innovating modes. For example, working-class speakers in New York City use slightly higher vowels in *coffee, more, lost* in emphatic and affective expressions, even though they do not shift to lower vowels in formal style as middle-class speakers do (Labov 1966:256). We thus observe in their speech the

---

these deal primarily with the two-valued consonantal variables of nonstandard Negro English with considerable contextual and grammatical conditioning, embedded in a more comprehensive set of sixteen phonological rules of English. The rules given here symbolize the relations of multivalued variables within a Cartesian vowel space, relations which are currently being investigated in an instrumental study of sound change in progress.

differentiation of innovating and archaic variants of this variable (oh):

(7)   (oh) = f(age, style).

The Embedding Problem. Linguists are naturally suspicious of any account of change which fails to show the influence of the structural environment upon the feature in question: it is reasonable to assume that the feature is embedded in a linguistic matrix which changes with it. Furthermore, we can argue that external factors have less effect upon a feature which is a member of a system in equilibrium than upon isolated features. Detailed studies of intimate covariation among linguistic variables in process of change provide the most persuasive empirical evidence of such systematic effects, although accounts of completed changes are not without value in this respect.

Thus in the New York City vowel system (Labov 1966:507 ff.) we find a variable (ah), representing the degree of backing of the long and ingliding vowel in *father, pa, car, guard, bar.* This variable is a function of another linguistic variable (oh), mentioned above. We can represent this covariation by the abbreviated notation:

(8)   (ah) = f(oh).

This expression can be related to a more analytical feature notation at the point where the binary set of features in a generative phonology is replaced by a smaller set of linear dimensions. For reasons outlined above (§ 2.41), the distinctive feature apparatus must be replaced here by a homogeneous set of dimensions which define locations in phonological space; however, we cannot outline the quantitative basis for such dimensions here and we will therefore retain the binary. The rules given below apply only to tense vowels generated in an *r*-less system after [r] becomes vocalized and preceding vowels lengthened, and therefore the features [+tense, +vocalic, −consonantal] are understood for each segment operated on.[57]

---

[57] In order to interpret Rules (11) and (13), one must understand the feature [grave] as equivalent to the dimension of fronting and backing, and [compact] as equivalent to the dimension of height; these two dimensions form a Cartesian space in which the distance between two pairs of coordinates can be interpreted as a straight line. The use of the variable notation is here, naturally, extended beyond the binary choice of + or − to indicate a linear series of values in the same manner as the treatment of stress in current generative phonology. Whether or not the dimensions indicated by the features are continu-

Rule (9) defines the variable (oh) and (10) defines (ah). The systematic status of (ah) is established by (11), for without this relationship, (10) would merely state that the gravity of (ah) varies.

$$
\text{(9)} \qquad \overset{3}{\begin{bmatrix} +\text{comp.} \\ -\text{diff.} \\ +\text{round} \end{bmatrix}} \rightarrow \overset{\text{(oh)}}{\begin{bmatrix} \alpha\ \text{comp.} \\ \rho\ \text{round} \end{bmatrix}} \quad / \quad \left[+\overline{\text{grave}} \right]
$$

where $1 \leqslant \alpha \leqslant 5$ and $\rho = \kappa\alpha$

$$
\text{(10)} \qquad \overset{\bar{a}}{[+\text{grave}]} \rightarrow \overset{\text{(ah)}}{[\gamma\text{grave}]} \quad / \quad \begin{bmatrix} +\overline{\text{comp.}} \\ -\text{diff.} \\ -\text{round} \end{bmatrix}
$$

$$
\text{(11)} \qquad \gamma = f[\alpha] = \sqrt{\kappa^2 - \alpha^2} \qquad \text{i.e., (ah)} = f(\text{oh})
$$

Rules such as (11) are not predictions about individual utterances of individual speakers. A large number of small effects contribute to a base level of fluctuation which makes such predictions impossible. But the level of fluctuation or random variability is relatively low: (11) applies to small numbers of utterances of small numbers of speakers,[58] in such a way that the mean value of the variable approaches the limit predicted by the rule. Thus, (11) is a rule of grammar of a speech community, not of an idiolect.

When we look further into the system of long and ingliding vowels, we find that (ah) can be determined by a simpler and more precise rule involving a third variable (eh), the height of the vowel in *bad, bared, dance*. We can replace the distance formula of (11) with

$$
\text{(12)} \qquad \overset{\text{æ}}{\begin{bmatrix} +\text{comp.} \\ -\text{diff.} \end{bmatrix}} \rightarrow \overset{\text{(eh)}}{[\beta\ \text{comp.}]} \quad / \quad \begin{bmatrix} -\overline{\text{grave}} \\ -\text{round} \end{bmatrix}
$$

$$
\text{(13)} \qquad \gamma = f'(\alpha, \beta) = \kappa'(\beta - \alpha) \quad \text{i.e., (ah)} = g'((\text{eh})(\text{oh})).
$$

Rule (13) states that if (eh) is higher than (oh), then (ah) is relatively front; but if (oh) is higher than (eh), (ah) moves to the back.

Vowels from other subsystems are involved as well: (ah) exhibits

---

ous or discrete is not decided here and is not crucial to the argument. (11) represents the finding that the distance between (ah) and (oh) tends to be constant.

[58] We find, for example, that stable values consistent with the over-all consistent structure are derived from groups as small as five speakers with five to ten utterances apiece (Labov 1966:113–131, 207–237).

strict co-occurrence with (ay), which represents the backing of the first element of the vowel in *my, side*.[59]

(14)   (ah) = (ay) = $g'((\text{eh})(\text{oh}))$

No additional feature rule is needed here, since (ay) is equivalent to [γ grave] and is therefore governed by (11). Similarly, (oy), the height of the vowel in *boy, Lloyd*, shows strict co-occurrence with (oh) in the basic vernacular, and requires no additional treatment.[60] However, the relationship between (ah) and (aw), the backing of the vowel in *now, mouth*, is not that of strict co-occurrence. As a consequence of its structural position in the back-upgliding subsystem, (aw) covaries inversely with (ah) and (ay) (Labov 1966:540). In its simplest form, this relation would be expressed by (10′), which would precede (10):[61]

$$
(10')\quad [+\text{grave}] \rightarrow [-\gamma\ \text{grave}]\ /\ \begin{bmatrix} +\overline{\text{comp.}} \\ -\text{diff.} \\ -\text{round} \end{bmatrix} \begin{bmatrix} -\text{comp.} \\ +\text{grave} \\ +\text{round} \\ -\text{cons.} \end{bmatrix}
$$

The extraordinary complexity of the relations of (ah), (oh), and the rest illustrates the wealth of arguments of a purely linguistic nature that can be brought to bear upon the problems of linguistic structure within a differentiated model. But here there are strong implications for the theory of linguistic change as well. It appears that the first step

[59] Before voiced obstruents and finally (ay) has the same tense nucleus as (ah). Data on the situation before voiceless obstruents are still inadequate to specify these rules more precisely. The binary notation used for the variables here is infelicitous, since it seems certain that (ay) and (oy) are to be analyzed as two segments in the phonemic output, but (ah) and (oh) as one segment.

[60] Note, however, that in formal styles (oh) and (oy) are treated differently. The irregular correction of (oh), lowering from [ʊᵊ] to [ɒ] or even [ɑ] does not apply to (oy) at all. It is therefore not uncommon to hear utterances such as [ðæts ɒl mɑi bʊᴵ] but *boy* never appears as [bɒᴵ]. The rules given here apply to the most systematic level of New York City dialect, the basic vernacular; as noted below, social correction applies less systematically to particular words or sounds, but rarely to features.

[61] Considerations of simplicity would lead us to this ordering. However, further study of the fronting of (aw) may indicate that it is less advanced and is a later generalization of (ay). Note that this dialect differs from the Philadelphia dialect used by Chomsky in that *my* and *now* originally shared the same low-center nucleus and were not differentiated as [mɑᴵ] and [næᵁ]. For the systematic basis of the fronting of [aw] in terms of the back-upgliding subsystem, see Labov (1966:540).

in this complex chain of relations was the raising of (eh), entailing the parallel (generalized) raising of (oh), which led to an associated backing of (ah) and a parallel raising of (oy). The backing of (ah) and the raising of (oy) induced a backing of (ay), which was accompanied by an opposing fronting of (aw). This sequence of events can be supported by figures on their distribution through various age levels of the population, and independent evidence from earlier studies (Labov 1966:559–564).

This chain of events indicates that structural relations within language do not have the immediate, categorial, and instantaneous character which is sometimes implied in discussions of the homogeneous model. It is true that the raising of (eh) led to the raising of (oh): we recognize front-back symmetry as one of the near-universal conditions of linguistic change. But the generalization did not take place instantly; on the contrary, three or four decades passed before the raising of (oh) was in full swing. The associated changes show similar lags which can be traced in the data. Therefore we see that some structural relations are more remote and less compelling than others: an obvious, common-sense conclusion, but one which is difficult to handle without including linguistic variables in our view of structure.

The internal relationships of (eh), (oh), (ah), (ay), (aw), and (oy) are complex enough to satisfy any request for a demonstration of the systematic character of phonological systems. But they do not explain the process of linguistic change involved. Given the fact that γ is dependent upon α and β, and that α is indeed partly dependent upon β, we must still account for the behavior of β. This variable shows the most complex behavior and the greatest number of determinants. It is not possible to say that it is in turn dependent upon another linguistic variable. The system of changes is not mutually determining; the evidence rather points to

(15) (eh) = [β comp.] = f(age, style, class, sex, ethnic group).
While α, the variable feature of (oh), is not independent of β, it also shows a wide spectrum of social determinants by a similar rule (Labov 1966:254–258, 292–315). Linguists who wish to avoid the study of social factors will not be able to penetrate very far into this system: there is a social matrix in which the change is embedded as well as a linguistic one. Relations within the social context are no less complex

than the linguistic relations just outlined, and sophisticated techniques are required for their analysis. But for various reasons linguists have not pursued the explanation of linguistic change in this area with the energy and competence required. In the following section we will briefly consider the historical background for this reluctance.

The Embedding Problem: the need for social realism. One of the earliest and most eloquent claims for the role of social factors in language change was made by Meillet:

Language is an institution with an autonomy of its own; one must therefore determine the general conditions of development from a purely linguistic point of view; . . . but since language is [also] a social institution, it follows that linguistics is a social science, and the only variable element to which one may appeal in order to account for a linguistic change is social change, of which language variations are but the consequences—sometimes immediate and direct, and more often mediated and indirect. (1906a:17)

If the nineteenth century's attempts at explanation of language change had come to naught, Meillet felt, it was because the laws with which it operated stated only the possibilities, not the necessities of development. The stronger form of explanation would come from an analysis of social conditions.

But for Meillet this remained, to a large extent, a set of desiderata. When he did venture into a concrete exploration of social factors, it was in the "easy" domain of lexical change (1906b); even there, he dealt with the remote past, and the only socially determined process he considered was the formation of specialized trade vocabularies and their infusion of words into the general circulation.

In the historical study of more intimately linguistic domains of language, phonology and grammar, reference to social factors was of course never completely absent from the literature: Wyld (1936), for example, based his conclusions about the history of English on letters and documents written by a broad range of the English social classes; Joos (1952) argued cogently that the prestige-marking differential is essential to explain "phonetic drift" in Old French; the exemplary works of Kökeritz (1953) and Fónagy (1956) penetrate deeply into the social context of historical change. But from the vantage of organized, cumulative linguistic theory, these contributions remained peripheral. In the citadels of theory an inverse proportion was developing between the degrees to which an explanation of change could be regarded as linguistic or social. Meillet (1906a), not yet inured to structural purism, pleaded for linguistic-*cum*-social explanations; more modern theorists, flushed with the increasing success of structural explanations, understandably looked on excursions into the social matrix of language as amateurish by comparison. An extreme position was taken by Kuryłowicz: "One must explain linguistic facts by other linguistic facts, not by heterogeneous facts. . . . Explanation by means of social facts is a methodological derailment" (*Lingua* 1.84 [1948]; quoted by Pulgram 1961:324 n.). For Kuryłowicz, even the influence of other languages was irrelevant: "the substratum theory . . . has no importance for the linguist." A different, and less recalcitrant, delimitation of the domain of linguistics was drawn by Martinet (1955: 190–195).

The distaste for amateurish sociologizing shown by Kuryłowicz, Martinet, and others may have been justified by the facts then available. We believe, however, that, as a result of the recent studies of complex sociolinguistic structures and language change in American English which we have cited, a position of sociological agnosticism in structural linguistics has become obsolete. Sociological factors, solidly formulated, have now been adduced to explain distributions and shifts in linguistic phenomena which, from a structural point of view, would have been seen as random. It would follow that the enlightened linguist examining language change will find it difficult to avoid enlarging the area of his competence, or enlisting colleagues to bring in new sources of reliable data.

A number of the linguistic variables that have been studied reveal a complex *sociolinguistic structure,* in which the value of the variable is determined by several social and linguistic factors as suggested by the schematic rules (3)–(4) above. The interpretation of the data in terms of language change depends upon the entire sociolinguistic structure, and not merely upon distribution in apparent or real time. The variable (r) in New York City provides one such example of the complexity of the data required for the analysis of linguistic change in progress.

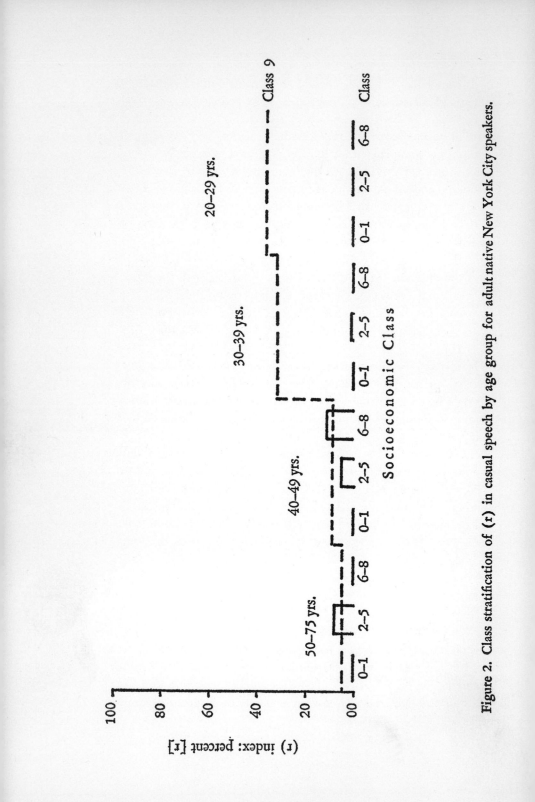

Figure 2. Class stratification of (r) in casual speech by age group for adult native New York City speakers.

Figure 2 shows mean (r) indexes—the frequency of constricted (r) in final and preconsonantal position—for a number of subgroups among adult native New York City speakers in casual speech. Along the horizontal axis are four age groups, each one subdivided into socioeconomic levels 0–1, 2–5, and 6–8, informally labeled "lower class," "working class," and "lower middle class." The level of the highest socioeconomic group, 9, "upper middle class," is indicated by a dotted line. There is no clear over-all trend toward an increase in *r*-pronunciation; the great majority of New Yorkers remain *r*-less, as one can hear at any time on the streets of the city. What Figure 2 shows is an increase in the *stratification* of (r): the distance between the upper middle class and the rest of the population is increasing. For the older age groups, there is no particular pattern in the distribution of (r): for the younger groups, [r] has evidently acquired the social significance of a prestige pronunciation.[62]

Figure 3 summarizes the situation for all age groups, and adds data on a wide range of styles. The horizontal axis shows casual speech, style *A*, on the left, followed by styles in which more and more attention is given to speech: at the extreme right is the context of minimal pairs in which the phonological variable itself is the focus of attention (*god* vs. *guard*). The status of [r] as a prestige marker is here indicated by the general upward direction of all subgroups from informal to formal contexts. Class 6–8, in particular, shows an extremely rapid increase, surpassing Class 9 level in the most formal styles. (For further detail, see Labov 1966:237–249, 342–355.)

How is a socially agnostic linguist to react to these facts? That we are dealing with a change in progress is apparent from the half-generational differences displayed in Figure 2 and independently confirmed in many other ways which we cannot develop here. That the behavior of socioeconomic subgroups is differentiated is also established (see pp. 154–204 for sampling procedures). A linguist excluding sociological factors would have to deal with New York City

---

[62] This change seems to mark a sharp break between those born in 1923 and before, and those born after. The overt development of the new prestige pattern appears to have followed shortly the end of World War II. It is not uncommon today to find teen-age upper-middle-class speakers who are almost consistent *r*-pronouncers. For the problem of the penetration of the entire population by a prestige pattern, see Labov (1966b).

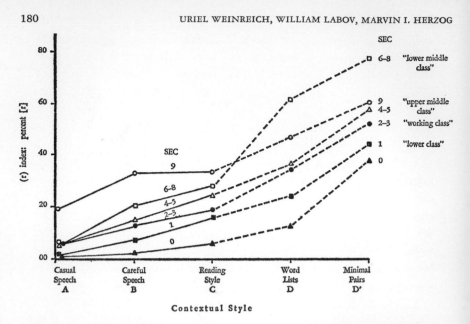

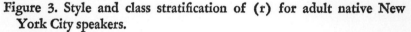

Figure 3. Style and class stratification of (r) for adult native New York City speakers.

English as a cluster of separate dialects which happen to be changing in parallel, or, ignoring socioeconomic differentiation, consider it as a single object characterized by massive free variation.[63] Either attitude, however, would deprive him of the most obvious *explanation* for the behavior of the majority—the fact that the change is originating in the highest ranking subgroup. And surely the behavior of each class in the several styles is not an indifferent switching between *random* styles: the character of (r) as a prestige feature is confirmed by the entire network of stylistic and social inequalities.

Finally, to underline the high level of structural organization in this diagram, we may consider what appears at first glance as a random irregularity of Figure 3: the "cross-over" of Class 6–8 in styles *D* and *D'*. In any one case, such a feature would remain an inexplicable deviation from the structural pattern. However, we observe the second highest status group switching ranks with the highest status group in formal style in two other cases of linguistic change in progress as

[63] This was in fact the alternative selected by several investigators of New York City speech in the 1940's and '50's (Labov 1966:35–38).

well.[64] This "hypercorrect" pattern also recurs in Levine and Crockett's independent study of *r*-pronunciation in North Carolina (1966: 223, cf. Table 7, "Education"). There is reason to believe that such hypercorrection is an important mechanism in the downward transmission of a prestige pattern and the completion of the linguistic change (Labov 1966b).

The Evaluation of Linguistic Variables. In Section 3.14 we considered the evaluation problem in relation to alternating codes or co-existent systems within a heterogeneous language structure. The evaluation of individual linguistic variables poses some special problems, but considerable progress has been made in their solution (Labov 1966:405 ff.). The "matched guises" presented to listeners must be controlled so as to differ only in the single linguistic variable under consideration.

The social evaluation of (r) in New York City has been studied in detail: the results indicate an extraordinary degree of agreement in subjective reactions to (r) as a [middle-class] prestige norm. But this agreement is characteristic of the younger age group only. For subjects over forty, there is considerable variation in subjective reactions; but *all* of the subjects under forty agreed in their [unconscious] positive evaluation of [r]. Comparison of Figure 4 with Figure 2 shows that this categorical change in evaluation coincides with the increase in the stratification of (r) discussed above. The change is more striking in the dimension of social evaluation than in the pattern of linguistic behavior.

In Figure 4, we are dealing with systematic evaluative reactions to linguistic features which the listener cannot consciously perceive. Such systematic evaluation is regularly associated with linguistic variables which show stylistic and social stratification. For some variables, the level of social awareness is so high that they are prominent topics in any discussion of speech. These linguistic "stereotypes" are not related to linguistic behavior in any one-to-one fashion; they are sharply focused on individual lexical items rather than on abstract categories. Correction in formal styles associated with such stereotypes is extreme

[64] This is the case with (eh) and (oh) discussed above, but not with (th) and (dh), which are not involved in change.

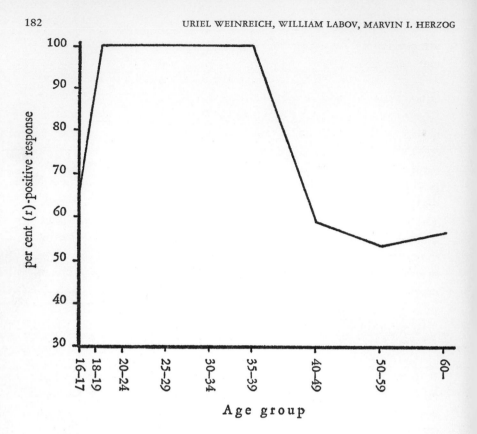

Figure 4. Subjective evaluation of (r) by age among native New York City speakers.

but bizarre in its distribution, and is accompanied by considerable psychological tension for most speakers: the results are the unsystematic and unstable set of contrasts characteristic of formal language. Thus the words *aunt* or *vase* inserted in a reading text are the cause of extraordinary vacillation and confusion;[65] heavily marked (oh) vowels in *office, chocolate,* and *coffee* are lowered irregularly to [ɒ] and thus contrast weakly with [ɑ] and [ɔˇ]; speakers who use [əɪʳ] in *bird* ridicule the stereotype [ɔɪ] which they perceive in others' *boid*; many who use high percentages of lenis stops for interdental fricatives

---

[65] Thus one speaker resolves the confusion: "These large ones are my [vɑziz] but these small ones are my [veziz]."

are deeply hurt if they are told that they have trouble with their *dems* and *doses*.[66]

The investigation of such social perceptions provides a rich body of data on late stages of language change, although it does not reveal the more systematic aspects of linguistic evolution. Overt social correction is sporadic, since, when a linguistic variable acquires social significance, speakers substitute the prestige norm for the basic vernacular as a control in audio-monitoring. The disjunction between production and perception, as studied through self-evaluation tests (Labov 1966:455–480), provides one more route to the analysis of change in progress. The study of overt statements about language yields many insights into the social factors which bear upon language change, and into the sources of irregularity which disturb the course of sound change; but to relate these data to the evolution of the basic vernacular is a matter which requires a detailed knowledge of the speech community and considerable sociolinguistic sophistication.

3.4. EMPIRICAL PRINCIPLES FOR THE THEORY OF LANGUAGE CHANGE

In the third part of this paper we have presented certain empirical findings which have significance for the theory of language change, and also certain conclusions drawn from these data as to the minimal complexity of a theory of linguistic structure which can account for this change. We are also concerned with methods for relating the concepts and statements of a theory of change to empirical evidence— that is, evidence based on rules for intersubjective agreement. In this final section, we will summarize certain principles concerning the empirical foundations for the theory of change; we will organize the discussion, as we have done previously, in terms of the problems to be solved.

The Constraints Problem. We have indicated that one possible goal of a theory of change is to determine the set of possible changes and possible conditions for change; to the extent that such a program springs from a close study of changes in progress, we believe that progress can be made. One such general constraint appears to apply

[66] See Whyte (1943:346) for a dramatic example.

to areas where a two-phoneme system is in contact with a merged one-phoneme system: we argue that, except under certain special conditions, the direction of change will be in favor of the one-phoneme system. We observe, as another example, many cases of correlated chain shifts where peripheral [tense] vowels rise, but none in the reverse direction.

We can also note that not every combination of linguistic and social factors has been observed in studies to date, nor has every possible combination of linguistic variables been observed. In no case, for example, have we found a variable which originated as a social stereotype with stylistic stratification and at a later stage emerged as a social variable without stylistic shift.

The Transition Problem. All of the changes submitted to careful empirical scrutiny so far have shown continuous distribution through successive age levels of the population. Between any two observed stages of a change in progress, one would normally attempt to discover the intervening stage which defines the path by which Structure *A* evolved into Structure *B*.

We find that the theory of language change can learn more from so-called transitional dialects than from "core" dialects (Herzog 1965: 1–5). Indeed, it stands to gain by considering every dialect as transitional. Consequently, there is no need to distinguish between intra-dialectal change and mixture of [jointly available] dialects.

By viewing some subsystems or variables as marked by the feature archaic/innovating, the theory of language can observe language change as it takes place. From observation *in vivo* it can learn things about language change that are simply lost in the monuments of the past.

This transition or transfer of features from one speaker to another appears to take place through the medium of bidialectal speakers, or more generally, speakers with heterogeneous systems characterized by orderly differentiation. Change takes place (1) as a speaker learns an alternate form, (2) during the time that the two forms exist in contact within his competence, and (3) when one of the forms becomes obsolete. The transfer seems to take place between peer groups of slightly differing age levels; all the empirical evidence gathered to date indicates that children do not preserve the dialect characteristics of their parents, but rather those of the peer group which dominates their preadolescent years.

The Embedding Problem. There can be little disagreement among linguists that language changes being investigated must be viewed as embedded in the linguistic system as a whole. The problem of providing sound empirical foundations for the theory of change revolves about several questions on the nature and extent of this embedding.

(a) *Embedding in the linguistic structure.* If the theory of linguistic evolution is to avoid notorious dialectic mysteries, the linguistic structure in which the changing features are located must be enlarged beyond the idiolect. The model of language envisaged here has (1) discrete, coexistent layers, defined by strict co-occurrence, which are functionally differentiated and jointly available to a speech community, and (2) intrinsic variables, defined by covariation with linguistic and extralinguistic elements. The linguistic change itself is rarely a movement of one entire system into another. Instead we find that a limited set of variables in one system shift their modal values gradually from one pole to another. The variants of the variables may be *continuous* or *discrete*; in either case, the variable itself has a continuous range of values, since it includes the frequency of occurrence of individual variants in extended speech. The concept of a variable as a structural element makes it unnecessary to view fluctuations in use as external to the system, for control of such variation is a part of the linguistic competence of members of the speech community.

(b) *Embedding in the social structure.* The changing linguistic structure is itself embedded in the larger context of the speech community, in such a way that social and geographic variations are intrinsic elements of the structure. In the explanation of linguistic change, it may be argued that social factors bear upon the system as a whole; but social significance is not equally distributed over all elements of the system, nor are all aspects of the system equally marked by regional variation. In the development of language change, we find linguistic structures embedded unevenly in the social structure; and in the earliest and latest stages of a change, there may be very little correlation with social factors. Thus it is not so much the task of the linguist to demonstrate the social motivation of a change as to determine the degree of social correlation which exists, and show how it bears upon the abstract linguistic system.

The Evaluation Problem. The theory of language change must establish empirically the subjective correlates of the several layers and variables in a heterogeneous structure. Such subjective correlates of evaluations cannot be deduced from the place of the variables within the linguistic structure. Furthermore, the level of social awareness is a major property of linguistic change which must be determined directly. Subjective correlates of change are more categorical in nature than the changing patterns of behavior: their investigation deepens our understanding of the ways in which discrete categorization is imposed upon the continuous process of change.

The Actuation Problem. The over-all process of linguistic change may involve stimuli and constraints both from society and from the structure of language. The difficulty of the actuation riddle is evident from the number of factors which influence change: it is likely that all explanations to be advanced in the near future will be after the fact. If we seriously consider the proposition that linguistic change is change in social behavior, then we should not be surprised that predictive hypotheses are not readily available, for this is a problem common to all studies of social behavior (Neurath 1944). Such considerations should not prevent us from examining as many cases as we can in enough detail to answer the problems raised above, and put these answers together into an over-all view of the process of change. One such proposal for the ways in which social factors bear upon linguistic features in a cyclical mechanism is based upon repeated patterns observed in a few well-studied cases (Labov 1965).

It is suggested that a linguistic change begins when one of the many features characteristic of speech variation spreads throughout a specific subgroup of the speech community. This linguistic feature then assumes a certain social significance—symbolizing the social values associated with that group (cf. Sturtevant 1947:81 ff.). Because the linguistic change is embedded in the linguistic structure, it is gradually generalized to other elements of the system. Such generalization is far from instantaneous, and change in the social structure of the community normally intervenes before the process is completed. New groups enter the speech community and reinterpret the on-going linguistic change in such a way that one of the secondary changes becomes primary. From such alternations of linguistic and social change proceed the extraordinary complexity of the sociolinguistic structures found in recent studies. The advancement of the linguistic change to completion may be accompanied by a rise in the level of social awareness of the change and the establishment of a social stereotype. Eventually, the completion of the change and the shift of the variable to the status of a constant is accompanied by the loss of whatever social significance the feature possessed. The high degree of regularity which sound change displays is the product of such loss of significance in the alternations involved, and the selection of one of the alternants as a constant.

3.5. SOME GENERAL PRINCIPLES FOR THE STUDY OF LANGUAGE CHANGE

Whether or not the particular mechanism of language changes suggested above holds true in most cases is not the important issue here. The aims of this paper are to put forward certain proposals concerning the empirical foundations of a theory of change. We have presented some empirical findings which such a theory must account for, and conclusions drawn from these findings as to the minimal complexity of linguistic structure involved; we are very much concerned with the methods for relating the theory of change to empirical evidence in ways that will lead to intersubjective agreement. Certain general statements about the nature of language change may be taken as central to our thinking on these problems:

1. Linguistic change is not to be identified with random drift proceeding from inherent variation in speech. Linguistic change begins when the generalization of a particular alternation in a given subgroup of the speech community assumes direction and takes on the character of orderly differentiation.

2. The association between structure and homogeneity is an illusion. Linguistic structure includes the orderly differentiation of speakers

and styles through rules which govern variation in the speech community; native command of the language includes the control of such heterogeneous structures.

3. Not all variability and heterogeneity in language structure involves change; but all change involves variability and heterogeneity.

4. The generalization of linguistic change throughout linguistic structure is neither uniform nor instantaneous; it involves the covariation of associated changes over substantial periods of time, and is reflected in the diffusion of isoglosses over areas of geographical space.

5. The grammars in which linguistic change occurs are grammars of the speech community. Because the variable structures contained in language are determined by social functions, idiolects do not provide the basis for self-contained or internally consistent grammars.

6. Linguistic change is transmitted within the community as a whole; it is not confined to discrete steps within the family. Whatever discontinuities are found in linguistic change are the products of specific discontinuities within the community, rather than inevitable products of the generational gap between parent and child.

7. Linguistic and social factors are closely interrelated in the development of language change. Explanations which are confined to one or the other aspect, no matter how well constructed, will fail to account for the rich body of regularities that can be observed in empirical studies of language behavior.

BIBLIOGRAPHY

Bailey, B. (1966). *Jamaican Creole Syntax.* London: Cambridge University Press.

Bally, C. (1944). *Linguistique générale et linguistique française.* Revised 2d ed. (Orig. 1932). Berne: A. Francke S.A.

Bellugi, U. (1967). "The Acquisition of Negation." Harvard University Dissertation.

Bloch, B. (1948). "A Set of Postulates for Phonemic Analysis," *Language* 24.3–46.

Bloomfield, L. (1927). "Literate and Illiterate Speech," *AS* 2.432–439. (1933). *Language.* New York: Holt.

Bright, W., and A. K. Ramanujan (1964). "Sociolinguistic Variation and Language Change" in Lunt (1964) 1107–1112.

Chomsky, N. (1965). *Aspects of the Theory of Syntax.* Cambridge, Mass.: The M.I.T. Press.

Closs, E. (1965). "Diachronic Syntax and Generative Grammar," *Language* 41.402–415.

Coseriu, E. (1958). *Sincronía, Diacronía e Historia.* Montevideo: Revista de la Facultad de Humanidades y Ciencias. Investigaciones y estudios. Serie Filología y lingüística, 2.

Deutsch, K. W. (1953). *Nationalism and Social Communication.* New York: Wiley.

de Groot, A. W. (1931). "Phonologie und Phonetik als Funktionswissenschaften," *TCLP* 4.

Ervin-Tripp, S. (1964). "An Analysis of the Interaction of Language, Topic and Listener" in J. Gumperz and D. Hymes. 86–102.

Ferguson, C. A. (1959). "Diglossia," *Word* 15.325–340; reprinted in Hymes (1964b). 429–438.
(1963). "Assumptions about Nasals" in Greenberg (1963a). 42–47.
———, and J. J. Gumperz (1960) (eds.). *Linguistic Diversity in South Asia: Studies in Regional, Social and Functional Variation.* Publication

of the Research Center in Anthropology, Folklore, and Linguistics, No. 13. Bloomington.

Fishman, J. A. (1967). "Bilingualism with and without Diglossia; Diglossia with and without Bilingualism," *Journal of Social Issues* 23:29–38.

Fónagy, I. (1956). "Über den Verlauf des Lautwandels," *Acta linguistica* [*hungarica.*] 6.173–278.

Frei, H. (1929). *Grammaire des fautes.* Paris: Geuthner.

     (1944). "Lois de passage," *Zeitschrift für romanische Philologie* 64.557–568.

Friedrich, P. (1966). "The Linguistic Reflex of Social Change: From Tsarist to Soviet Russian Kinship," *Sociological Inquiry* 36.159–185.

Fries, C. C., and K. Pike (1949). "Co-existent Phonemic Systems," *Language* 25.29–50.

Gauchat, L. (1905). *L'Unité phonétique dans le patois d'une commune.* Halle.

Geertz, C. (1960). "Linguistic Etiquette" in *The Religion of Java.* Glencoe: Free Press. 248–260.

Gilliéron, J., and M. Roques (1912). *Études de géographie linguistique d'après Atlas linguistique de la France.* Paris: Champion.

Greenberg, J. H. (1954). *Essays in Linguistics.* Chicago: The University of Chicago Press.

     (1959). "Language and Evolution" in *Evolution and Anthropology: A Centennial Appraisal.* Washington.

     (1963a) (ed.). *Universals of Language.* Cambridge, Mass.: The M.I.T. Press.

     (1963b). "Some Universals of Grammar with Particular Reference to the Order of Meaningful Elements," *ibid.* 58–90.

     (1966). "Synchronic and Diachronic Universals in Phonology," *Language* 42.508–517.

Gumperz, J. J. (1964). "Linguistic and Social Interaction in Two Communities" in Gumperz and Hymes (1964). 137–153.

     (1967). "On the Linguistic Markers of Bilingual Communication," *Journal of Social Issues* 23.48–57.

    ———, and D. Hymes (1964) (eds.). *The Ethnography of Communication=American Anthropologist* 66.6, Part 2.

Halle, M. (1959). *The Sound Pattern of Russian.* The Hague: Mouton.

     (1962). "Phonology in Generative Grammar," *Word* 18.54–72; quoted from the reprinted version in *The Structure of Language* (eds. J. A. Fodor and J. J. Katz). Englewood Cliffs, N. J. 1964. 334–352.

Harris, Z. S. (1951). *Structural Linguistics.* Chicago: University of Chicago Press.

Haugen, E. (1954). "Problems of Bilingual Description," *Georgetown University Monographs on Languages and Linguistics* 7.9–19.

(1957). *Bilingualism in the Americas=PADS* 26.

Herder, J. G. (1772). *Über den Ursprung der Sprache*. Berlin.

Hermann, E. (1929). "Lautveränderungen in der Individualsprache einer Mundart," *Nachrichten der Gesellschaft der Wissenschaften zu Göttingen, philos-hist. Kl.* 9.195–214.

Herzog, M. I. (1965). *The Yiddish Language in Northern Poland*. Bloomington & The Hague. (= *IJAL* 31.2, Part 2.)

(1968). "Yiddish in the Ukraine: Isoglosses and Historical Inferences"; to appear in *The Field of Yiddish*, Vol. III (eds. M. I. Herzog, W. Ravid, and U. Weinreich). The Hague.

Hill, A. A. (1936). "Phonetic and Phonemic Change," *Language* 12.15–22; Reprinted in *RiL*, I.

Hockett, C. F. (1958). *A Course in Modern Linguistics*. New York: Macmillan.

(1965). "Sound Change," *Language* 41.185–204.

(1966). "The Quantification of Functional Load: A Linguistic Problem." Santa Monica, Cal.: The Rand Corp.

Hoenigswald, H. M. (1960). *Language Change and Linguistic Reconstruction*. Chicago: University Press.

Hymes, D. (1961). "Functions of Speech: An Evolutionary Approach" in Gruber, Frederick C. (ed.). *Anthropology and Education*. Philadelphia: University of Pennsylvania Press. 55–83.

(1962). "The Ethnography of Speaking," *Anthropology and Human Behavior*. Washington, D.C. 13–53.

(1964a). "Toward Ethnographies of Communication" in J. Gumperz and D. Hymes. 1–34.

(1964b). (ed.). *Language in Culture and Society*. New York, Evanston & London: Harper & Row.

Jakobson, R. (1928). "The Concept of the Sound Law and the Teleological Criterion"; reprinted from *Časopis pro moderní filologii* 14 in his *Selected Writings*. I, 1–2.

(1931). "Prinzipien der historischen Phonologie," *TCLP* 4.257–267; reprinted in French in his *Selected Writings*. I, 202–220.

(1941). *Kindersprache, Aphasie und allgemeine Lautgesetze*. Uppsala; reprinted in his *Selected Writings*. I, 328–400.

(1958). "Typological Studies and Their Contribution to Historical Comparative Linguistics" in *Proceedings of the Eighth International Congress of Linguists. Oslo*. 17–25; reprinted in his *Selected Writings*. I, 523–531.

(1960). "Kazańska szkoła lingwistyki i jej miejsce w światowym rozwoju fonologii," *Biuletyn Polskiego Towarzystwa Językoznawczego* 19.1–34.

(1962). *Selected Writings*. I: *Phonological Studies*. The Hague: Mouton.

Joos, M. (1950). "Description of Language Design," *JASA* 22.701–708; reprinted in *RiL*, I.

(1952). "The Medieval Sibilants," *Language* 28.222–231.

Kelley, G. (1966). "The Status of Hindi as a Lingua Franca" in Bright, W. (ed.). *Sociolinguistics*. The Hague: Mouton. 299–305.

Keyser, S. J. (1963). "Review of H. Kurath and R. I. McDavid, Jr., *The Pronunciation of English in the Atlantic States*," *Language* 39.303–316.

King, R. D. (1965). "Functional Load: Its Measure and its Role in Sound Change." University of Wisconsin Ph.D. Dissertation.

Klima, E. S. (1964). "Relatedness between Grammatical Systems," *Language* 40.1–20.

Kökeritz, H. (1953). *Shakespeare's Pronunciation*. New Haven: Yale University Press.

Kraus, J. C. (1787). "Review of Pallas, *Sravnitel'nye slovari vsex jazykov i narečij* . . . , Vol. I" *Allgemeine Literatur-Zeitung*, Oct. 1, 2, 3 (a, b).

Kruszewski, N. (1881). *Über die Lautabwandlungen*. Kazan'. [An English translation by R. Austerlitz of this prophetic booklet, now rare, is scheduled for publication in 1968.]

Kuryłowicz, J. (1949). "La Nature des procès dits 'analogiques'," *Acta Linguistica* 5.15–37 (1945–1949).

(1964). "On the Methods of Internal Reconstruction" in Lunt (1964), 9–31.

Labov, W. (1963). "The Social Motivation of a Sound Change," *Word* 19.273–309.

(1965). "On the Mechanism of Linguistic Change," *Georgetown University Monographs on Languages and Linguistics* 18.91–114.

(1966). *The Social Stratification of English in New York City*. Washington, D.C.: Center for Applied Linguistics.

(1966b). "Hypercorrection by the Lower Middle Class as a Factor in Linguistic Change": in Bright, W. (ed.). *Sociolinguistics*. The Hague. 84–101.

(1966c). "The Linguistic Variable as a Structural Unit," *Washington Linguistics Review* 3:4–22.

———, and P. Cohen (1967). "Systematic Relation of Standard and Non-Standard Rules in the Grammars of Negro Speakers," *Project Literacy*, Report No. 7. Ithaca: Cornell University.

Labov, W., P. Cohen, C. Robins, and J. Lewis. (1968). *A Study of the Non-*

standard English of Negro and Puerto Rican Speakers in New York City. Cooperative Research Project 3288 Final Report, Volume I. Washington, D.C.: U. S. Office of Education.

Lambert, W. E. (1967). "A Social Psychology of Bilingualism," *Journal of Social Issues* 23.91–109.

———— et al. (1960). "Evaluational Reactions to Spoken Languages," *Journal of Abnormal and Social Psychology* 60.44–51.

Lehmann, W. P. (1962). *Historical Linguistics: An Introduction.* New York: Holt, Rinehart and Winston.

Leskien, A. (1876). *Die Declination im Slavisch-Litauischen* . . . Leipzig: Hirzel.

Levine, L., and H. J. Crockett, Jr. (1966). "Speech Variation in a Piedmont Community: Postvocalic *r*," *Sociological Inquiry* 36.186–203.

Lunt, H. (1964) (ed.). *Proceedings of the Ninth International Congress of Linguists.* The Hague: Mouton.

Malkiel, Y. (1957–1958). "Diachronic Hypercharacterization in Romance," *Archivum Linguisticum.* 9.79–113, 10.1–36.

Mańczak, W. (1958). "Tendences générales des changements analogiques," *Lingua* 7.298–325, 387–420.

Martin, S. (1964). "Speech Levels in Japan and Korea" in Hymes (1964b). 407–415.

Martinet, A. (1955). *Économie des changements phonétiques.* Berne: Francke.

(1964). "Structural Variation in Language" in Lunt (1964). 521–529.

Mathesius, V. (1911). "O potenciálnosti jevů jazykových," *Věstník Král. české společnosti nauk, tř. filos.-hist.,* Sec. II, English translation in Vachek (1964b). 1–32.

(1931). "Zum Problem der Belastungs- und Kombinationsfähigkeit der Phoneme," *TLCP* 4.148–152; reprinted in Vachek (1964b), 177–182.

(1934). "Zur synchronischen Analyse fremden Sprachguts," *Englische Studien* 70.21–35; reprinted in Vachek (1964b). 398–412.

Meillet, A. (1906a). "L'État actuel des études de linguistique générale"; reprinted in his *Linguistique historique et linguistique générale.* I, 1–18. Paris: Champion. (1926).

(1906b). "Comment les mots changent de sens," *L'Année sociologique* (1905–1906); reprinted in his *Linguistique historique et linguistique générale.* I, 230–271.

Miller, W., and S. Ervin (1964). "The Development of Grammar in Child

Language" in U. Bellugi and R. Brown (eds.) *The Acquisition of Language. Child Development Monographs* 29.9–34.

Moulton, W. G. (1961). "Lautwandel durch innere Kausalität: die ostschweizerische Vokalspaltung," *Zeitschrift für Mundartforschung* 28.227–252.

———. (1962). "Dialect Geography and the Concept of Phonological Space," *Word* 18.23–33.

Neurath, O. (1944). *"Foundations of the Social Sciences," International Encyclopedia of Unified Science.* Vol. II, No. 1. Chicago: University of Chicago Press.

Neustupný, J. V. (1961). "The Asymmetry of Phonological Oppositions," *The Bulletin of the Phonetic Society of Japan* (ONSEI GAKKAI KAIHO). 106.1–6.

———. (1966). "On the Analysis of Linguistic Vagueness," *Travaux linguistiques de Prague 2.*

Osgood, C. E., and T. A. Sebeok (1954) (eds.). *Psycholinguistics.* Baltimore. (= Supplement to *IJAL* 20:4.)

Osthoff, H., and K. Brugmann (1878). Introduction to *Morphologische Untersuchungen.* Leipzig.

Paul, H. (1880). *Prinzipien der Sprachgeschichte.* Halle: Niemeyer. Fourth edition, 1909; fifth, 1920.

Pulgram, E. (1961). "French /ə/: Statics and Dynamics of Linguistic Subcodes," *Lingua* 10.305–325.

Reichstein, R. (1960). "Étude des variations sociales et géografiques des faits linguistiques (observations faites à Paris en 1956–1957)," *Word* 16.55–95 (André Martinet's Post-script: 96–99).

Rona, J. P. (1966). "The Social and Cultural Status of Guaraní in Paraguay" in Bright, W. (ed.). *Sociolinguistics.* The Hague: Mouton. 277–292.

Sapir, E. (1907). "Herder's 'Ursprung der Sprache'," *Modern Philology* 5.109–142.

———. (1921). *Language.* New York: Harcourt, Brace and Company.

Saporta, S. (1965). "Ordered Rules, Dialect Differences, and Historical Processes," *Language* 41.218–224.

Saussure, F. de (1916). *Cours de linguistique générale.* Paris. Second edition, 1922.

Sechehaye, A. (1940). "Les trois linguistiques saussuriennes," *Vox romanica* 5.1–48.

Siversten, E. (1960). *Cockney Phonology.* London, Oslo: Oslo University Press.

Stewart, W. E. (1966). "Social Dialect" in *Research Planning Conferences on Language Development in Disadvantaged Children.* New York: Yeshiva University. 53–61.

Sturtevant, E. H. (1947). *An Introduction to Linguistics.* New Haven: Yale University Press.

Vachek, J. (1964a). "On Peripheral Phonemes of Modern English," *Brno Studies in English.* 4.7–110.

(1964b). comp. *A Prague School Reader in Linguistics.* Bloomington: Indiana University Press.

Wang, W. S-Y. (1967). "The Measurement of Functional Load," *Phonetica* 16.36–54.

Weinreich, U. (1953). *Languages in Contact.* New York: Publications of the Linguistic Circle of New York.

(1954). "Is a Structural Dialectology Possible?" *Word* 10.388–400.

(1957a). "On the Description of Phonic Interference," *Word* 13.1–11.

(1957b). "Functional Aspects of Indian Bilingualism," *Word* 13.203–233.

(1958). "A Retrograde Sound Shift in the Guise of a Survival," *Miscelánea Homenaje a André Martinet.* Canarias: Biblioteca Filológica. Universidad de la Laguna. II, 221–267.

(1960). "Mid-Century Linguistics: Achievements and Frustrations" (review of Hockett 1958), *Romance Philology* 13.320–341.

(1968). "The Geographic Makeup of Belorussian Yiddish"; to appear in *The Field of Yiddish,* Vol. III (eds. M. I. Herzog, W. Ravid, and U. Weinreich). The Hague.

Whyte, W. F. (1943). *Street Corner Society.* Chicago: University of Chicago Press.

Winteler, J. (1876). *Die Kerenzer Mundart.* Leipzig.

Wyld, H. C. (1936). *A History of Modern Colloquial English.* Oxford: Blackwell.

Žirmunskij, V. M. (1958). "O sinxronii i diaxronii v jazykoznanii," *Voprosy Jazykoznanija* 5:43–52.

INDEX